Oliver Goldsmith

POEMS AND PLAYS

Edited and introduced by
TOM DAVIS
University of Birmingham

EVERYMAN
J. M. DENT · LONDON
CHARLES E. TUTTLE
VERMONT

For Esther and Naomi

First published in 1975
New edition 1990
This edition first published in Everyman in 1993
Introduction, textual editing and critical apparatus
© J. M. Dent 1975, 1990 and 1993

J. M. Dent
Orion Publishing Group
Orion House
5 Upper St Martin's Lane
London WC2H 9EA
and
Charles E. Tuttle Co. Inc.
28 South Main Street
Rutland, Vermont 05701
USA

Printed in Great Britain by
The Guernsey Press Co. Ltd
Guernsey, C.I.

British Library Cataloguing-in-Publication Data
is available upon request.

ISBN 0 460 87390 3

CONTENTS

CONTENTS

NOTE ON THE AUTHOR AND EDITOR

OLIVER GOLDSMITH, the second son of an Anglo-Irish clergyman, is thought to have been born at Pallas, Co. Longford, in 1730. Educated at Trinity College, Dublin, he graduated in 1750 and entered Edinburgh University in 1752 to study medicine, though he took no degree. His literary career began in 1757, after travels on the continent, when he became a reviewer and hack-writer for Griffith's *Monthly Review*. In 1759 he published his first substantial work, *An Enquiry into the Present State of Polite Learning in Europe*. By now Goldsmith was contributing to a number of periodicals and in 1762 his 'Chinese letters', written for Newbery's *Public Ledger*, were published as *The Citizen of the World*. Two years later *The Traveller*, a poem which met with some critical acclaim, appeared, and two years after that, *The Vicar of Wakefield*. Goldsmith's first comedy, *The Good-Natur'd Man*, was produced at Covent Garden in 1768 with moderate success. His best-known poem, *The Deserted Village*, appeared in 1770, and he also wrote well-received light verse, such as *Retaliation* and *The Haunch of Venison*. *She Stoops to Conquer* (1773) was Goldsmith's triumph but the following year he became seriously ill and he died on 4 April 1774.

TOM DAVIS is Lecturer in bibliography and palaeography at the School of English at the University of Birmingham. He is also a forensic handwriting expert and has done extensive research into that subject.

CHRONOLOGY OF GOLDSMITH'S LIFE

Year	Age	Life
1730		Born, probably at Pallas, County Westmeath, Ireland, on November 10th
1732	2	
1733	3	
1737	7	
1738	8	
1739	9	
1740	10	
1741	11	
1742	12	
1743	13	
1744	14	
1745	15	Enters Trinity College, Dublin
1746		
1747	17	Takes part in a student riot, earning a public admonishment
1748	18	
1749	19	
1750–2	20	Graduates B.A. Unsuccessful attempts to enter the Anglican Church, to leave Ireland and study law in London, and possibly to emigrate to America. Employed as a private tutor
1751	21	
1752	22	Enters University of Edinburgh to study medicine
1754	24	Leaves Edinburgh to study medicine at Leyden
1755	25	Wanders through France, Germany, Switzerland and Italy
1756-	26	Arrives in London and takes various jobs: apothecary's assistant, physician, proof-reader,

CHRONOLOGY OF HIS TIMES

Year	Artistic Events	Historical Events
1730		
1732	Covent Garden Opera House opens	
1733	Pope, *Essay on Man and Imitation of Horace*	
1737	Johnson comes to London	Death of Queen Caroline
1738	Johnson, *London*	Treaty of Vienna
1739		War of Jenkins' Ear
1740	Richardson, *Pamela 1–2*	
1741	Handel, *Messiah*	War of Austrian Succession
1742	Fielding, *Joseph Andrews*	Resignation of Robert Walpole
1743	Pope, *Dunciad*	
1744	Johnson, *Life of Savage*	
1745		Jacobite rebellion
1746	Collins, *Odes*	Defeat of Jacobites at Culloden
1747		
1748	Richardson, *Clarissa* Smollett, *Roderick Random*	End of War of Austrian Succession
1749	Johnson, *Vanity of Human Wishes* Fielding, *Tom Jones*	
1750		
1751	Smollett, *Peregrine Pickle*	
1752		
1754		
1755	Johnson, *Dictionary*	
1756		Seven Years War begins Indian Mutiny begins

Year	Age	Life
		usher at a boys' school. Perhaps obtains medical degree from Dublin.
1757–9	27	Begins career as a writer with hack work: reviews, articles and translations
1759	29	Publishes *An Enquiry into the Present State of Learning in Europe*, and begins to become the friend of eminent literary men: Percy, Johnson, Burke and Smollett. Writes *The Bee*.
1760	30	Begins the 'Chinese Letters'
1761	31	Probably meets Joshua Reynolds
1762	32	The 'Chinese Letters' published in collected form as *The Citizen of the World*
1763		
1764	34	A founder member of Dr Johnson's Club
		The Traveller published
1765		
1766	36	*The Vicar of Wakefield* published
1768	38	*The Good Natur'd Man* performed and published
1770	40	*The Deserted Village* published
1771		
1772	42	Performance of *Threnodia Augustalis*
1773	43	*She Stoops to Conquer* performed and published
1774	44	Seriously ill with kidney trouble and fever; dies on April 4th
		Retaliation posthumously published
1775		
1776		Monument with Johnson's Latin epitaph erected in Westminster Abbey

Year	Artistic Events	Historical Events
1757		
1759	Johnson, *Rasselas* Voltaire, *Candide*	British capture Quebec
1760	Sterne, *Tristram Shandy 1–2*	Accession of George III
1761		
1762		
1763	Boswell meets Johnson	End of Seven Years War
1764	Horace Walpole, *The Castle of Otranto*	
1765		Stamp duty imposed on American colonists
1766		
1768	Sterne, *Sentimental Journey*	Captain Cook's first voyage
1770		
1771	Smollet, *Humphry Clinker*	
1772		
1773		'Boston Tea Party'
1774		
1775	Johnson, *Journey to the Western Isles of Scotland* Sheridan, *The Rivals*	American War of Independence
1776	Sheridan, *School for Scandal* Gibbon, *Decline and Fall Vol. 1*	American Declaration of Independence

INTRODUCTION

Oliver Goldsmith was and is still a paradoxical figure. His contemporaries could not understand why he was a great writer, and neither, apparently, can we. If we judge by the standard of how often it is performed, then *She Stoops to Conquer* is one of our greatest plays. But the critical discussion it has provoked is worse than non-existent: it is, on the whole, negligible. Goldsmith's formal, serious, public works, *The Deserted Village* and *The Traveller*, have received their due: their elegance and professionalism are open to analysis, and their intellectual and social content can be discussed with the kind of (rather limiting) seriousness which they present and represent. But *Retaliation*, which I take to be Goldsmith's finest poem, and his finest mode, the brilliant light conversation of the verse letters, are hardly mentioned.

Perhaps the difficulty we encounter is that felt by the poet's friends. They found it hard to *identify* Goldsmith, to reconcile the shifting images of him that they found in his life: writer of genius, 'a very great man', 'inspired idiot', laughable failure, bad doctor, buffoon. We too, looking at what we know of his life, and reading the works, are faced always with the same shape-shifting variety of poses and pretences. Goldsmith's fame came from his brilliant success at estimating the moods and needs of his contemporary audience, and this explains part of the problem: he was always quick to adapt to what the audience needed. But beyond this there is a further shift, as if the author was continually protecting himself from his audience, with irony, parody, buffoonery. This ironic stance is one of the principal sources of Goldsmith's greatness; but I shall try to show that his highest claim to our admiration is based on those works in which the ironies are left behind, and we see, for a moment, a face behind the faces: an extraordinary integrity and directness. For perhaps what the masks of irony cover is simply an uncertainty in Goldsmith as to the extent and nature of his talent: Johnson said Goldsmith 'would have been a great man had he known the real value of his own internal resources' (Rousseau, 190)[1]. So only when we are presented with this realisation can the truest genius of Oliver Goldsmith be revealed.

Goldsmith's tendency to irony and self-protection was first pointed out by Robert Hopkins, in the most interesting and challenging work on Goldsmith now available. Having made this important contribution, however, he goes on to distort it. He is concerned, as will be seen in detail later, to reinstate Goldsmith's reputation by showing that his ironies are those of Pope and Swift: the *côterie* satire, that fools the many for the entertainment of the few. Thus he is, for instance, concerned to show that *The Vicar of Wakefield* contains 'corrosive . . . satire against hypocrisy' (191). But it has always been recognised that Goldsmith was entirely free of malice of any kind in his writings – that in fact he never goes in for the kind of covert personal savagery with which Hopkins credits him.

He was, curiously, too much of a gentleman. His characteristic response was much more straightforward and, characteristically, much less competent. When, towards the end of his life, he was viciously attacked by Kenrick in the *London Packet*, his immediate reaction was to take a stout stick and go and thrash whoever was responsible. Since this is Goldsmith, we must add that he attacked the wrong man, and since the wrong man was bigger than the diminutive Irishman, Goldsmith was in fact thrashed himself: he had an unfortunate talent for farce. But we should not dismiss the incident for all that; it is the essential, central, rectitude of the age that Goldsmith is clumsily imitating. When Johnson was threatened by MacPherson for exposing his spurious *Ossian*, he too bought himself a stout stick. This is one of the qualities in Johnson that we admire; it is no less admirable in Goldsmith, for all his absurdity.

The comparison with Johnson is vital. Hopkins, in defining Goldsmith's irony, quotes Swift, who distinguishes two kinds

---

[1] In this introduction, references to books have been made simply by the author's name and a page number. The titles can be found in the bibliography. References to Boswell's *Life of Johnson* are given by date rather than page number, so that any of the available editions may be used.

of satire (12). One is Swift's own, written to mock coxcombs
for 'no other Reward than that of laughing with a few Friends
in a Corner'. The other is that of 'a *publick Spirit*, prompting
Men of *Genius* and Virtue, to mend the World as far as they
are able'. This is the Johnsonian stance, but it is also
Goldsmith's. Johnson's nobility is repeated as farce, but it is
none the less effective for that. Goldsmith's humour reconciles;
his optimism heals; his comedy recommends the good and is
innocent – the physician's art. Goldsmith was of course a
terrible doctor – by perversely administering bad drugs he
succeeded in killing his most important patient: himself. But in
his writings the farce of his life is transformed, as ever, into
purity and elegance by the medicinal kindness of his satire.

In surveying Goldsmith's life we are immediately aware of
the basic problem of identifying the man behind the rôles.
Goldsmith was in a sense classless, elevated by his genius to the
company of the aristocratic and talented, but independent of
the patronage of the rich because of his close relationship with
his paying audience. This classlessness forced him at different
times to propose different rôles and images for himself, and
much of his most important art is concerned with a similar
kind of rôle-playing. One of the poses is that of the wit, dandy,
gentleman. A disastrous failure, this; his extravagant clothes
and attempts to shine in conversation gave Boswell several
malicious anecdotes, and his gambling was notoriously
unsuccessful. But in his art his own ineptness in polite society is
presented with marvellous irony – the verse letter to the
Bunburys (212) is the best example, and it is this theme, as I
shall show, that became the deeply serious centre of *She Stoops
to Conquer*. A good deal of Goldsmith's important work is
designed to establish another pose: the idea that the decent
clerical provincial obscurity of his birth is the highest good. The
serious and moving preface to *The Traveller* (160) establishes
this as the overt theme of the poem, and the famous description
of the Vicar of Auburn (184) gives it a rather sentimental
reinforcement. But the polarities embodied in these two poems
split Goldsmith's life: the strength of *The Traveller* is its vivid
evocation of foreignness, and the return to England is the
return to a foreign country – very like Byron's return at the end
of *Don Juan*. But we know that Goldsmith in fact fought with
considerable energy to *escape* from provincial obscurity, and

this, presumably, is why Auburn, allegedly the place of his birth, hardly exists in the poem as a reality.[1] Goldsmith at the end of *The Deserted Village* affects to weep that poetry must desert our shores (line 407 ff.); but one of his claims to excellence is that he made poetry into a citizen of the world. Only in *The Vicar of Wakefield* are these divisions reconciled: the loving detachment of its portrayal of Primrose, the strengths and weaknesses of his decent provinciality, exemplify Goldsmith's healing (but not, apparently, self-healing) art.

Where in all this can we find Goldsmith? The answer, perhaps, is in the gambler – the bad gambler. Impulsive, irresolute, extravagant; splashing out on hopeless risks, refusing certainties, hopelessly in debt to circumstance, and invariably redeemed by the immense security of his talent. The financial disasters of Primrose in *The Vicar* and Honeywood in *The Good-Natured Man* are redeemed by benevolent fortune at the last moment. Goldsmith is in each case dramatising the bad gambler's optimism: something turns up. What invariably turned up for Goldsmith was his skill as a writer. Johnson wrote two different epitaphs on Goldsmith, each of them, in their different ways, referring to this. '*Nullum fere scribendi genus non tetigit, nullum quod tetigit non ornavit*' (*Life*, 22 June 1776). 'There was hardly any kind of writing that he did not touch upon, and he touched none that he did not adorn.' Which sums up his skill with professional admiration: he was a professional, a handyman; he could turn his hand to anything. This was the only gamble he could win; in his art he could adopt any rôle, any pose, with success. The other comment is more succinct. He died, Johnson reported in a letter to Boswell, owing no less than £2,000. 'Was ever poet so trusted before?' (*Life*, 4 July 1774). Johnson's unique generosity turns disaster into praise: the extent of the debt is the extent of the collateral, the huge resource of Goldsmith's talent.

The Traveller was the first of Goldsmith's works to be published under his own name: it was 'his first serious claim on the attention of posterity' (Wardle, 157). And posterity has, on the whole, treated it rather favourably – though less favourably than did Goldsmith's contemporaries. Johnson himself

---

[1] This point was originally made by the contemporary reviewers: 'If Dr. Goldsmith had hitherto passed his life at Auburn, he would not have been so conspicuous, nor, we hope, so happy a man as he is in London.'

congratulated the public 'on a production to which, since the death of Pope, it will not be easy to find any thing equal' (Rousseau, 33). *The London Chronicle* likewise found in it 'a degree of poetical merit beyond what we have seen for several years' and approved more specifically of its 'strength and connexion of thought' (Rousseau, 34). But the public, after a slow start, was more emphatic. Says Reynolds, in his affectionate retrospective of Goldsmith, 'his Traveller produced an eagerness unparalleled to see the author. He was sought after with greediness' (Wardle, 161). And the literary elite of the day paid him the interesting tribute of refusing to believe he wrote it: it was so good, they thought, it must be Johnson's. Throughout the poem the personal is played off against the political, just as the sentimental individualism that we associate with Romanticism is balanced against the impersonal generalising wisdom of Augustanism. Its contemporary success derived from Goldsmith's professional acuteness in catching the changing mood of the time: he produced, as the poem that would make his name, a blend of *Rasselas* and *Childe Harold*, and the puzzles about which of these moods predominate are a tribute to his tact in blending them. The subjective narrator is announced immediately, a man of feeling, interestingly miserable, 'remote, unfriended, melancholy, slow' (line 1) but also blessed with the rewards of sentimental cosmopolitanism: 'Creation's heir, the world, the world is mine' (line 50). But sense, as Hopkins points out (76), immediately redresses the sensibility: the narrator is a miser (line 51), with a miser's besotted narrowness of vision and greed – greed for emotional experience. Behind this balancing is a sad understanding: that loneliness, and the wisdom it brings, is irreversible. The brother's domestic happiness and generosity are, with wry irony, described in almost the same terms as the specifically limited happiness of the Swiss peasant: the lines 'And haply too some pilgrim, thither led,/With many a tale repays the nightly bed' (lines 197-8) could come from either section. The Traveller's happiness is that he can take part in each of these local blessings, but the perspective of his wanderings prevents him from believing in them: he can 'find no spot of all the world my own' (line 30). The poem's essential strength is its dramatisation of this state of mind: it is, as its title points out, about its narrator. Its commentary, political, social, and poetic,

xviii   INTRODUCTION

has the principal function of creating this complex image of the exile, who can participate imaginatively or directly (as in the French idyll, lines 240-54), but is condemned to generalise, to *judge* this romantic participation.

'His *Traveller* is a very fine performance; ay, and so is his *Deserted Village*, were it not sometimes too much the echo of his *Traveller*' (*Life*, 30 April 1773). Johnson was right; not only was the theme of the latter poem taken from lines 397-422 of the earlier work, but also the two prevailing moods, sentimental melancholy and discursive meditation, are repeated, again balancing, as Lonsdale emphasises (673), round the central figure of the narrator. And criticism has followed rather similar lines of approach to the two poems. The *Gentleman's Magazine* actually echoed Johnson's praise of The Traveller, promising the reader 'more pleasure than he has received from poetry since the days of Pope' (Friedman, iv, 279). The *Critical Review* agreed, but with a qualification: 'few ruined villages are to be met with except on poetical ground' (see p. 254). Friedman sums up the contemporary response: 'the more extended reviews distinguish between the political doctrine, which they find in some measure deficient or erroneous, and the poetical execution, to which they give high praise' (iv, 279). It can be argued that Goldsmith's political thoughts in this poem did indeed have an objective validity, and convincing defences of his views on rural depopulation have been prepared, for instance, by H. J. Bell and Earl Miner; but this does not directly affect the poetry, as the eighteenth-century critics knew.[3] The criticism is important nonetheless, since it leads us to wonder whether the poem has any relation at all to real and realisable experience. No-one would deny that *The Traveller* is based on Goldsmith's travels, and its recollections are vivid and real, whatever one might think of the political commentary; but the non-existence of Auburn has been clearly demonstrated by the number of (equally convincing) attempts to prove that it existed as different places. What these attempts prove is not that Auburn is or was somewhere particular, but that large numbers of people have

[3] 'That luxury is at present depopulating our country, not only by preventing marriage, but driving our villagers over the Western Ocean, we may perhaps be disposed to deny with the best and wisest of Dr. Goldsmith's friends, but we do not therefore read his poem with the less pleasure.'

wanted it to be. The poem's self-pleasing dream has communicated itself directly, and one feels – how nice, how vital to a proper life it is that Auburn does or did exist. (Indeed Donald Davie points out in his essay published in *The Art of Oliver Goldsmith* [1984] that not only are there now cities or settlements named after Auburn in no less than fifteen of the United States of America, but there is even an Auburn University in Auburn, Alabama.)

That the non-existence of a contemporary Auburn is perhaps damaging to the poem – or, at least, to parts of it – was first pointed out in a snappish but continuously interesting close reading of 1785, by John Scott (p. 259). He quotes the first paragraph of the poem and comments with acrimony on the over-use of clichés and the repetition of certain words. Another example of his sharpness: he quotes the lines 128-9: 'For all the bloomy flush of life is fled./All but yon widowed, solitary thing' and comments: 'after mentioning the general privation of the "*bloomy flush of life*," the exceptionary, "*all but*," includes, as part of that "*bloomy flush*," an "*aged decrepid matron*;" that is to say, in plain prose, "*the bloomy flush of life is all fled but one old woman*." ' This point sounds unfair, but its point is clear and true: Goldsmith is not thinking, but daydreaming: those who desert this ideal village can only be young and bloomy, those who stay can only be decrepit, whatever logic tells us.

There is an opposite point of view: Lonsdale (673) finds that the overworked words, such as 'sweet' and 'smiling', constitute a 'technique of echoing repetitions', which 'when reinforced by alliteration, assonance, firm syntax and Goldsmith's increasing metrical skill . . . can achieve at best a rhetorical elevation of some force'. The force is undeniable; but Raymond Williams, in his recent discussion of pastoral, is not sympathetic to what the poem is trying to force us into. While he believes in the rightness of the attack on enclosures, he feels that the poem is responding, not to a place, but to an entirely literary artefact, built from powerful poetic platitudes (74-9). With some ingenuity, he finds in this an explanation for the odd banishment of poetry with the villagers to unsympathetic shores (lines 407-30). Luxury and commerce are hostile, not to villages so much as to pastoral poetry, and thus the emigration of poetry is the only emigration that the poem is really talking about. One might add that, read in this way, the poem has the virtue of being right: in the nineteenth century the literary pastoral is predominantly an American art-form.

What can we make of these disagreements? The appeal of the poetry is powerful, but its power lacks substance. One must remember, as usual with Goldsmith, his sensitivity to the market. Poetry, 'that found'st me poor at first, and keep'st me so' (line 414) in fact repaid Goldsmith for *The Deserted Village* at the rate of nearly five shillings a couplet — a considerable sum. Obviously the poem found buyers, and in 1770 the buyers were more single-mindedly romantic and less comfortable with irony than when *The Traveller* was published. Goldsmith was a great writer in his day because he judged the market so exactly; he is considered a great writer now because the popularising is presented in his best work with careful intelligence and irony. In *The Deserted Village* this is not so. It echoes and emphasises the earlier poem to repeat its success, and the emphasis distorts and simplifies. Dr Johnson was right.

It is this relationship with a market that has hindered critics in judging the merits and demerits of the rest of Goldsmith's poems. The critical position is easy to summarise: it has not progressed in essentials beyond Hazlitt, who in 1824 wrote: 'his verse flows like a limpid stream. His ease is quite unconscious. Everything in him is spontaneous, unstudied, yet elegant, harmonious, graceful, nearly faultless. Without the point of refinement of Pope, he has more natural tenderness, a greater suavity of manner, a more genial spirit' (Rousseau, 258). What sold was easy and smooth poetry, and this Goldsmith produced with remarkable skill; so remarkable that it is hard now to penetrate beyond it to its real merits. What is behind it is the relationship with an audience. Goldsmith's important poems fall into three categories, and the contents of each can be judged in the light of this relationship.

The first category is the formal self-consciously serious mode of *The Traveller*, *The Deserted Village*, *Threnodia Augustalis* and *The Captivity*. The last two are bad poems, but they are essentially the same kind of serious public verse as the two great poems, and their tedious absence of an ironic stance points out the same limiting factor in *The Deserted Village*. The next group is of poems that can be called, however serious their content, light verse. These include the supremely skillful quatrain poems like the 'Elegy on the Death of a Mad Dog', 'When lovely woman stoops to folly', and the ballad 'Turn, gentle hermit of the dale'. The two serious poems, the Ballad and 'When lovely woman' can only now be taken seriously if they are read as jokes — in fact, light verse. Their compelling ease and smooth regularity only accentuate this:

> 'And there forlorn despairing hid,
>   I'll lay me down and die:
> 'Twas so for me that Edwin did,
>   And so for him will I.'
>
> 'Forbid it heaven!' the hermit cry'd,
>   And clasp'd her to his breast:
> The wondering fair one turn'd to chide,
>   'Twas Edwin's self that prest.

(Ballad, lines 137-44)

Read as light verse this is marvellously absurd. Was it meant to be so? Probably not; but once more we are faced with the problem of the attitude behind the poetry. It is exactly like a dilemma that has puzzled Goldsmith's biographers: his foolishness, if any of it were intentional, would be extremely witty. 'I am sure,' Goldsmith's friend Mary Horneck told Prior, 'that on many occasions, from the peculiar manner of his humour and assumed frown of countenance, that what was often uttered in jest, was mistaken by those who did not know him for earnest' (ii. 379). Wardle, pondering on this problem, quotes among others an incident noted waspishly by Mrs Piozzi: Goldsmith, hearing that a sentimental comedy by Hugh Kelly was doing far better than his own anti-sentimental *Good-Natured Man,* was seen gazing into a mirror and heard to say 'A handsomer Fellow than Kelly however' (8). What do we make of this? We know Goldsmith was startlingly ugly; we know *Goldsmith* knew this (see, for instance, the verse-letter to Mrs Bunbury, line 50). If this is a joke, it has the marvellous inspired inconsequentiality that one can only find in two other places in eighteenth-century literature: one is in Blake's *An Island in the Moon,* and the other can be exemplified by

> This dog and man at first were friends;
> But when a pique began,
> The dog, to gain some private ends,
> Went mad and bit the man.

Which is, of course, by Goldsmith ('Elegy on the Death of a Mad Dog', lines 17-20). Where does this leave the stanzas quoted from the Ballad? Brilliant light verse or absurd serious poetry? There is no ready resolution; one is left to wonder at the complexity of the central issue, which is Goldsmith's relationship with his audience.

The third group are the conversation poems, the letter to Mrs Bunbury, *The Haunch of Venison,* the verses in reply to an invitation to dinner, and *Retaliation.* All of these are distinct in that they were not written primarily for publication and the mass audience: they were written for a limited audience of friends, and the easy intimacy they portray allows the irony and self-irony that marks Goldsmith's best work to run freely. This tone is typified by the letter to Mrs Bunbury, which is almost entirely a remarkable exercise in the ironic portrayal of a bad gambler – Goldsmith himself.

> Yet still I set snugg and continue to sigh on
> Till made by my losses as bold as a lion
> I venture at all, while my avarice regards
> The whole pool as my own. Come give me five cards.
> Well done cry the ladies. Ah Doctor that's good.
> The pool's very rich. Ah. The Doctor is lood.

(Lines 21-6)

The most important thing here is the quality of the verse, which effortlessly catches tones of voice that themselves create the milieu of the poem: the ladies' attitude to the poet, the poet's attitude to this attitude – his willingness to play along with it, but also to play with it, which shows itself in his remarkable ability to contain it in these pellucid couplets. In this poem the skill and intelligence – we can realise, as his contemporaries did not, that the two are indistinguishable – are controlled; the talent for mockery is subdued, in kindness and friendship, into self-mockery. Once more the nature of the two-way relationship between audience and poet governs the poem.

Only in one of his poems did Goldsmith drop the varieties of cover that protect the poet from his audience, and that is the *Retaliation*. It is for this reason that this is, to my mind, his finest poem, in spite of its lack of finish and its unevenness. In it the narrator is not dramatised or disguised: he is strongly and completely there, confronting the giants, Burke, Garrick, Reynolds, as an equal. We are not used to this kind of satire: we expect satire to be devoted to denigration, and thus read any praise in such poetry as ironic. This mistake was made by Mrs Piozzi, who used to quote 'as an instance of the danger of *irony*, the character of Cumberland in Goldsmith's Retaliation; which had, by all who did not know the doctor, been taken for serious commendation. He drew the characters which were to mend the *hearts* of the community, not from his contemporaries, but *himself*.' (Quoted by Hopkins, 10.) This is rather puzzling: where is the covert bitterness that Cumberland missed? The reference is to a clear, gentle, and obvious rebuke. Hopkins, for whom Mrs Piozzi's judgement is an important substantiation of his own view, undertakes to explain. He claims that the line 'He grew lazy at last and drew from himself' (line 78) is 'seen in its true satirical light as an echo of lines 71-72: "And coxcombs alike in their failings alone,/Adopting his portraits are pleas'd with their own." *Ergo* – Cumberland himself is a coxcomb!. . . the technique of blame by praise must have been a very rich source of amusement to Goldsmith's closest friends who, like Mrs Piozzi, understood perfectly well what was going on' (11). This entirely misses the point. The poem was not written – as we expect satires to be written – at the expense of those whom it depicts, but *for* them: *they* were the close friends for whom the poem was immediately composed. And it simply does not follow that because fools took the paragons that Cumberland drew from himself as depictions of themselves, that Cumberland was a fool: clearly, it is the coxcombs who are mocked, not the author. What is criticised is the fact that Cumberland's comedy lacks moral effect, which is a rather more serious and worthwhile thing to say than that its author is an idiot.

This satire is remarkable because it is the satire of judgement and balance, not hiding behind its ironies but exposing itself with some courage to the censure of those whom it censures, demanding that they recognise the wisdom of its praise, the justice of its attack. The technique is essentially the same as that of *The Traveller*, though it is handled more subtly: the praiseworthy qualities are also the qualities attacked. Cumberland is such a good man that he cannot depict fools. Garrick is such a great actor that he cannot stop acting. The genius of Burke is so remarkable that we owe it the tribute of the severest criticism: 'Here lies our good Edmund, whose genius was such,/We scarcely can praise it, or blame it too much' (lines 29-30). The intelligence of the praise enforces its acceptance; accepting this, the target must accept the criticism, because the two are inseparable. There is no defence against this. Nor should there be: who looks for a defence against a surgeon? It is a devastating gentleness.

Goldsmith's first play, *The Good-Natured Man*, has attracted adverse criticism since its first performance. It was on the whole a success, at least in financial terms, but the audience was not yet ready for its attack on sentimental comedy. This uncertainty in his audience creates here, as in *The Deserted Village*, a corresponding and fatal uncertainty in Goldsmith. He hedges his bets. One strong line of critical opinion has pointed out that although the play mocks the sententious moralising of sentimental comedy, its own happy ending is conducted with exactly the same moralising flatness. R. B. Heilman in an important article has attacked this view, but it is hard to avoid the fact that Sir William Honeywood is presented, without irony, as coming out with statements like 'he who seeks only for applause from without, has all his happiness in another's keeping' (60) – which is, as Quintana points out (148), the stuff of sentimentalism.

The tangle of attitudes seems to centre on Honeywood, the good-natured man. Here the theme of *The Traveller* and *Retaliation* – excess of virtue is a vice – is presented clumsily, without sharpness or definition. Honeywood's vices are extravagance and moral weakness, but to present these vices as the excesses of virtue is to excuse them, and thus fatally to weaken the mainspring of the whole play. Honeywood is never in serious trouble, because there is, as we are kept aware, always money in the background to redeem him, and when this redemption takes place, we tend to see it as financial, not moral. Perhaps the weakness lies in a (for once) self-indulgent self-portrayal. It was clear to Leigh Hunt (Rousseau, 318) that Honeywood was a personification of Goldsmith's own 'accommodating careless temper', and for this reason it fails: it is too accommodating, towards sentimentality and weakness, and too careless.

She Stoops to Conquer is a different matter. As far as actors and audiences are concerned, it is one of the best plays in our literature. It has a marvellous pace, and it makes you laugh, and has done so since it was first performed. But criticism has hardly begun to explain why it appeals so deeply, so completely, and so enduringly. The answer, or at least the beginnings of an answer, must lie in the fact that there are two plays: Tony Lumpkin's, and Kate Hardcastle's. One appeals to deep and ancient responses, and the other, since it deals with the conflict between social forms and the imperatives of love, is perpetually modern. On another level, Tony Lumpkin is Goldsmith, in one of his most devious disguises; while Kate Hardcastle's play is about the stripping away of disguise.

'This play is a paradox: its characters are all as natural as were ever drawn, and yet they do nothing probable nor possible from the beginning of the play to the end. No house of a gentleman was ever thus mistaken for an inn; nor did any change of dress ever disguise the acquaintance of the morning into a stranger in the evening' (*Bell's British Theatre*, 1791). The first of these paradoxes is created by Tony Lumpkin, and it is into his world that, like the two gentlemen down from London, we are plunged. Lumpkin is in a real sense the author of this play: the play as a whole was originally entitled 'The Novel', a reference to the fiction – Lumpkin's changing of the house to an inn – that sets the whole play in motion and keeps it going. His energy and wit and incompetence have a long lineage: partly from the wise servant in Molière and the *Commedia dell' Arte,* but what he most reminds us of is Puck, in *A Midsummer Night's Dream,* and behind him the ancient irresponsibility of Robin Goodfellow, here creating, as in the earlier play, the framework of disguise and misunderstanding the shapes the lovers' own disguises and reveals to them who they are. Lumpkin's puckish energy drives the play on – he reappears whenever the whole preposterous plot is likely to founder, speeds up the pace, and allows neither the characters nor the audience the moment's pause for reflection that would allow them to realise the absurdity of the whole business.

Another part of Lumpkin's hold on us is that he is the subtlest and most critical and self-critical of all the disguises that Goldsmith put on to encounter his audience. He is, as I said, clearly the author of most of the play; yet he is made a fool of by it. Like Goldsmith he is both child-like and mature; he is provincial, like Goldsmith, and this is both a strength and an absurdity. He is a gentleman, and a buffoon, happiest, as Goldsmith was, when singing comic songs at an inn. He sums up the paradox of Goldsmith's character: he is a fool, a booby, and yet has the sharp satiric intelligence that penetrates the shams and snobberies of the other characters.

The initial impetus of the play comes from this intelligence. Marlow and Hastings mistake him for a bumpkin: their narrow social vision tells them that the young squire cannot be at a low inn, and he uses this narrow perspective to trap them. Because they are gentlemen, they can talk perfectly naturally and without the disguise of politeness in an inn, and so tell him with complete honesty what they think of Tony Lumpkin. Incensed, he determines to enforce this undisguised honesty on them, so that they will betray themselves to Hardcastle and Kate. It is the old theme of pastoral, given an ironic twist: in the country, you find out who you really are.

But part of the play is taken over by Kate Hardcastle, and given a different shape. She takes Lumpkin's 'novel' and uses it for her own ends: she stoops to conquer. There is a further level of honesty beneath the snobbish frankness that Marlow and Hastings reveal to Hardcastle: it is this further place, this bedrock of personality on which love can build, that she intends to expose. The two gentlemen talk, disastrously, in front of one of the intended fathers-in-law, of the false mechanics of conquest, of laying siege to the ladies; but it is she who lays siege, and conquers.

Marlow's barriers are social, and expressed through language: Kate Hardcastle's is a play about that English topic, the language of class. Lumpkin exposes the falsities of this, with mocking destructiveness. Kate builds, redirecting the play from his satire towards the integration of comedy, as the lovers learn to talk to one another.

Marlow can conceive of only two ways of talking to women. Women of his own class must be addressed in the language of 'sentiment' that denies the reality of feeling, and symbolically robs him of speech. 'Females of another class', as he puts it, are to be patronised, pursued, and seduced. Both transactions involve disguise and falsity, both use false language as a protection against the exposures of a real relationship.

What Kate does is to present him with her own paradox. She puts on a disguise to encircle his disguises, and then gradually and imperceptibly changes the false speech into real communication. Step by step he is seduced without realising it into talking to her as a real person. By the end of their last interview they are both using the language of their class, but without affectation. The deceits fall away, and he finds her to be his equal.

It is at this point in the play, where disguise is discarded and equals meet and recognise each other, through the medium of comedy, that *She Stoops to Conquer* matches *Retaliation,* and reveals the essential greatness of Oliver Goldsmith.

Tom Davis

NOTE ON THE TEXT

This edition contains in full, in chronological order, all the plays and poems that Goldsmith is known to have written, omitting only the short play *The Grumbler*, which is an abridgement with very little alteration of Sedley's translation of De Bruey's *Le Grondeur*, and a few poems which may or may not be Goldsmith's – all of which are of only doubtful literary value.

The texts of the plays and poems have been determined according to modern methods of textual scholarship in order to present, as closely as possible, the form in which Goldsmith may have wished his work to appear, in spelling and punctuation as well as in the words of the text. This 'old spelling' is fortunately very close to modern usage, and thus there is little risk of the reader being distracted by it. What difficulties there are, are explained in the notes. Editorial intervention in the text of the original copies has been kept to a minimum; and this minimum is recorded in an appendix, to enable the reader, if he or she wishes, to reconstruct the original versions in spelling, punctuation and text.

POEMS AND PLAYS

THE
GOOD NATUR'D MAN:
A
COMEDY.

As Performed at the

THEATRE-ROYAL
IN
COVENT-GARDEN.

BY MR. GOLDSMITH.

LONDON:
Printed for W. GRIFFIN, in Catharine-Street, Strand.
MDCCLXVIII.

DRAMATIS PERSONAE

MEN

Sir Charles Marlow,   Mr. Gardner
Young Marlow (his Son),   Mr. Lewes
Hardcastle,   Mr. Shuter
Hastings,   Mr. Dubellamy
Tony Lumpkin,   Mr. Quick
Diggory,   Mr. Saunders

WOMEN

Mrs. Hardcastle,   Mrs. Green
Miss Hardcastle,   Mrs. Bulkely
Miss Neville,   Mrs. Kniveton
Maid,   Miss Willems

Landlord, Servants, &c. &c.

PREFACE

When I undertook to write a comedy, I confess I was strongly prepossessed in favour of the poets of the last age, and strove to imitate them. The term, *genteel comedy*, was then unknown amongst us, and little more was desired by an audience, than nature and humour, in whatever walks of life they were most conspicuous. The author of the following scenes never imagined that more would be expected of him, and therefore to delineate character has been his principal aim. Those who know any thing of composition, are sensible, that in pursuing humour, it will sometimes lead us into the recesses of the mean; I was even tempted to look for it in the master of a spunging-house: but in deference to the public taste, grown of late, perhaps, too delicate; the scene of the bailiffs was retrenched in the representation. In deference also to the judgment of a few friends, who think in a particular way, the scene is here restored. The author submits it to the reader in his closet; and hopes that too much refinement will not banish humour and character from our's, as it has already done from the French theatre. Indeed the French comedy is now become so very elevated and sentimental, that it has not only banished humour and *Moliere* from the stage, but it has banished all spectators too.

Upon the whole, the author returns his thanks to the public for the favourable reception which the Good Natur'd Man has met with: and to Mr. Colman in particular, for his kindness to it. It may not also be improper to assure any, who shall hereafter write for the theatre, that merit, or supposed merit, will ever be a sufficient passport to his protection.

PROLOGUE

WRITTEN BY

DR. JOHNSON

SPOKEN BY

MR. BENSLEY

Prest by the load of life, the weary mind
Surveys the general toil of human kind;
With cool submission joins the labouring train,
And social sorrow, loses half it's pain:
Our anxious Bard, without complaint, may share   10
This bustling season's epidemic care.
Like Caesar's pilot, dignified by fate,
Tost in one common storm with all the great;
Distrest alike, the statesman and the wit,
When one a borough courts, and one the pit.
The busy candidates for power and fame,
Have hopes, and fears, and wishes, just the same;
Disabled both to combat, or to fly,
Must hear all taunts, and hear without reply.
Uncheck'd on both, loud rabbles vent their rage,   20
As mongrels bay the lion in a cage.
Th' offended burgess hoards his angry tale,
For that blest year when all that vote may rail;
Their schemes of spite the poet's foes dismiss,
Till that glad night, when all that hate may hiss.
This day the powder'd curls and golden coat,
Says swelling Crispin, begg'd a cobler's vote.
This night, our wit, the pert apprentice cries,
Lies at my feet, I hiss him, and he dies.
The great, 'tis true, can charm th' electing tribe;   30
The bard may supplicate, but cannot bribe.
Yet judg'd by those, whose voices ne'er were sold,
He feels no want of ill persuading gold;
But confident of praise, if praise be due,
Trusts without fear, to merit, and to you.

THE GOOD NATUR'D MAN

ACT I

Scene, *An Apartment in* YOUNG HONEYWOOD'S *Hous*

Enter SIR WILLIAM HONEYWOOD, JARVIS

SIR WILL. Good Jarvis, make no apologies for this honest bluntness. Fidelity, like yours, is the best excuse for every freedom.

JARVIS. I can't help being blunt, and being very angry too, when I hear you talk of disinheriting so good, so worthy a young gentleman as your nephew, my master. All the world loves him.

SIR WILL. Say rather, that he loves all the world; that is his fault.   10

JARVIS. I'm sure there is no part of it more dear to him than you are, tho' he has not seen you since he was a child.

SIR WILL. What signifies his affection to me, or how can I be proud of a place in a heart where every sharper and coxcomb find an easy entrance?

JARVIS. I grant you that he's rather too good natur'd; that he's too much every man's man; that he laughs this minute with one, and cries the next with another; but whose instructions may he thank for all this?

SIR WILL. Not mine, sure? My letters to him during my employment   20 in Italy, taught him only that philosophy which might prevent, not defend his errors.

JARVIS. Faith, begging your honour's pardon, I'm sorry they taught him any philosophy at all; it has only serv'd to spoil him. This same philosophy is a good horse in the stable, but an errant jade on a journey. For my own part, whenever I hear him mention the name on't, I'm always sure he's going to play the fool.

SIR WILL. Don't let us ascribe his faults to his philosophy, I entreat you. No, Jarvis, his good nature arises rather from his fears of

5

offending the importunate, than his desire of making the deserving happy.

JARVIS. What it rises from, I don't know. But, to be sure, every body has it, that asks it.

SIR WILL. Ay, or that does not ask it. I have been now for some time a concealed spectator of his follies, and find them as boundless as his dissipation.

JARVIS. And yet, faith, he has some fine name or other for them all. He calls his extravagance, generosity; and his trusting every body, universal benevolence. It was but last week he went security for a 10 fellow whose face he scarce knew, and that he call'd an act of exalted mu—mu—munificence; ay, that was the name he gave it.

SIR WILL. And upon that I proceed, as my last effort, tho' with very little hopes to reclaim him. That very fellow has just absconded, and I have taken up the security. Now, my intention is to involve him in fictitious distress, before he has plunged himself into real calamity. To arrest him for that very debt, to clap an officer upon him, and then let him see which of his friends will come to his relief.

JARVIS. Well, if I could but any way see him thoroughly vexed, every 20 groan of his would be music to me; yet faith, I believe it impossible. I have tried to fret him myself every morning these three years; but, instead of being angry, he sits as calmly to hear me scold, as he does to his hair-dresser.

SIR WILL. We must try him once more, however, and I'll go this instant to put my scheme into execution; and I don't despair of succeeding, as, by your means, I can have frequent opportunities of being about him, without being known. What a pity it is, Jarvis, that any man's good will to others should produce so much neglect of himself, as to require correction. Yet, we must touch his weaknesses 30 with a delicate hand. There are some faults so nearly allied to excellence, that we can scarce weed out the vice without eradicating the virtue.   [Exit.

JARVIS. Well, go thy ways, Sir William Honeywood. It is not without reason that the world allows thee to be the best of men. But here comes his hopeful nephew; the strange good natur'd, foolish, open hearted—And yet, all his faults are such that one loves him still the better for them.

Enter HONEYWOOD

HONEYW. Well, Jarvis, what messages from my friends this morning? 40
JARVIS. You have no friends.

HONEYW. Well; from my acquaintance then?

JARVIS. (*Pulling out bills*) A few of our usual cards of compliment, that's all. This bill from your taylor; this from your mercer; and this from the little broker in Crooked-lane. He says he has been at a great deal of trouble to get back the money you borrowed.

HONEYW. That I don't know; but I'm sure we were at a great deal of trouble in getting him to lend it.

JARVIS. He has lost all patience.

HONEYW. Then he has lost a very good thing.

JARVIS. There's that ten guineas you were sending to the poor gentle- 10 man and his children in the Fleet. I believe that would stop his mouth for a while, at least.

HONEYW. Ay, Jarvis, but what will fill their mouths in the mean time? Must I be cruel because he happens to be importunate; and, to relieve his avarice, leave them to insupportable distress?

JARVIS. 'Sdeath! Sir, the question now is how to relieve yourself. Yourself—Hav'nt I reason to be out of my senses, when I see things going at sixes and sevens?

HONEYW. Whatever reason you may have for being out of your senses, I hope you'll allow that I'm not quite unreasonable for continuing 20 in mine.

JARVIS. You're the only man alive in your present situation that could do so—Every thing upon the waste. There's Miss Richland and her fine fortune gone already, and upon the point of being given to your rival.

HONEYW. I'm no man's rival.

JARVIS. Your uncle in Italy preparing to disinherit you; your own fortune almost spent; and nothing but pressing creditors, false friends, and a pack of drunken servants that your kindness has made unfit for any other family. 30

HONEYW. Then they have the more occasion for being in mine.

JARVIS. Soh! What will you have done with him that I caught stealing your plate in the pantry? In the fact; I caught him in the fact.

HONEYW. In the fact! If so, I really think that we should pay him his wages, and turn him off.

JARVIS. He shall be turn'd off at Tyburn, the dog; we'll hang him, if it be only to frighten the rest of the family.

HONEYW. No, Jarvis: it's enough that we have lost what he has stolen, let us not add to it the loss of a fellow creature!

JARVIS. Very fine; well, here was the footman just now, to complain 40 of the butler; he says he does most work, and ought to have most wages.

HONEYW. That's but just; tho' perhaps here comes the butler to complain of the footman.

JARVIS. Ay, its the way with them all, from the scullion to the privy-
counsellor. If they have a bad master, they keep quarrelling with
him; if they have a good master, they keep quarrelling with one
another.

Enter BUTLER, *drunk*

BUTLER. Sir, I'll not stay in the family with Jonathan; you must part
with him, or part with me, that's the ex-ex-exposition of the matter,
Sir.   10

HONEYW. Full and explicit enough. But what's his fault, good Philip?

BUTLER. Sir, he's given to drinking, Sir, and I shall have my morals
corrupted, by keeping such company.

HONEYW. Ha! Ha! He has such a diverting way—

JARVIS. O quite amusing.

BUTLER. I find my wines a going, Sir, and liquors don't go without
mouths, Sir; I hate a drunkard, Sir.

HONEYW. Well, well, Philip, I'll hear you upon that another time, so go
to bed now.

JARVIS. To bed! Let him go to the devil.   20

BUTLER. Begging your honour's pardon, and begging your pardon
master Jarvis, I'll not go to bed, nor to the devil neither. I have
enough to do to mind my cellar. I forgot, your honour, Mr. Croaker
is below. I came on purpose to tell you.

HONEYW. Why didn't you shew him up, blockhead?

BUTLER. Shew him up, Sir? With all my heart, Sir. Up or down, all's one
to me.   [*Exit.*

JARVIS. Ay, we have one or other of that family in this house from
morning till night. He comes on the old affair I suppose. The match
between his son, that's just returned from Paris, and Miss Richland, 30
the young lady he's guardian to.

HONEYW. Perhaps so. Mr. Croaker, knowing my friendship for the
young lady, has got it into his head that I can persuade her to what
I please.

JARVIS. Ah! If you lov'd yourself but half as well as she loves you,
we should soon see a marriage that would set all things to rights
again.

HONEYW. Love me! Sure, Jarvis, you dream. No, no; her intimacy
with me never amounted to more than friendship—mere friendship.
That she is the most lovely woman that ever warm'd the human   40
heart with desire, I own. But never let me harbour a thought of

making her unhappy, by a connection with one so unworthy her merits as I am. No, Jarvis, it shall be my study to serve her, even in spite of my wishes; and to secure her happiness, tho' it destroys my own.

JARVIS. Was ever the like! I want patience.

HONEYW. Besides, Jarvis, tho' I could obtain Miss Richland's consent, do you think I could succeed with her guardian, or Mrs. Croaker his wife; who, tho' both very fine in their way, are yet a little opposite in their dispositions you know.

JARVIS. Opposite enough, Heaven knows; the very reverse of each 10 other; she all laugh and no joke; he always complaining, and never sorrowful; a fretful poor soul that has a new distress for every hour in the four and twenty—

HONEYW. Hush, hush, he's coming up, he'll hear you.

JARVIS. One whose voice is a passing bell—

HONEYW. Well, well, go, do.

JARVIS. A raven that bodes nothing but mischief; a coffin and cross bones; a bundle of rue; a sprig of deadly night shade; a— (*Honeywood stopping his mouth at last, pushes him off*) [*Exit* JARVIS.

HONEYW. I must own my old monitor is not entirely wrong. There is 20 something in my friend Croaker's conversation that quite depresses me. His very mirth is an antidote to all gaiety, and his appearance has a stronger effect on my spirits than an undertaker's shop.—Mr. Croaker, this is such a satisfaction—

Enter CROAKER

CROAKER. A pleasant morning to Mr. Honeywood, and many of them. How is this! You look most shockingly to day my dear friend. I hope this weather does not affect your spirits. To be sure, if this weather continues—I say nothing—But God send we be all better this day three months.   30

HONEYW. I heartily concur in the wish, tho' I own not in your apprehensions.

CROAKER. May be not! Indeed what signifies what weather we have in a country going to ruin like ours? Taxes rising and trade falling. Money flying out of the kingdom and Jesuits swarming into it. I know at this time no less than an hundred and twenty-seven Jesuits between Charing-cross and Temple-bar.

HONEYW. The Jesuits will scarce pervert you or me I should hope.

CROAKER. May be not. Indeed what signifies whom they pervert in a country that has scarce any religion to lose? I'm only afraid for our 40 wives and daughters.

HONEYW. I have no apprehensions for the ladies I assure you.

CROAKER. May be not. Indeed what signifies whether they be perverted or no? The women in my time were good for something. I have seen a lady drest from top to toe in her own manufactures formerly. But now a-days the devil a thing of their own manufactures about them, except their faces.

HONEYW. But, however these faults may be practised abroad, you don't find them at home, either with Mrs. Croaker, Olivia or Miss Richland.

CROAKER. The best of them will never be canoniz'd for a saint when she's dead. By the bye, my dear friend, I don't find this match between Miss Richland and my son much relish'd, either by one side or t'other.

HONEYW. I thought otherwise.

CROAKER. Ah, Mr Honeywood, a little of your fine serious advice to the young lady might go far: I know she has a very exalted opinion of your understanding.

HONEYW. But would not that be usurping an authority that more properly belongs to yourself?

CROAKER. My dear friend you know but little of my authority at home. People think, indeed, because they see me come out in a morning thus, with a pleasant face, and to make my friends merry, that all's well within. But I have cares that would break an heart of stone. My wife has so encroach'd upon every one of my privileges, that I'm now no more than a mere lodger in my own house.

HONEYW. But a little spirit exerted on your side might perhaps restore your authority.

CROAKER. No, tho' I had the spirit of a lion! I do rouze sometimes. But what then! Always hagling and hagling. A man is tired of getting the better before his wife is tired of losing the victory.

HONEYW. It's a melancholy consideration indeed, that our chief comforts often produce our greatest anxieties, and that an encrease of our possessions is but an inlet to new disquietudes.

CROAKER. Ah, my dear friend, these were the very words of poor Dick Doleful to me not a week before he made away with himself. Indeed, Mr. Honeywood, I never see you but you put me in mind of poor— Dick. Ah there was merit neglected for you! and so true a friend; we lov'd each other for thirty years, and yet he never asked me to lend him a single farthing.

HONEYW. Pray what could induce him to commit so rash an action at last?

CROAKER. I don't know, some people were malicious enough to say it

was keeping company with me; because we us'd to meet now and
then and open our hearts to each other. To be sure I lov'd to hear
him talk, and he lov'd to hear me talk; poor dear Dick. He us'd to say
that Croaker rhim'd to joker; and so we us'd to laugh—Poor Dick.
                                                    (*Going to cry*)

HONEYW. His fate affects me.

CROAKER. Ay, he grew sick of this miserable life, where we do nothing
  but eat and grow hungry, dress and undress, get up and lie down;
  while reason, that should watch like a nurse by our side, falls as fast
  asleep as we do.   10

HONEYW. To say truth, if we compare that part of life which is to come,
  by that which we have past, the prospect is hideous.

CROAKER. Life at the greatest and best is but a froward child, that must
  be humour'd and coax'd a little till it falls asleep, and then all the care
  is over.

HONEYW. Very true, Sir, nothing can exceed the vanity of our existence, but the folly of our pursuits. We wept when we came into the
  world, and every day tells us why.

CROAKER. Ah, my dear friend, it is a perfect satisfaction to be miserable
  with you. My son Leontine shan't lose the benefit of such fine con-   20
  versation. I'll just step home for him. I am willing to shew him so
  much seriousness in one scarce older than himself—And what if I
  bring my last letter to the Gazetteer on the encrease and progress of
  earthquakes? It will amuse us I promise you. I there prove how the
  late earthquake is coming round to pay us another visit from London
  to Lisbon, from Lisbon to the Canary Islands, from the Canary
  Islands to Palmyra, from Palmyra to Constantinople, and so from
  Constantinople back to London again.   [*Exit.*

HONEYW. Poor Croaker! His situation deserves the utmost pity. I
  shall scarce recover my spirits these three days. Sure to live upon   30
  such terms is worse than death itself. And yet, when I consider
  my own situation; a broken fortune, an hopeless passion, friends in
  distress; the wish but not the power to serve them——(*pausing and
  sighing*)

                        Enter BUTLER

BUTLER. More company below, Sir; Mrs. Croaker and Miss Richland;
  shall I shew them up? But they're shewing up themselves.   [*Exit.*

              Enter MRS. CROAKER *and* MISS RICHLAND

MISS RICH. You're always in such spirits.

MRS. CROAKER. We have just come, my dear Honeywood, from the   40 auction. There was the old deaf dowager, as usual, bidding like a fury against herself. And then so curious in antiques! Herself the most genuine piece of antiquity in the whole collection.

HONEYW. Excuse me, ladies, if some uneasiness from friendship makes me unfit to share in this good humour: I know you'll pardon me.

MRS. CROAKER. I vow he seems as melancholy as if he had taken a dose of my husband this morning. Well, if Richland here can pardon you, I must.

MISS RICH. You would seem to insinuate, madam, that I have particular reasons for being dispos'd to refuse it. 10

MRS. CROAKER. Whatever I insinuate, my dear, don't be so ready to wish an explanation.

MISS RICH. I own I should be sorry, Mr. Honeywood's long friendship and mine should be misunderstood.

HONEYW. There's no answering for others madam. But I hope you'll never find me presuming to offer more than the most delicate friendship may readily allow.

MISS RICH. And I shall be prouder of such a tribute from you than the most passionate professions from others. 20

HONEYW. My own sentiments, Madam: friendship is a disinterested commerce between equals; love, an abject intercourse between tyrants and slaves.

MISS RICH. And, without a compliment, I know none more disinterested or more capable of friendship than Mr. Honeywood.

MRS. CROAKER. And indeed I know nobody that has more friends, at least among the ladies. Miss Fruzz, Miss Odbody and Miss Winterbottom, praise him in all companies. As for Miss Biddy Bundle, she's his professed admirer.

MISS RICH. Indeed! an admirer! I did not know, Sir, you were such a favourite there. But is she seriously so handsome? Is she the mighty thing talk'd of? 30

HONEYW. The town, Madam, seldom begins to praise a lady's beauty, till she's beginning to lose it. (*Smiling*)

MRS. CROAKER. But she's resolved never to lose it, it seems. For as her natural face decays, her skill improves in making the artificial one. Well, nothing diverts me more than one of those fine old dressy things, who thinks to conceal her age, by every where exposing her person; sticking herself up in the front of a side-box; trailing thro' a minuet at Almack's; and then, in the public gardens; looking for all the world like one of the painted ruins of the place. 40

HONEYW. Every age has its admirers, ladies. While you, perhaps, are trading among the warmer climates of youth; there ought to be some to carry on an useful commerce in the frozen latitudes beyond fifty.

MISS RICH. But then the mortifications they must suffer before they can be fitted out for traffic. I have seen one of them fret an whole morning at her hair-dresser, when all the fault was her face.

HONEYW. And yet I'll engage has carried that face at last to a very good market. This good natur'd town, Madam, has husbands, like spectacles, to fit every age, from fifteen to fourscore.

MRS. CROAKER. Well, you're a dear good-natur'd creature. But you 10 know you're engaged with us this morning upon a stroling party. I want to shew Olivia the town, and the things; I believe I shall have business for you for the whole day.

HONEYW. I am sorry, Madam, I have an appointment with Mr. Croaker, which it is impossible to put off.

MRS. CROAKER. What! with my husband! Then I'm resolved to take no refusal. Nay, I protest you must. You know I never laugh so much as with you.

HONEYW. Why, if I must, I must. I'll swear you have put me into such spirits. Well, do you find jest, and I'll find laugh, I promise you. 20 We'll wait for the chariot in the next room.   [Exeunt.

Enter LEONTINE and OLIVIA

LEONT. There they go, thoughtless and happy. My dearest Olivia, what would I give to see you capable of sharing in their amusements, and as chearful as they are.

OLIVIA. How, my Leontine, how can I be chearful, when I have so many terrors to oppress me? The fear of being detected by this family, and the apprehensions of a censuring world, when I must be detected—

LEONT. The world! my love, what can it say? At worst it can only say 30 that being compelled by a mercenary guardian to embrace a life you disliked, you formed a resolution of flying with the man of your choice; that you confided in his honour, and took refuge in my father's house; the only one where your's could remain without censure.

OLIVIA. But consider, Leontine, your disobedience and my indiscretion: your being sent to France to bring home a sister; and, instead of a sister, bringing home————

LEONT. One dearer than a thousand sisters. One that I am convinc'd will be equally dear, to the rest of the family, when she comes to be 40 known.

OLIVIA. And that, I fear, will shortly be.

LEONT. Impossible, 'till we ourselves think proper to make the discovery. My sister, you know, has been with her aunt, at Lyons, since she was a child, and you find every creature in the family takes you for her.

OLIVIA. But may'nt she write, may'nt her aunt write?

LEONT. Her aunt scarce ever writes, and all my sister's letters are directed to me.

OLIVIA. But won't your refusing Miss Richland, for whom you know the old gentleman intends you, create a suspicion?   10

LEONT. There, there's my master-stroke. I have resolved not to refuse her; nay, an hour hence I have consented to go with my father, to make her an offer of my heart and fortune.

OLIVIA. Your heart and fortune!

LEONT. Don't be alarm'd, my dearest. Can Olivia think so meanly of my honour, or my love, as to suppose I could ever hope for happiness from any but her? No, my Olivia, neither the force, nor, permit me to add, the delicacy of my passion, leave any room to suspect me. I only offer Miss Richland an heart, I am convinc'd she will refuse; as I am confident, that, without knowing it, her affections are fixed upon Mr.   20 Honeywood.

OLIVIA. Mr. Honeywood! You'll excuse my apprehensions; but when your merits come to be put in the ballance—

LEONT. You view them with too much partiality. However, by making this offer, I shew a seeming compliance with my father's commands, and perhaps upon her refusal I may have his consent to chuse for myself.

OLIVIA. Well, I submit. And yet, my Leontine, I own, I shall envy her even your pretended addresses. I consider every look, every expression of your esteem, as due only to me. This is folly perhaps: I   30 allow it; but it is natural to suppose, that merit which has made an impression on ones own heart, may be powerful over that of another.

LEONT. Don't, my life's treasure, don't let us make imaginary evils, when you know we have so many real ones to encounter. At worst, you know, if Miss Richland should consent, or my father refuse his pardon, it can but end in a trip to Scotland; and——

Enter CROAKER

CROAKER. Where have you been, boy? I have been seeking you. My friend Honeywood here, has been saying such comfortable things.   40 Ah! he's an example indeed; where is he? I left him here.

LEONT. Sir, I believe you may see him, and hear him too in the next room, he's preparing to go out with the ladies.

CROAKER. Good gracious, can I believe my eyes or my ears! I'm struck dumb with his vivacity, and stunn'd with the loudness of his laugh. Was there ever such a transformation! (*A laugh behind the scenes,* CROAKER *mimics it*) Ha! ha! ha! there it goes, a plague take their balderdash; yet I could expect nothing less, when my precious wife was of the party. On my conscience, I believe, she could spread an horse-laugh thro' the pews of a tabernacle.

LEONT. Since you find so many objections to a wife, Sir, how can you 10 be so earnest in recommending one to me?

CROAKER. I have told you, and tell you again, boy, that Miss Richland's fortune must not go out of the family; one may find comfort in the money, whatever one does in the wife.

LEONT. But, Sir, tho', in obedience to your desire, I am ready to marry her; it may be possible, she has no inclination to me.

CROAKER. I'll tell you once for all how it stands. A good part of Miss Richland's large fortune consists in a claim upon government, which my good friend, Mr. Lofty, assures me the treasury will allow. One half of this she is to forfeit, by her father's will, in case she refuses to 20 marry you. So, if she rejects you, we seize half her fortune; if she accepts you, we seize the whole, and a fine girl into the bargain.

LEONT. But, Sir, if you will but listen to reason——

CROAKER. Come, then, produce your reasons. I tell you I'm fix'd, determined, so now produce your reasons. When I'm determined, I always listen to reason, because it can then do no harm.

LEONT. You have alledged that a mutual choice was the first requisite in matrimonial happiness.

CROAKER. Well, and you have both of you a mutual choice. She has her choice—to marry you, or lose half her fortune; and you have your 30 choice—to marry her, or pack out of doors without any fortune at all.

LEONT. An only Son, Sir, might expect more indulgence.

CROAKER. An only father, Sir, might expect more obedience; besides, has not your sister here, that never disobliged me in her life, as good a right as you? He's a sad dog, Livy, my dear, and would take all from you. But he shan't, I tell you he shan't, for you shall have your share.

OLIVIA. Dear Sir, I wish you'd be convinced that I can never be happy in any addition to my fortune, which is taken from his. 40

CROAKER. Well, well, its a good child, so say no more, but come with me, and we shall see something that will give us a great deal of pleasure, I promise you; old Ruggins, the curry-comb-maker, lying in state; I'm told he makes a very handsome corpse, and becomes his coffin prodigiously. He was an intimate friend of mine, and these are friendly things we ought to do for each other. [*Exeunt.*

END OF THE FIRST ACT

ACT II

SCENE, CROAKER'S *House*

MISS RICHLAND, GARNET

MISS RICH. Olivia not his sister? Olivia not Leontine's sister? You amaze me!

GARNET. No more his sister than I am; I had it all from his own servant; I can get any thing from that quarter.

MISS RICH. But how? Tell me again, Garnet.

GARNET. Why, Madam, as I told you before, instead of going to Lyons to bring home his sister, who has been there with her aunt these ten years; he never went further than Paris; there he saw and fell in love with this young lady; by the bye, of a prodigious family. 10

MISS RICH. And brought her home to my guardian, as his daughter?

GARNET. Yes, and daughter she will be; if he don't consent to their marriage, they talk of trying what a Scotch parson can do.

MISS RICH. Well, I own they have deceived me—And so demurely as Olivia carried it too!—Would you believe it, Garnet, I told her all my secrets; and yet the sly cheat concealed all this from me?

GARNET. And, upon my word, Madam, I don't much blame her; she was loath to trust one with her secrets, that was so very bad at keeping her own. 20

MISS RICH. But, to add to their deceit, the young gentleman, it seems, pretends to make me serious proposals. My guardian and he are to be here presently, to open the affair in form. You know I am to lose half my fortune if I refuse him.

GARNET. Yet, what can you do? For being, as you are, in love with Mr. Honeywood, Madam—

MISS RICH. How! ideot; what do you mean? In love with Mr. Honeywood! Is this to provoke me?

17

GAR. That is, Madam, in friendship with him; I meant nothing more
than friendship, as I hope to be married; nothing more.

MIS RICH. Well, no more of this! As to my guardian, and his son, they
shall find me prepared to receive them; I'm resolved to accept their
proposal with seeming pleasure, to mortify them by compliance, and
so throw the refusal at last upon them.

GAR. Delicious! and that will secure your whole fortune to yourself.
Well, who could have thought so innocent a face could cover so
much cuteness.

MISS RICH. Why, girl, I only oppose my prudence to their cunning, and 10
practise a lesson they have taught me against themselves.

GAR. Then you're likely not long to want employment, for here they
come, and in close conference.

Enter CROAKER, LEONTINE

LEON. Excuse me, Sir, if I seem to hesitate upon the point of putting
the lady so important a question.

CROAKER. Lord! good Sir, moderate your fears; you're so plaguy shy,
that one would think you had changed sexes. I tell you we must have
the half or the whole. Come, let me see with what spirit you begin?
Well, why don't you? Eh! What? Well then—I must, it seems— 20
Miss Richland, my dear, I believe you guess at our business; an affair
which my son here comes to open, that nearly concerns your happiness.

MISS RICH. Sir, I should be ungrateful not to be pleased with any thing
that comes recommended by you.

CROAKER. How, boy, could you desire a finer opening? Why don't you
begin, I say?   (*To* LEONT.)

LEONT. 'Tis true, Madam, my father, Madam, has some intentions—
hem—of explaining an affair—which—himself—can best explain,
Madam.   30

CROAKER. Yes, my dear; it comes intirely from my son; it's all a request
of his own, Madam. And I will permit him to make the best of it.

LEONT. The whole affair is only this, Madam; my father has a proposal
to make, which he insists none but himself shall deliver.

CROAKER. My mind misgives me, the fellow will never be brought on.
(*Aside.*) In short, Madam, you see before you one that loves you; one
whose whole happiness is all in you.

MISS RICH. I never had any doubts of your regard, Sir; and I hope you
can have none of my duty.

CROAKER. That's not the thing, my little sweeting; my love! No, no, 40
another guess lover than I; there he stands, Madam; his very looks

declare the force of his passion—Call up a look, you dog—But then, had you seen him, as I have, weeping, speaking soliloquies and blank verse, sometimes melancholy, and sometimes absent—

MISS RICH. I fear, Sir, he's absent now; or such a declaration would have come most properly from himself.

CROAKER. Himself, Madam! he would die before he could make such a confession; and if he had not a channel for his passion thro' me, it would ere now have drowned his understanding.

MISS RICH. I must grant, Sir, there are attractions in modest diffidence, above the force of words. A silent address is the genuine eloquence 10 of sincerity.

CROAKER. Madam, he has forgot to speak any other language; silence is become his mother tongue.

MISS RICH. And it must be confessed, Sir, it speaks very powerfully in his favour. And yet, I shall be thought too forward in making such a confession; shan't I Mr. Leontine?

LEONT. Confusion! my reserve will undo me. But, if modesty attracts her, impudence may disgust her. I'll try. (Aside.) Don't imagine from my silence, Madam, that I want a due sense of the honour and happiness intended me. My father, Madam, tells you, your humble servant 20 is not totally indifferent to you. He admires you; I adore you; and when we come together, upon my soul I believe we shall be the happiest couple in all St. James's.

MISS RICH. If I could flatter myself, you thought as you speak, Sir——

LEONT. Doubt my sincerity, Madam? By your dear self I swear. Ask the brave if they desire glory; ask cowards if they covet safety——

CROAKER. Well, well, no more questions about it.

LEONT. Ask the sick if they long for health, ask misers if they love money, ask——

CROAKER. Ask a fool if he can talk nonsense! What's come over the 30 boy? What signifies asking, when there's not a soul to give you an answer? If you would ask to the purpose, ask this lady's consent to make you happy.

MISS RICH. Why indeed, Sir, his uncommon ardour almost compels me, forces me, to comply. And yet I'm afraid he'll despise a conquest gain'd with too much ease; wont you Mr. Leontine?

LEONT. Confusion! (Aside.) O by no means, Madam, by no means. And yet, Madam, you talk'd of force. There is nothing I would avoid so much as compulsion in a thing of this kind. No, Madam, I will still be generous, and leave you at liberty to refuse. 40

CROAKER. But I tell you, Sir, the lady is not at liberty. Its a match. You see she says nothing. Silence gives consent.

LEONT. But, Sir, she talk'd of force. Consider, Sir, the cruelty of con-
straining her inclinations.

CROAKER. But I say there's no cruelty. Don't you know, blockhead,
that girls have always a roundabout way of saying yes before company? So get you both gone together into the next room, and hang
him that interrupts the tender explanation. Get you gone, I say; I'll
not hear a word.

LEONT. But Sir, I must beg leave to insist—

CROAKER. Get off you puppy, or I'll beg leave to insist upon knocking
you down. Stupid whelp. But I don't wonder, the boy takes entirely 10
after his mother.   [*Exeunt* MISS RICH. *and* LEONT.

Enter MRS. CROAKER

MRS. CROAKER. Mr. Croaker, I bring you something, my dear, that I
believe will make you smile.

CROAKER. I'll hold you a guinea of that, my dear.

MRS. CROAKER. A letter; and, as I knew the hand, I ventured to open it.

CROAKER. And how can you expect your breaking open my letters
should give me pleasure?

MRS. CROAKER. Poo, its from your sister at Lyons, and contains good
news: read it.   20

CROAKER. What a Frenchified cover is here! That sister of mine has
some good qualities, but I could never teach her to fold a letter.

MRS. CROAKER. Fold a fiddlestick. Read what it contains.

CROAKER, *reading*

DEAR NICK,

*An English gentleman, of large fortune, has for some time made private, tho'
honourable proposals to your daughter Olivia. They love each other tenderly,
and I find she has consented, without letting any of the family know, to crown
his addresses. As such good offers don't come every day, your own good sense,
his large fortune, and family considerations, will induce you to forgive her—* 30
Yours ever—RACHEL CROAKER.

My daughter, Olivia, privately contracted to a man of large fortune!
This is good news indeed. Oh! My heart never foretold me of this.
And yet, how slily the little baggage has carried it since she came
home. Not a word on't to the old ones for the world. Yet, I thought,
I saw something she wanted to conceal.

MRS. CROAKER. Well, if they have concealed their amour, they shan't
conceal their wedding; that shall be public, I'm resolved.

CROAKER. I tell thee, woman, the wedding is the most foolish part of the ceremony. I can never get this woman to think of the more serious part of the nuptial engagement.

MRS. CROAKER. What, would you have me think of their funeral? But come, tell me, my dear, don't you owe more to me than you care to confess? Would you have ever been known to Mr. Lofty, who has undertaken Miss Richland's claim at the treasury, but for me? Who was it first made him an acquaintance at Lady Shabbaroon's route? who got him to promise us his interest? Is not he a back-stairs favourite, one that can do what he pleases with those that do what they please? Isn't he an acquaintance that all your groaning and 10 lamentations could never have got us?

CROAKER. He is a man of importance, I grant you. And yet, what amazes me is, that while he is giving away places to all the world, he can't get one for himself.

MRS. CROAKER. That perhaps may be owing to his nicety. Great men are not easily satisfied.

Enter FRENCH SERVANT

SERVANT. An expresse from Monsieur Lofty. He vil be vait upon your honours instammant. He be only giving four five instruction, read two tree memorial, call upon von ambassadeur. He vill be vid you 20 in one tree minutes.

MRS. CROAKER. You see now, my dear. What an extensive department! Well, friend, let your master know, that we are extremely honoured by this honour. Was there any thing ever in a higher style of breeding! All messages among the great are now done by express.

CROAKER. To be sure, no man does little things with more solemnity, or claims more respect than he. But he's in the right on't. In our bad world, respect is given, where respect is claim'd.

MRS. CROAKER. Never mind the world, my dear; you were never in a pleasanter place in your life. Let us now think of receiving him with 30 proper respect (*a loud rapping at the door*) and there he is by the thundering rap.

CROAKER. Ay, verily, there he is, as close upon the heels of his own express, as an indorsement upon the back of a bill. Well, I'll leave you to receive him, whilst I go to chide my little Olivia for intending to steal a marriage without mine or her aunt's consent. I must seem to be angry, or she too may begin to despise my authority. [*Exit.*

Enter LOFTY, *speaking to his servant*

LOFTY. And if the Venetian ambassador, or that teazing creature the Marquis, should call, I'm not at home. Dam'me, I'll be pack horse 40

to none of them. My dear Madam, I have just snatched a moment—
And if the expresses to his grace be ready, let them be sent off; they're
of importance. Madam, I ask a thousand pardons.

MRS. CROAKER. Sir, this honour——

LOFTY. And Dubardieu! If the person calls about the commission, let
him know that it is made out. As for Lord Cumbercourt's stale request, it can keep cold: you understand me. Madam, I ask ten thousand pardons.

MRS. CROAKER. Sir, this honour——

LOFTY. And, Dubardieu! If the man comes from the Cornish borough, 10
you must do him; you must do him, I say. Madam, I ask ten thousand pardons. And if the Russian ambassador calls: but he will scarce
call to-day, I believe. And now, Madam, I have just got time to
express my happiness in having the honour of being permitted to
profess myself your most obedient humble servant.

MRS. CROAKER. Sir, the happiness and honour are all mine; and yet,
I'm only robbing the public while I detain you.

LOFTY. Sink the public, Madam, when the fair are to be attended. Ah,
could all my hours be so charmingly devouted! Sincerely, don't you
pity us poor creatures in affairs? Thus it is eternally; solicited for 20
places here, teized for pensions there, and courted every where. I
know you pity me. Yes, I see you do.

MRS. CROAKER. Excuse me, Sir. Toils of empires pleasures are, as Congrave says.

LOFTY. Congrave, Congrave; is he of the House?

MRS. CROAKER. The modern poet of that name, Sir.

LOFTY. Oh, a modern! We men of business despise the moderns; and as
for the ancients, we have no time to read them. Poetry is a pretty
thing enough for our wives and daughters; but not for us. Why now,
here I stand that know nothing of books. I say, Madam, I know 30
nothing of books; and yet, I believe, upon a land carriage fishery, a
stamp act, or a jaghire, I can talk my two hours without feeling the
want of them.

MRS. CROAKER. The world is no stranger to Mr. Lofty's eminence in
every capacity.

LOFTY. I vow to Gad, Madam, you make me blush. I'm nothing, nothing, nothing in the world; a mere obscure gentleman. To be sure,
indeed, one or two of the present ministers are pleased to represent
me as a formidable man. I know they are pleased to be-spatter me at
all their little dirty levees. Yet, upon my soul, I wonder what they 40
see in me to treat me so! Measures, not men, have always been my
mark; and I vow, by all that's honourable, my resentment has never

done the men, as mere men, any manner of harm—That is as mere men.

MRS. CROAKER. What importance, and yet what modesty!

LOFTY. Oh, if you talk of modesty, Madam! There I own, I'm accessible to praise. Modesty is my foible: It was so, the Duke of Brentford used to say of me. I love Jack Lofty, he used to say: no man has a finer knowledge of things; quite a man of information; and when he speaks upon his legs, by the lord he's prodigious, he scouts them; and yet all men have their faults; too much modesty is his, says his Grace.   10

MRS. CROAKER. And yet, I dare say, you don't want assurance when you come to solicit for your friends.

LOFTY. O, there indeed I'm in bronze. Apropos, I have just been mentioning miss Richland's case to a certain personage; we must name no names. When I ask, I am not to be put off, madam. No, no, I take my friend by the button. A fine girl, sir; great justice in her case. A friend of mine. Borough interest. Business must be done, Mr. Secretary. I say, Mr. Secretary, her business must be done, sir. That's my way, madam.

MRS. CROAKER. Bless me! you said all this to the Secretary of State, did   20
you?

LOFTY. I did not say the Secretary, did I? Well, curse it, since you have found me out I will not deny it. It was to the Secretary.

MRS. CROAKER. This was going to the fountain head at once, not applying to the understrappers, as Mr. Honeywood would have had us.

LOFTY. Honeywood! he! he! he! He was, indeed, a fine solicitor. I suppose you have heard what has just happened to him?

MRS. CROAKER. Poor dear man; no accident, I hope.

LOFTY. Undone, madam, that's all. His creditors have taken him into   30
custody. A prisoner in his own house.

MRS. CROAKER. A prisoner in his own house! How! At this very time! I'm quite unhappy for him.

LOFTY. Why so am I. The man, to be sure, was immensely good natur'd. But then I could never find that he had any thing in him.

MRS. CROAKER. His manner, to be sure, was excessive harmless; some, indeed, thought it a little dull. For my part, I always concealed my opinion.

LOFTY. It can't be conceal'd, madam; the man was dull, dull as the last new comedy! A poor impracticable creature! I tried once or twice   40
to know if he was fit for business; but he had scarce talents to be groom-porter to an orange barrow.

MRS CROAKER. How differently does miss Richland think of him! For, I believe, with all his faults, she loves him.

LOFTY. Loves him! Does she? You should cure her of that by all means. Let me see, what if she were sent to him this instant, in his present doleful situation? My life for it that works her cure. Distress is a perfect antidote to love. Suppose we join her in the next room? Miss Richland is a fine girl, and has a fine fortune—two very fine things—and must not be thrown away. Upon my honour, Madam, I have a regard for Miss Richland; and, rather than she should be thrown away, I should think it no indignity to marry her myself.   10

[*Exeunt.*

Enter OLIVIA *and* LEONTINE

LEONT. And yet, trust me, Olivia, I had every reason to expect Miss Richland's refusal, as I did every thing in my power to deserve it. Her indelicacy surprises me.

OLIVIA. Sure, Leontine, there's nothing so indelicate in being sensible of your merit. If so, I fear, I shall be the most guilty thing alive.

LEONT. But you mistake, my dear. The same attention I used to advance my merit with you, I practised to lessen it with her. What more could I do?   20

OLIVIA. Let us now rather consider what's to be done. We have both dissembled too long—I have always been asham'd—I am now quite weary of it. Sure I could never have undergone so much for any other but you.

LEONT. And you shall find my gratitude equal to your kindest compliance. Tho' our friends should totally forsake us, Olivia, we can draw upon content for the deficiencies of fortune.

OLIVIA. Then why should we defer our scheme of humble happiness, when it is now in our power? I may be the favourite of your father, it is true; but can it ever be thought, that his present kindness to a   30 suppos'd child, will continue to a known deceiver?

LEONT. I have many reasons to believe it will; as his attachments are but few, they are lasting. His own marriage was a private one, as our's may be. Besides, I have sounded him already at a distance, and find all his answers exactly to our wish. Nay, by an expression or two that drop'd from him, I am induced to think he knows of this affair.

OLIVIA. Indeed! But that would be an happiness too great to be expected.

LEONT. However it be, I'm certain you have power over him; and am persuaded, if you inform'd him of our situation, that he would be   40 disposed to pardon it.

OLIVIA. You had equal expectations, Leontine, from your last scheme with Miss Richland, which you find has succeeded most wretchedly.

LEONT. And that's the best reason for trying another.

OLIVIA. If it must be so, I submit.

LEONT. As we could wish, he comes this way. Now, my dearest Olivia, be resolute. I'll just retire within hearing, to come in at a proper time, either to share your danger, or confirm your victory.   [*Exit.*

Enter CROAKER

CROAKER. Yes, I must forgive her; and yet not too easily, neither. It will be proper to keep up the decorums of resentment a little, if it be only to impress her with an idea of my authority.

OLIVIA. How I tremble to approach him!—Might I presume, Sir—If I interrupt you—

CROAKER. No, child, where I have an affection, it is not a little thing can interrupt me. Affection gets over little things.

OLIVIA. Sir, you're too kind. I'm sensible how ill I deserve this partiality. Yet Heaven knows there is nothing I would not do to gain it.

CROAKER. And you have but too well succeeded, you little hussey, you. With those endearing ways of yours, on my conscience, I could be brought to forgive any thing, unless it were a very great offence indeed.

OLIVIA. But mine is such an offence—When you know my guilt.—Yes, you shall know it, tho' I feel the greatest pain in the confession.

CROAKER. Why then, if it be so very great a pain, you may spare yourself the trouble, for I know every syllable of the matter before you begin.

OLIVIA. Indeed! Then I'm undone.

CROAKER. Ay, Miss, you wanted to steal a match, without letting me know it, did you! But I'm not worth being consulted, I suppose, when there's to be a marriage in my own family. No, I'm to have no hand in the disposal of my own children. No, I'm nobody. I'm to be a mere article of family lumber; a piece of crack'd china to be stuck up in a corner.

OLIVIA. Dear Sir, nothing but the dread of your authority could induce us to conceal it from you.

CROAKER. No, no, my consequence is no more; I'm as little minded as a dead Russian in winter, just stuck up with a pipe in his mouth till there comes a thaw.—It goes to my heart to vex her.

OLIVIA. I was prepar'd, Sir, for your anger, and despair'd of pardon, even while I presum'd to ask it. But your severity shall never abate my affection, as my punishment is but justice.

CROAKER. And yet you should not despair neither, Livy. We ought to hope all for the best.

OLIVIA. And do you permit me to hope, Sir! Can I ever expect to be forgiven! But hope has too long deceiv'd me.

CROAKER. Why then, child, it shan't deceive you now, for I forgive you this very moment. I forgive you all; and now you are indeed my daughter.

OLIVIA. O transport! This kindness overpowers me.

CROAKER. I was always against severity to our children. We have been young and giddy ourselves, and we can't expect boys and girls to be 10 old before their time.

OLIVIA. What generosity! But can you forget the many falshoods, the dissimulation——

CROAKER. You did indeed dissemble, you urchin you; but where's the girl that won't dissemble for an husband! My wife and I had never been married, if we had not dissembled a little before hand.

OLIVIA. It shall be my future care never to put such generosity to a second trial. And as for the partner of my offence and folly, from his native honour, and the just sense he has of his duty, I can answer for him that—— 20

Enter LEONTINE

LEONT. Permit him thus to answer for himself. (*Kneeling*) Thus, Sir, let me speak my gratitude for this unmerited forgiveness. Yes, Sir, this even exceeds all your former tenderness: I now can boast the most indulgent of fathers. The life he gave, compared to this, was but a trifling blessing.

CROAKER. And, good Sir, who sent for you, with that fine tragedy face, and flourishing manner? I don't know what we have to do with your gratitude upon this occasion.

LEONT. How, Sir! is it possible to be silent when so much oblig'd! 30 Would you refuse me the pleasure of being grateful! Of adding my thanks to my Olivia's! Of sharing in the transports that you have thus occasion'd!

CROAKER. Lord, Sir, we can be happy enough, without your coming in to make up the party. I don't know what's the matter with the boy all this day; he has got into such a rhodomontade manner all the morning!

LEONT. But, Sir, I that have so large a part in the benefit, is it not my duty to shew my joy? Is the being admitted to your favour so slight an obligation? Is the happiness of marrying my Olivia so small a 40 blessing?

CROAKER. Marrying Olivia! marrying Olivia! marrying his own sister!
Sure the boy is out of his senses. His own sister!

LEONT. My sister!

OLIVIA. Sister! How have I been mistaken!   [*Aside*

LEONT. Some curs'd mistake in all this I find.   [*Aside*

CROAKER. What does the booby mean, or has he any meaning. Eh, what
do you mean, you blockhead you?

LEONT. Mean, Sir—why, Sir—only when my sister is to be married, that
I have the pleasure of marrying her, Sir; that is, of giving her away,
Sir—I have made a point of it.   10

CROAKER. O, is that all. Give her away. You have made a point of it.
Then you had as good make a point of first giving away yourself, as
I'm going to prepare the writings between you and miss Richland
this very minute. What a fuss is here about nothing! Why, what's the
matter now? I thought I had made you at least as happy as you could
wish.

OLIVIA. O! yes, Sir, very happy.

CROAKER. Do you foresee any thing, child? You look as if you did. I
think if any thing was to be foreseen, I have as sharp a look out as
another: and yet I foresee nothing.   [*Exit.* 20

LEONTINE, OLIVIA

OLIVIA. What can it mean?

LEONT. He knows something, and yet for my life I can't tell what.

OLIVIA. It can't be the connexion between us, I'm pretty certain.

LEONT. Whatever it be, my dearest, I'm resolv'd to put it out of Fortune's
power to repeat our mortification. I'll haste, and prepare for our
journey to Scotland this very evening. My friend Honeywood has
promis'd me his advice and assistance. I'll go to him, and repose our
distresses on his friendly bosom: and I know so much of his honest
heart, that if he can't relieve our uneasinesses, he will at least share   30
them.   [*Exeunt.*

END OF THE SECOND ACT

ACT III

Scene, YOUNG HONEYWOOD'S *House*

BAILIFF, HONEYWOOD, FOLLOWER

BAILIFF. Looky, Sir, I have arrested as good men as you in my time: no disparagement of you neither. Men that would go forty guineas on a game of cribbage. I challenge the town to shew a man in more genteeler practice than myself.

HONEYW. Without all question, Mr. ——. I forget your name, Sir?

BAILIFF. How can you forget what you never knew? he, he, he.

HONEYW. May I beg leave to ask your name? 10

BAILIFF. Yes, you may.

HONEYW. Then, pray, Sir, what is your name, Sir?

BAILIFF. That I didn't promise to tell you. He, he, he. A joke breaks no bones, as we say among us that practice the law.

HONEYW. You may have reason for keeping it a secret perhaps?

BAILIFF. The law does nothing without reason. I'm asham'd to tell my name to no man, Sir. If you can shew cause, as why, upon a special capus, that I should prove my name. But, come, Timothy Twitch is my name. And, now you know my name, what have you to say to that? 20

HONEYW. Nothing in the world, good Mr. Twitch, but that I have a favour to ask, that's all.

BAILIFF. Ay, favours are more easily asked than granted, as we say among us that practice the law. I have taken an oath against granting favours. Would you have me perjure myself?

HONEYW. But my request will come recommended in so strong a manner, as, I believe you'll have no scruple (*pulling out his purse*). The thing is only this: I believe I shall be able to discharge this trifle in two or three days at farthest; but, as I would not have the affair known for the world, I have thoughts of keeping you, and your 30 good friend here, about me till the debt is discharged; for which, I shall be properly grateful.

BAILIFF. Oh! that's another maxum, and altogether within my oath. For certain, if an honest man is to get any thing by a thing, there's no reason why all things should not be done in civility.

HONEYW. Doubtless, all trades must live, Mr. Twitch; and your's is a necessary one. (*Gives him money*.)

BAILIFF. Oh! your honour; I hope your honour takes nothing amiss as I does, as I does nothing but my duty in so doing. I'm sure no man can say I ever give a gentleman, that was a gentleman, ill usage. If I 10 saw that a gentleman was a gentleman, I have taken money not to see him for ten weeks together.

HONEYW. Tenderness is a virtue, Mr. Twitch.

BAILIFF. Ay, Sir, its a perfect treasure. I love to see a gentleman with a tender heart. I don't know, but I think I have a tender heart myself. If all that I have lost by my heart was put together, it would make a —but no matter for that.

HONEYW. Don't account it lost, Mr. Twitch. The ingratitude of the world can never deprive us of the conscious happiness of having acted with humanity ourselves.   20

BAILIFF. Humanity, Sir, is a jewel. Its better than gold. I love humanity. People may say that we, in our way, have no humanity; but I'll shew you my humanity this moment. There's my follower here, little Flanigan, with a wife and four children, a guinea or two would be more to him, than twice as much to another. Now, as I can't shew him any humanity myself, I must beg leave you'll do it for me.

HONEYW. I assure you, Mr. Twitch, your's is a most powerful recommendation (*giving money to the follower*).

BAILIFF. Sir, you're a gentleman. I see you know what to do with your money. But, to business: we are to be with you here as your friends, 30 I suppose. But set in case company comes.—Little Flanigan here, to be sure, has a good face; a very good face: but then, he is a little seedy, as we say among us that practice the law. Not well in cloaths. Smoke the pocket holes.

HONEYW. Well, that shall be remedied without delay.

Enter SERVANT

SERVANT. Sir, Miss Richland is below.

HONEYW. How unlucky. Detain her a moment. We must improve, my good friend, little Mr. Flanigan's appearance first. Here, let Mr. Flanigan have a suit of my cloaths—quick—the brown and silver— 40 Do you hear?

SERVANT. That your honour gave away to the begging gentleman that makes verses, because it was as good as new.

HONEYW. The white and gold then.

SERVANT. That your honour, I made bold to sell, because it was good for nothing.

HONEYW. Well, the first that comes to hand then. The blue and gold. I believe Mr. Flanigan will look best in blue.   [Exit FLANIGAN.

BAILIFF. Rabbit me, but little Flanigan will look well in any thing. Ah, if your honour knew that bit of flesh as well as I do, you'd be perfectly in love with him. There's not a prettier scout in the four counties   10 after a shy-cock than he. Scents like a hound; sticks like a weazle. He was master of the ceremonies to the black queen of Moroco when I took him to follow me (Re-enter FLANIGAN). Hch, ecod, I think he looks so well, that I don't care if I have a suit from the same place for myself.

HONEYW. Well, well, I hear the lady coming. Dear Mr. Twitch, I beg you'll give your friend directions not to speak. As for yourself, I know you will say nothing without being directed.

BAILIFF. Never you fear me, I'll shew the Lady that I have something to say for myself as well as another. One man has one way of talking,   20 and another man has another, that's all the difference between them.

Enter MISS RICHLAND *and her* MAID

MISS RICH. You'll be surprised, Sir, with this visit. But you know I'm yet to thank you for chusing my little library.

HONEYW. Thanks, Madam, are unnecessary, as it was I that was obliged by your commands. Chairs here. Two of my very good friends, Mr. Twitch and Mr. Flanigan. Pray, gentlemen, sit without ceremony.

MISS RICH. Who can these odd looking men be! I fear it is as I was informed. It must be so.   [*Aside* 30

BAILIFF. (*after a pause*) Pretty weather, very pretty weather for the time of the year, Madam.

FOLLOWER. Very good circuit weather in the country.

HONEYW. You officers are generally favourites among the ladies. My friends, Madam, have been upon very disagreeable duty, I assure you. The fair should, in some measure, recompence the toils of the brave.

MISS RICH. Our officers do indeed deserve every favour. The gentlemen are in the marine service, I presume, Sir.

HONEYW. Why, Madam, they do—occasionally serve in the Fleet, Madam. A dangerous service.   40

MISS RICH. I'm told so. And I own, it has often surprised me, that, while we have had so many instances of bravery there, we have had so few of wit at home to praise it.

HONEYW. I grant, Madam, that our poets have not written as our soldiers have fought; but, they have done all they could, and Hawke or Amherst could do no more.

MISS RICH. I'm quite displeased when I see a fine subject spoiled by a dull writer.

HONEYW. We should not be so severe against dull writers, Madam. It is ten to one, but the dullest writer exceeds the most rigid French critic who presumes to despise him.   10

FOLLOWER. Damn the French, the parle vous, and all that belongs to them.

MISS RICH. Sir!

HONEYW. Ha, ha, ha, honest Mr. Flanigan. A true English officer, Madam; he's not contented with beating the French, but he will scold them too.

MISS RICH. Yet, Mr. Honeywood, this does not convince me but that severity in criticism is necessary. It was our first adopting the sever-ity of French taste, that has brought them in turn to taste us.

BAILIFF. Taste us! By the Lord, Madam, they devour us. Give Mon-   20
seers but a taste, and I'll be damn'd, but they come in for a bellyful.

MISS RICH. Very extraordinary this.

FOLLOWER. But very true. What makes the bread rising, the parle vous that devour us. What makes the mutton fivepence a pound, the parle vous that eat it up. What makes the beer three pence halfpenny a pot—

HONEYW. Ah; the vulgar rogues, all will be out. Right, gentlemen, very right upon my word, and quite to the purpose. They draw a parallel, Madam, between the mental taste, and that of our senses. We are injur'd as much by French severity in the one, as by French rapacity   30
in the other. That's their meaning.

MISS RICH. Tho' I don't see the force of the parallel, yet, I'll own, that we should sometimes pardon books, as we do our friends, that have now and then agreeable absurdities to recommend them.

BAILIFF. That's all my eye. The King only can pardon, as the law says: for set in case——

HONEYW. I'm quite of your opinion, Sir. I see the whole drift of your argument. Yes, certainly our presuming to pardon any work, is arrogating a power that belongs to another. If all have power to condemn, what writer can be free?   40

BAILIFF. By his habus corpus. His habus corpus can set him free at any time. For set in case——

HONEYW. I'm obliged to you, Sir, for the hint. If, Madam, as my friend
observes, our laws are so careful of a gentleman's person, sure we
ought to be equally careful of his dearer part, his fame.

FOLLOWER. Ay, but if so be a man's nabb'd, you know——

HONEYW. Mr. Flanigan, if you spoke for ever, you could not improve
the last observation. For my own part, I think it conclusive.

BAILIFF. As for the matter of that, mayhap——

HONEYW. Nay, Sir, give me leave in this instance to be positive. For
where is the necessity of censuring works without genius, which
must shortly sink of themselves: what is it, but aiming our   10
unnecessary blow against a victim already under the hands of
justice?

BAILIFF. Justice! O, by the elevens, if you talk about justice, I think I
am at home there; for, in a course of law——

HONEYW. My dear Mr. Twitch, I discern what you'd be at perfectly, and
I believe the lady must be sensible of the art with which it is introduced. I suppose you perceive the meaning, Madam, of his course
of law.

MISS RICH. I protest, Sir, I do not. I perceive only that you answer one
gentleman before he has finished, and the other before he has well   20
begun.

BAILIFF. Madam, you are a gentlewoman, and I will make the matter
out. This here question is about severity and justice, and pardon,
and the like of they. Now to explain the thing—

HONEYW. O! curse your explanations.   [*Aside*

Enter SERVANT

SERVANT. Mr. Leontine, Sir, below, desires to speak with you upon
earnest business.

HONEYW. That's lucky (*aside*). Dear Madam, you'll excuse me, and my
good friends here, for a few minutes. There are books, Madam, to   30
amuse you. Come, gentlemen, you know I make no ceremony with
such friends. After you, Sir. Excuse me. Well, if I must. But, I know
your natural politeness.

BAILIFF. Before and behind, you know.

FOLLOWER. Ay, ay, before and behind, before and behind.

              [*Exeunt* HONEYWOOD, BAILIFF, *and* FOLLOWER.

MISS RICH. What can all this mean, Garnet?

GARNET. Mean, Madam, why, what should it mean, but what Mr. Lofty
sent you here to see? These people he calls officers, are officers sure
enough: sheriff's officers; bailiffs, Madam.   40

MISS RICH. Ay, it is certainly so. Well, tho' his perplexities are far from giving me pleasure; yet, I own there's something very ridiculous in them, and a just punishment for his dissimulation.

GARNET. And so they are. But I wonder, Madam, that the lawyer you just employed to pay his debts, and set him free, has not done it by this time. He ought at least to have been here before now. But lawyers are always more ready to get a man into troubles, than out of them.

Enter SIR WILLIAM

SIR WILL. For Miss Richland to undertake setting him free, I own, was quite unexpected. It has totally unhinged my schemes to reclaim 10 him. Yet, it gives me pleasure to find, that among a number of worthless friendships, he has made one acquisition of real value; for there must be some softer passion on her side that prompts this generosity. Ha! here before me. I'll endeavour to sound her affections. Madam, as I am the person that have had some demands upon the gentleman of this house, I hope you'll excuse me, if, before I enlarged him, I wanted to see yourself.

MISS RICH. The precaution was very unnecessary, Sir. I suppose your wants were only such as my agent had power to satisfy.

SIR WILL. Partly, Madam. But, I was also willing you should be fully 20 apprized of the character of the gentleman you intended to serve.

MISS RICH. It must come, Sir, with a very ill grace from you. To censure it, after what you have done, would look like malice; and to speak favourably of a character you have oppressed, would be impeaching your own. And sure, his tenderness, his humanity, his universal friendship, may atone for many faults.

SIR WILL. That friendship, Madam, which is exerted in too wide a sphere, becomes totally useless. Our bounty, like a drop of water, disappears when diffused too widely. They, who pretend most to this universal benevolence, are either deceivers, or dupes. Men who de- 30 sire to cover their private ill-nature, by a pretended regard for all; or, men who, reasoning themselves into false feelings are more earnest in pursuit of splendid, than of useful virtues.

MISS RICH. I am surprised, Sir, to hear one who has probably been a gainer by the folly of others, so severe in his censure of it.

SIR WILL. Whatever I may have gained by folly, Madam, you see I am willing to prevent your losing by it.

MISS RICH. Your cares for me, Sir, are unnecessary. I always suspect those services which are denied where they are wanted, and offered, perhaps, in hopes of a refusal. No, Sir, my directions have been 40 given, and I insist upon their being complied with.

SIR WILL. Thou amiable woman. I can no longer contain the expressions of my gratitude: my pleasure. You see before you, one who has been equally careful of his interest: one, who has for some time been a concealed spectator of his follies, and only punished, in hopes to reclaim them—His uncle.

MISS RICH. Sir William Honeywood! You amaze me. How shall I conceal my confusion? I fear, Sir, you'll think I have been too forward in my services. I confess I ———

SIR WILL. Don't make any apologies, Madam. I only find myself unable to repay the obligation. And yet, I have been trying my interest of 10 late to serve you. Having learnt, Madam, that you had some demands upon government, I have, tho' unasked, been your solicitor there.

MISS RICH. Sir, I'm infinitely obliged to your intentions. But my guardian has employed another gentleman who assures him of success.

SIR WILL. Who, the important little man that visits here! Trust me, Madam, he's quite contemptible among men in power, and utterly unable to serve you. Mr. Lofty's promises are much better known to people of fashion, than his person, I assure you.

MISS RICH. How have we been deceived! As sure as can be, here he 20 comes.

SIR WILL. Does he! Remember I'm to continue unknown. My return to England has not as yet been made public. With what impudence he enters!

Enter LOFTY

LOFTY. Let the chariot—let my chariot drive off, I'll visit to his grace's in a chair. Miss Richland here before me! Punctual, as usual, to the calls of humanity. I'm very sorry, Madam, things of this kind should happen, especially to a man I have shewn every where, and carried amongst us as a particular acquaintance.   30

MISS RICH. I find, Sir, you have the art of making the misfortunes of others your own.

LOFTY. My dear Madam, what can a private man like me do? One man can't do every thing; and then, I do so much in this way every day: Let me see, something considerable might be done for him by subscription; it could not fail if I carried the list. I'll undertake to set down a brace of Dukes, two dozen Lords, and half the lower house, at my own peril.

SIR WILL. And after all, its more than probable, Sir, he might reject the offer of such powerful patronage.   40

LOFTY. Then, Madam, what can we do? You know I never make promises. In truth, I once or twice tried to do something with him in the way of business; but as I often told his uncle, Sir William Honeywood, the man was utterly impracticable.

SIR WILL. His uncle! then that gentleman, I suppose, is a particular friend of yours.

LOFTY. Meaning me, Sir?—Yes, Madam, as I often said, my dear Sir William, you are sensible I would do any thing as far as my poor interest goes, to serve your family; but what can be done; there's no procuring first rate places, for ninth rate abilities.

MISS RICH. I have heard of Sir William Honeywood; he's abroad in employment; he confided in your judgement, I suppose.

LOFTY. Why, yes, Madam; I believe Sir William had some reason to confide in my judgement; one little reason, perhaps.

MISS RICH. Pray, Sir, what was it?

LOFTY. Why, Madam—but let it go no further—it was I procured him his place.

SIR WILL. Did you, Sir?

LOFTY. Either you or I, Sir.

MISS RICH. This, Mr. Lofty, was very kind, indeed.

LOFTY. I did love him, to be sure; he had some amusing qualities; no man was fitter to be toastmaster to a club, or had a better head.

MISS RICH. A better head?

LOFTY. Ay, at a bottle; to be sure, he was as dull as a choice spirit; but hang it, he was grateful, very grateful; and gratitude hides a multitude of faults.

SIR WILL. He might have reason, perhaps. His place is pretty considerable, I'm told.

LOFTY. A trifle, a mere trifle, among us men of business; the truth is, he wanted dignity to fill up a greater.

SIR WILL. Dignity of person, do you mean, Sir? I'm told he's much about my size and figure, Sir.

LOFTY. Ay, tall enough for a marching regiment; but then he wanted a something—a consequence of form—a kind of a—I believe the Lady perceives my meaning.

MISS RICH. O perfectly; you courtiers can do any thing, I see.

LOFTY. My dear Madam, all this is but a mere exchange; we do greater things for one another every day. Why, as thus, now: let me suppose you the first lord of the treasury, you have an employment in you that I want; I have a place in me that you want; do me here, do you there: interest of both sides, few words, flat, done and done, and its over.

SIR WILL. A thought strikes me. (*Aside.*) Now you mention Sir William

Honeywood, Madam; and as he seems, Sir, an acquaintance of yours; you'll be glad to hear he's arrived from Italy; I had it from a friend who knows him as well as he does me, and you may depend on my information.

LOFTY. The devil he is! If I had known that, we should not have been quite so well acquainted. (*Aside*)

SIR WILL. He is certainly return'd; and as this gentleman is a friend of yours, he can be of signal service to us, by introducing me to him; there are some papers relative to your affairs, that require dispatch and his inspection.   10

MISS RICH. This gentleman, Mr. Lofty, is a person employed in my affairs: I know you'll serve us.

LOFTY. My dear Madam, I live but to serve you. Sir William shall even wait upon him, if you think proper to command it.

SIR WILL. That would be quite unnecessary.

LOFTY. Well, we must introduce you then. Call upon me—let me see— ay, in two days.

SIR WILL. Now, or the opportunity will be lost for ever.

LOFTY. Well, if it must be now, now let it be. But damn it, that's unfortunate; my lord Grig's curs'd Pensacola business comes on this very   20 hour, and I'm engaged to attend—another time—

SIR WILL. A short letter to Sir William will do.

LOFTY. You shall have it; yet, in my opinion, a letter is a very bad way of going to work; face to face, that's my way.

SIR WILL. The letter, Sir, will do quite as well.

LOFTY. Zounds, Sir, do you pretend to direct me? direct me in the business of office? do you know me, Sir? who am I?

MISS RICH. Dear Mr. Lofty, this request is not so much his as mine; if my commands—but you despise my power.

LOFTY. Delicate creature! your commands could even controle a debate   30 at midnight; to a power so constitutional, I am all obedience and tranquility. He shall have a letter; where is my secretary? Dubardieu! And yet, I protest I don't like this way of doing business. I think if I spoke first to Sir William—But you will have it so.

[*Exit with* MISS RICH.

SIR WILLIAM, *alone*

SIR WILL. Ha, ha, ha! This too is one of my nephew's hopeful associates. O vanity, thou constant deceiver, how do all thy efforts to exalt, serve but to sink us. Thy false colourings, like those employed to heighten beauty, only seem to mend that bloom which they contri-   40 bute to destroy. I'm not displeased at this interview; exposing this fellow's impudence to the contempt it deserves may be of use to my design; at least, if he can reflect, it will be of use to himself.

Enter JARVIS

SIR WILL. How now, Jarvis, where's your master, my nephew?

JARVIS. At his wits end, I believe; he's scarce gotten out of one scrape, but he's running his head into another.

SIR WILL. How so?

JARVIS. The house has but just been cleared of the bailiffs, and now he's again engaging tooth and nail in assisting old Croaker's son to patch up a clandestine match with the young lady that passes in the house 10 for his sister.

SIR WILL. Ever busy to serve others.

JARVIS. Ay, any body but himself. The young couple, it seems, are just setting out for Scotland, and he supplies them with money for the journey.

SIR WILL. Money! how is he able to supply others, who has scarce any for himself?

JARVIS. Why, there it is; he has no money, that's true; but then, as he never said no to any request in his life, he has given them a bill drawn by a friend of his upon a merchant in the city, which I am to 20 get chang'd; for you must know that I am to go with them to Scotland myself.

SIR WILL. How!

JARVIS. It seems the young gentleman is obliged to take a different road from his mistress, as he is to call upon an uncle of his that lives out of the way, in order to prepare a place for their reception, when they return; so they have borrowed me from my master, as the properest person to attend the young lady down.

SIR WILL. To the land of matrimony! A pleasant journey, Jarvis.

JARVIS. Ay, but I'm only to have all the fatigues on't. 30

SIR WILL. Well, it may be shorter, and less fatiguing, than you imagine. I know but too much of the young lady's family and connexions, whom I have seen abroad. I have also discover'd that Miss Richland is not indifferent to my thoughtless nephew; and will endeavour, tho' I fear in vain, to establish that connexion. But, come, the letter I wait for must be almost finish'd; I'll let you further into my intentions, in the next room.   [*Exeunt.*

END OF THE THIRD ACT

ACT IV

SCENE, CROAKER'S *House*

LOFTY

LOFTY. Well, sure the devil's in me of late, for running my head into such defiles, as nothing but a genius like my own could draw me from. I was formerly contented to husband out my places and pensions with some degree of frugality; but, curse it, of late I have given away the whole Court Register in less time than they could print the title page; yet, hang it, why scruple a lie or two to come at a fine girl, when I every day tell a thousand for nothing. Ha! Honeywood here before me. Could Miss Richland have set him at liberty? 10

Enter HONEYWOOD

Mr. Honeywood, I'm glad to see you abroad again. I find my concurrence was not necessary in your unfortunate affairs. I had put things in a train to do your business; but it is not for me to say what I intended doing.

HONEYW. It was unfortunate indeed, Sir. But what adds to my uneasiness is, that while you seem to be acquainted with my misfortune, I, myself, continue still a stranger to my benefactor.

LOFTY. How! not know the friend that served you? 20

HONEYW. Can't guess at the person.

LOFTY. Enquire.

HONEYW. I have, but all I can learn is, that he chuses to remain concealed, and that all enquiry must be fruitless.

LOFTY. Must be fruitless?

HONEYW. Absolutely fruitless.

LOFTY. Sure of that?

HONEYW. Very sure.

LOFTY. Then I'll be damn'd if you shall ever know it from me.

HONEYW. How, Sir!

LOFTY. I suppose now, Mr. Honeywood, you think my rent-roll very considerable, and that I have vast sums of money to throw away; I know you do. The world to be sure says such things of me.

HONEYW. The world, by what I learn, is no stranger to your generosity. But where does this tend?

LOFTY. To nothing; nothing in the world. The town, to be sure, when it makes such a thing as me the subject of conversation, has asserted, that I never yet patronized a man of merit.

HONEYW. I have heard instances to the contrary, even from yourself. 10

LOFTY. Yes, Honeywood, and there are instances to the contrary, that you shall never hear from myself.

HONEYW. Ha, dear Sir, permit me to ask you but one question.

LOFTY. Sir, ask me no questions: I say, Sir, ask me no questions; I'll be damn'd, if I answer them.

HONEYW. I will ask no further. My friend, my benefactor, it is, it must be here, that I am indebted for freedom, for honour. Yes, thou worthiest of men, from the beginning I suspected it, but was afraid to return thanks; which, if undeserved, might seem reproaches.

LOFTY. I protest I don't understand all this, Mr. Honeywood. You treat 20 me very cavalierly. I do assure you, Sir.—Blood, Sir, can't a man be permitted to enjoy the luxury of his own feelings without all this parade?

HONEYW. Nay, do not attempt to conceal an action that adds to your honour. Your looks, your air, your manner, all confess it.

LOFTY. Confess it! Sir. Torture itself, Sir, shall never bring me to confess it. Mr. Honeywood, I have admitted you upon terms of friendship. Don't let us fall out; make me happy, and let this be buried in oblivion. You know I hate ostentation; you know I do. Come, come, Honeywood, you know I always lov'd to be a friend, and not a 30 patron. I beg this may make no kind of distance between us. Come, come, you and I must be more familiar—Indeed we must.

HONEYW. Heavens! Can I ever repay such friendship! Is there any way! Thou best of men, can I ever return the obligation?

LOFTY. A bagatelle, a mere bagatelle. But I see your heart is labouring to be grateful. You shall be grateful. It would be cruel to disappoint you.

HONEYW. How! Teach me the manner. Is there any way?

LOFTY. From this moment you're mine. Yes, my friend, you shall know it—I'm in love.   40

HONEYW. And can I assist you?

LOFTY. Nobody so well.

HONEYW. In what manner? I'm all impatience.

LOFTY. You shall make love for me.

HONEYW. And to whom shall I speak in your favour?

LOFTY. To a lady with whom you have great interest, I assure you. Miss Richland.

HONEYW. Miss Richland!

LOFTY. Yes, Miss Richland. She has struck the blow up to the hilt, in my bosom, by Jupiter.

HONEYW. Heavens! was ever any thing more unfortunate! It is too much to be endur'd.   10

LOFTY. Unfortunate indeed! And yet I can endure it, till you have opened the affair to her for me. Between ourselves, I think she likes me. I'm not apt to boast, but I think she does.

HONEYW. Indeed! But do you know the person you apply to?

LOFTY. Yes, I know you are her friend and mine: that's enough. To you, therefore, I commit the success of my passion. I'll say no more, let friendship do the rest. I have only to add, that if at any time my little interest can be of service—but, hang it, I'll make no promises—you know my interest is your's at any time. No apologies, my friend, I'll not be answered, it shall be so.   [*Exit.* 20

HONEYW. Open, generous, unsuspecting man! He little thinks that I love her too; and with such an ardent passion!—But then it was ever but a vain and hopeless one; my torment, my persecution! What shall I do! Love, friendship, a hopeless passion, a deserving friend! Love, that has been my tormentor; a friend, that has, perhaps, distress'd himself, to serve me. It shall be so. Yes, I will discard the fondling hope from my bosom, and exert all my influence in his favour. And yet to see her in the possession of another!—Insupportable. But then to betray a generous, trusting friend!—Worse, worse. Yes, I'm resolv'd. Let me but be the instrument of their happiness,   30 and then quit a country, where I must for ever despair of finding my own.   [*Exit.*

Enter OLIVIA *and* GARNET, *who carries a Milliner's Box*

OLIVIA. Dear me, I wish this journey were over. No news of Jarvis yet? I believe the old peevish creature delays purely to vex me.

GARNET. Why, to be sure, Madam, I did hear him say, a little snubbing before marriage, would teach you to bear it the better afterwards.

OLIVIA. To be gone a full hour, tho' he had only to get a bill changed in the city! How provoking!

GARNET. I'll lay my life, Mr. Leontine, that had twice as much to do, is   40 setting off by this time from his inn; and here you are left behind.

OLIVIA. Well, let us be prepar'd for his coming, however. Are you sure you have omitted nothing, Garnet?

GARNET. Not a stick, madam—all's here. Yet I wish you could take the white and silver to be married in. It's the worst luck in the world, in any thing but white. I knew one Bett Stubbs, of our town, that was married in red; and, as sure as eggs is eggs, the bridegroom and she had a miff before morning.

OLIVIA. No matter. I'm all impatience till we are out of the house.

GARNET. Bless me, madam, I had almost forgot the wedding ring!— The sweet little thing—I don't think it would go on my little finger. 10 And what if I put in a gentleman's night cap, in case of necessity, madam? But here's Jarvis.

Enter JARVIS

OLIVIA. O, Jarvis, are you come at last? We have been ready this half hour. Now let's be going. Let us fly!

JARVIS. Aye, to Jericho; for we shall have no going to Scotland this bout, I fancy.

OLIVIA. How! What's the matter?

JARVIS. Money, money, is the matter, Madam. We have got no money. What the plague do you send me of your fool's errand for? My 20 master's bill upon the city is not worth a rush. Here it is, Mrs. Garnet may pin up her hair with it.

OLIVIA. Undone! How could Honeywood serve us so! What shall we do? Can't we go without it?

JARVIS. Go to Scotland without money! To Scotland without money! Lord how some people understand geography! We might as well set sail for Patagonia upon a cork jacket.

OLIVIA. Such a disappointment! What a base insincere man was your master, to serve us in this manner. Is this his good nature?

JARVIS. Nay, don't talk ill of my master, Madam. I won't bear to hear 30 any body talk ill of him but myself.

GARNET. Bless us! now I think on't, Madam, you need not be under any uneasiness, I saw Mr. Leontine receive forty guineas from his father just before he set out, and he can't yet have left the inn. A short letter will reach him there.

OLIVIA. Well remember'd, Garnet; I'll write immediately. How's this! Bless me, my hand trembles so I can't write a word. Do you write, Garnet; and, upon second thought it will be better from you.

GARNET. Truly, madam, I write and indite but poorly. I never was kute at my larning. But I'll do what I can to please you. Let me see. All out 40 of my own head, I suppose?

OLIVIA. Whatever you please.

GARNET (*Writing*) Muster Croaker—Twenty guineas, Madam?

OLIVIA. Ay, twenty will do.

GARNET. At the bar of the Talbot till call'd for. Expedition—will be
blown up—All of a flame—Quick, dispatch—Cupid, the little God
of Love—I conclude it, madam, with Cupid, I love to see a love letter
end like poetry.

OLIVIA. Well, well, what you please, any thing. But how shall we send
it? I can trust none of the servants of this family.

GARNET. Odso, Madam, Mr. Honeywood's butler is in the next room; 10
he's a dear, sweet man; he'll do any thing for me.

JARVIS. He! the dog, he'll certainly commit some blunder. He's drunk
and sober ten times a day.

OLIVIA. No matter. Fly, Garnet; any body we can trust will do. [*Exit
GARNET.*] Well, Jarvis, now we can have nothing more to interrupt
us. You may take up the things, and carry them on to the inn. Have
you no hands, Jarvis?

JARVIS. Soft and fair, young lady. You, that are going to be married,
think things can never be done too fast: but we that are old, and
know what we are about, must elope methodically, Madam.   20

OLIVIA. Well, sure, if my indiscretions were to be done over again——

JARVIS. My life for it you would do them ten times over.

OLIVIA. Why will you talk so? If you knew how unhappy they make
me—

JARVIS. Very unhappy, no doubt: I was once just as unhappy when I
was going to be married myself. I'll tell you a story about that——

OLIVIA. A story! when I'm all impatience to be away. Was there ever
such a dilatory creature!——

JARVIS. Well, Madam, if we must march, why we will march; that's all.
Tho', odds bobs we have still forgot one thing we should never 30
travel without—a case of good razors, and a box of shaving-powder.
But no matter, I believe we shall be pretty well shaved by the way.

[*Going*

Enter GARNET

GARNET. Undone, undone, Madam. Ah, Mr. Jarvis, you said right
enough. As sure as death Mr. Honeywood's rogue of a drunken
butler, drop'd the letter before he went ten yards from the door.
There's old Croaker has just pick'd it up, and is this moment reading
it to himself in the hall.

OLIVIA. Unfortunate! We shall be discover'd.   40

GARNET. No, Madam: don't be uneasy, he can make neither head nor

tail of it. To be sure he looks as if he was broke loose from Bedlam
about it, but he can't find what it means for all that. O Lud, he is
coming this way all in the horrors!

OLIVIA. Then let us leave the house this instant, for fear he should ask
farther questions. In the mean time, Garnet, do you write and send
off just such another.   [*Exeunt.*

Enter CROAKER

CROAKER. Death and destruction! Are all the horrors of air, fire and
water to be levelled only at me! Am I only to be singled out for gun-
powder-plots, combustibles and conflagration! Here it is—An incen-   10
diary letter drop'd at my door. *To Muster Croaker, these, with speed.*
Ay, ay, plain enough the direction: all in the genuine incendiary
spelling, and as cramp as the devil. *With speed.* O, confound your
speed. But let me read it once more. (*Reads*)
  *Mustar Croakar as sone as yoew see this leve twenty gunnes at the bar of
the Talboot tell caled for or yowe and yower experetion will be al blown up.*
Ah, but too plain. Blood and gunpowder in every line of it. Blown
up! murderous dog! All blown up! Heavens! what have I and my
poor family done, to be all blown up! (*reads*) *Our pockets are low, and
money we must have.* Ay, there's the reason: they'll blow us up, because   20
they have got low pockets. (*Reads*) *It is but a short time you have to consider; for if this takes wind, the house will quickly be all of a flame.* Inhuman
monsters! blow us up, and then burn us. The earthquake at Lisbon
was but a bonfire to it. (*Reads*) *Make quick dispatch, and so no more at
present. But may Cupid, the little God of Love, go with you wherever you go.*
The little God of Love! Cupid, the little God of Love go with me!
Go you to the devil, you and your little Cupid together; I'm so
frightned, I scarce know whether I sit, stand, or go. Perhaps this
moment I'm treading on lighted matches, blazing brimstone and
barrels of gunpowder. They are preparing to blow me up into the   30
clouds. Murder! We shall be all burnt in our beds; we shall be all
burnt in our beds.

Enter MISS RICHLAND

MISS RICH. Lord, Sir, what's the matter?

CROAKER. Murder's the matter. We shall be all blown up in our beds
before morning.

MISS RICH. I hope not, Sir.

CROAKER. What signifies what you hope, Madam, when I have a cer-
tificate of it here in my hand. Will nothing alarm my family! Sleeping
and eating, sleeping and eating is the only work from morning till   40

night in my house. My insensible crew could sleep, tho' rock'd by an earthquake; and fry beef steaks at a volcano.

MISS RICH. But, Sir, you have alarmed them so often already, we have nothing but earthquakes, famines, plagues and mad dogs from year's end to year's end. You remember, Sir, it is not above a month ago, you assur'd us of a conspiracy among the bakers, to poison us in our bread; and so kept the whole family a week upon potatoes.

CROAKER. And potatoes were too good for them. But why do I stand talking here with a girl, when I should be facing the enemy without? 10 Here, John, Nicodemus, search the house. Look into the cellars, to see if there be any combustibles below; and above in the apartments, that no matches be thrown in at the windows. Let all the fires be put out, and let the engine be drawn out in the yard, to play upon the house in case of necessity.   [*Exit.*

MISS RICHLAND *alone*

MISS RICH. What can he mean by all this? Yet, why should I enquire, when he alarms us in this manner almost every day! But Honeywood has desired an interview with me in private. What can he mean; or, rather, what means this palpitation at his approach! It is the first time 20 he ever shewed any thing in his conduct that seem'd particular. Sure he cannot mean to —— but he's here.

Enter HONEYWOOD

HONEYW. I presum'd to solicit this interview, Madam, before I left town, to be permitted—

MISS RICH. Indeed! Leaving town, Sir?——

HONEYW. Yes, Madam; perhaps the kingdom. I have presumed, I say, to desire the favour of this interview—in order to disclose something which our long friendship prompts. And yet my fears—

MISS RICH. His fears! What are his fears to mine! (*Aside.*) We have 30 indeed been long acquainted, Sir; very long. If I remember, our first meeting was at the French ambassador's.—Do you recollect how you were pleas'd to rally me upon my complexion there?

HONEYW. Perfectly, madam; I presum'd to reprove you for painting: but your warmer blushes soon convinc'd the company, that the colouring was all from nature.

MISS RICH. And yet you only meant it, in your good natur'd way, to make me pay a compliment to myself. In the same manner you danc'd that night with the most aukward woman in company, because you saw nobody else would take her out.   40

HONEYW. Yes; and was rewarded the next night, by dancing with the finest woman in company, whom every body wish'd to take out.

MISS RICH. Well, Sir, if you thought so then, I fear your judgment has since corrected the errors of a first impression. We generally shew to most advantage at first. Our sex are like poor tradesmen, that put all their best goods to be seen at the windows.

HONEYW. The first impression, Madam, did indeed deceive me. I expected to find a woman with all the faults of conscious flattered beauty. I expected to find her vain and insolent. But every day has since taught me that it is possible to possess sense without pride, and 10 beauty without affectation.

MISS RICH. This, Sir, is a style very unusual with Mr. Honeywood; and I should be glad to know why he thus attempts to encrease that vanity, which his own lessons taught me to despise.

HONEYW. I ask pardon, Madam. Yet, from our long friendship, I presumed I might have some right to offer, without offence, what you may refuse without offending.

MISS RICH. Sir! I beg you'd reflect; tho', I fear, I shall scarce have any power to refuse a request of yours; yet, you may be precipitate: consider, Sir.   20

HONEYW. I own my rashness; but, as I plead the cause of friendship, of one who loves—Don't be alarmed, Madam—Who loves you with the most ardent passion; whose whole happiness is placed in you—

MISS RICH. I fear, Sir, I shall never find whom you mean, by this description of him.

HONEYW. Ah, Madam, it but too plainly points him out; tho' he should be too humble himself to urge his pretensions, or you too modest to understand them.

MISS RICH. Well; it would be affectation any longer to pretend ignorance; and, I will own, Sir, I have long been prejudiced in his favour. 30 It was but natural to wish to make his heart mine, as he seem'd himself ignorant of its value.

HONEYW. I see she always lov'd him (aside). I find, Madam, you're already sensible of his worth, his passion. How happy is my friend, to be the favourite of one with such sense to distinguish merit, and such beauty to reward it.

MISS RICH. Your friend! Sir. What friend?

HONEYW. My best friend—My friend Mr. Lofty, Madam.

MISS RICH. He, Sir!

HONEYW. Yes, he Madam. He is, indeed, what your warmest wishes 40 might have form'd him. And to his other qualities, he adds that of the most passionate regard for you.

MISS RICH. Amazement!—No more of this, I beg you, Sir.

HONEYW. I see your confusion, Madam, and know how to interpret it.
  And since I so plainly read the language of your heart, shall I make
  my friend happy, by communicating your sentiments?

MISS RICH. By no means.

HONEYW. Excuse me; I must; I know you desire it.

MISS RICH. Mr. Honeywood, let me tell you, that you wrong my sentiments and yourself. When I first applied to your friendship, I expected advice and assistance; but now, Sir, I see that it is vain to
  expect happiness from him, who has been so bad an œconomist of 10
  his own; and that I must disclaim his friendship, who ceases to be a
  friend to himself.   [Exit.

HONEYW. How is this! she has confessed she lov'd him, and yet she
  seemed to part in displeasure. Can I have done any thing to reproach
  myself with? No; I believe not; yet, after all, these things should not
  be done by a third person; I should have spared her confusion. My
  friendship carried me a little too far.

Enter CROAKER, *with the Letter in his Hand, and* MRS. CROAKER

MRS. CROAKER. Ha, ha, ha! And so, my dear, it's your supreme wish
  that I should be quite wretched upon this occasion? Ha, ha.   20

CROAKER. (*Mimicking*) Ha, ha, ha! and so my dear it's your supreme
  pleasure to give me no better consolation?

MRS. CROAKER. Positively, my dear, what is this incendiary stuff and
  trumpery to me? Our house may travel thro' the air like the house
  of Loretto, for ought I care, if I'm to be miserable in it.

CROAKER. Would to Heaven it were converted into an house of correction for your benefit. Have we not every thing to alarm us? Perhaps,
  this very moment the tragedy is beginning.

MRS. CROAKER. Then let us reserve our distress till the rising of the
  curtain, or give them the money they want, and have done with 30
  them.

CROAKER. Give them my money!—And pray, what right have they to
  my money?

MRS. CROAKER. And pray, what right then have you to my good
  humour?

CROAKER. And so your good humour advises me to part with my
  money? Why then, to tell your good humour a piece of my mind,
  I'd sooner part with my wife. Here's Mr. Honeywood, see what he'll
  say to it. My dear Honeywood, look at this incendiary letter dropped
  at my door. It will freeze you with terror; and yet lovey here can 40
  read it—Can read it, and laugh.

MRS. CROAKER. Yes, and so will Mr. Honeywood.

CROAKER. If he does, I'll suffer to be hanged the next minute in the rogue's place, that's all.

MRS. CROAKER. Speak, Mr. Honeywood; is there any thing more foolish than my husband's fright upon this occasion?

HONEYW. It would not become me to decide, Madam; but doubtless, the greatness of his terrors now, will but invite them to renew their villainy another time.

MRS. CROAKER. I told you, he'd be of my opinion.

CROAKER. How, Sir! do you maintain that I should lie down under 10 such an injury, and shew, neither by my tears, or complaints, that I have something of the spirit of a man in me?

HONEYW. Pardon me, Sir. You ought to make the loudest complaints, if you desire redress. The surest way to have redress, is to be earnest in the pursuit of it.

CROAKER. Ay, whose opinion is he of now?

MRS. CROAKER. But don't you think that laughing off our fears is the best way?

HONEYW. What is the best, Madam, few can say; but I'll maintain it to be a very wise way. 20

CROAKER. But we're talking of the best. Surely the best way is to face the enemy in the field, and not wait till he plunders us in our very bed-chamber.

HONEYW. Why, Sir, as to the best, that—that's a very wise way too.

MRS. CROAKER. But can any thing be more absurd, than to double our distresses by our apprehensions, and put it in the power of every low fellow, that can scrawl ten words of wretched spelling, to torment us?

HONEYW. Without doubt, nothing more absurd.

CROAKER. How! would it not be more absurd to despise the rattle till 30 we are bit by the snake?

HONEYW. Without doubt, perfectly absurd.

CROAKER. Then you are of my opinion?

HONEYW. Entirely.

MRS. CROAKER. And you reject mine?

HONEYW. Heavens forbid, Madam. No, sure no reasoning can be more just than yours. We ought certainly to despise malice if we cannot oppose it, and not make the incendiary's pen as fatal to our repose as the highwayman's pistol.

MRS. CROAKER. O! then you think I'm quite right? 40

HONEYW. Perfectly right.

CROAKER. A plague of plagues, we can't be both right. I ought to be sorry, or I ought to be glad. My hat must be on my head, or my hat must be off.

MRS. CROAKER. Certainly, in two opposite opinions, if one be perfectly reasonable, the other can't be perfectly right.

HONEYW. And why may not both be right, Madam: Mr. Croaker in earnestly seeking redress, and you in waiting the event with good humour? Pray let me see the letter again. I have it. This letter requires twenty guineas to be left at the bar of the Talbot inn. If it be indeed an incendiary letter, what if you and I, Sir, go there; and, when the writer comes to be paid his expected booty, seize him?   10

CROAKER. My dear friend its the very thing; the very thing. While I walk by the door, you shall plant yourself in ambush near the bar; burst out upon the miscreant like a masqued battery; extort a confession at once, and so hang him up by surprise.

HONEYW. Yes; but I would not chuse to exercise too much severity. It is my maxim, Sir, that crimes generally punish themselves.

CROAKER. Well, but we may upbraid him a little, I suppose? (*Ironically*)

HONEYW. Ay, but not punish him too rigidly.

CROAKER. Well, well, leave that to my own benevolence.

HONEYW. Well, I do: but remember that universal benevolence is the   20
first law of nature.

[*Exeunt* HONEYWOOD *and* MRS. CROAKER.

CROAKER. Yes; and my universal benevolence will hang the dog, if he had as many necks as a hydra.

END OF THE FOURTH ACT

ACT V

Scene, *An Inn*

Enter OLIVIA, JARVIS

OLIVIA. Well, we have got safe to the inn, however. Now, if the post-chaise were ready—

JARVIS. The horses are just finishing their oats; and, as they are not going to be married, they chuse to take their own time.

OLIVIA. You are for ever giving wrong motives to my impatience.

JARVIS. Be as impatient as you will, the horses must take their own time; besides, you don't consider, we have got no answer from our 10 fellow traveller yet. If we hear nothing from Mr. Leontine, we have only one way left us.

OLIVIA. What way?

JARVIS. The way home again.

OLIVIA. Not so. I have made a resolution to go, and nothing shall induce me to break it.

JARVIS. Ay; resolutions are well kept when they jump with inclination. However, I'll go hasten things without. And I'll call too at the bar to see if any thing should be left for us there. Don't be in such a plaguy hurry, Madam, and we shall go the faster, I promise you. 20

[Exit JARVIS.

Enter LANDLADY

LANDLADY. What! Solomon; why don't you move? Pipes and tobacco for the Lamb there.—Will no body answer? To the Dolphin; quick. The Angel has been outrageous this half hour. Did your ladyship call, Madam?

OLIVIA. No, Madam.

LANDLADY. I find, as you're for Scotland, Madam—But, that's no business of mine; married, or not married, I ask no questions. To

be sure, we had a sweet little couple set off from this two days ago
for the same place. The Gentleman, for a Taylor, was, to be sure, as
fine a spoken taylor, as ever blew froth from a full pot. And the
young lady so bashful, it was near half an hour before we could get
her to finish a pint of rasberry between us.

OLIVIA. But this gentleman and I are not going to be married, I assure
you.

LANDLADY. May be not. That's no business of mine; for certain, Scotch
marriages seldom turn out. There was, of my own knowledge, Miss
Macfag, that married her father's footman.—Alack-a-day, she and her   10
husband soon parted, and now keep separate cellars in Hedge-Lane.

OLIVIA. A very pretty picture of what lies before me.   [*Aside*

Enter LEONTINE

LEONT. My dear Olivia, my anxiety till you were out of danger, was too
great to be resisted. I could not help coming to see you set out, tho'
it exposes us to a discovery.

OLIVIA. May every thing you do prove as fortunate. Indeed, Leontine,
we have been most cruelly disappointed. Mr. Honeywood's bill upon
the city has it seems been protested, and we have been utterly at a
loss how to proceed.   20

LEONT. How! An offer of his own too. Sure, he could not mean to
deceive us.

OLIVIA. Depend upon his sincerity; he only mistook the desire for the
power of serving us. But let us think no more of it. I believe the post-
chaise is ready by this.

LANDLADY. Not quite yet: and, begging your ladyship's pardon, I don't
think your ladyship quite ready for the post-chaise. The north road
is a cold place, Madam. I have a drop in the house of as pretty rasberry as ever was tipt over tongue. Just a thimble full to keep the
wind off your stomach. To be sure, the last couple we had here, they   30
said it was a perfect nosegay. Ecod, I sent them both away as good
natur'd—Up went the blinds, round went the wheels, and drive
away post-boy, was the word.

Enter CROAKER

CROAKER. Well, while my friend Honeywood is upon the post of danger
at the bar, it must be my business to have an eye about me here. I
think I know an incendiary's look; for, wherever the devil makes a
purchase, he never fails to set his mark. Ha! who have we here? My
son and daughter! What can they be doing here!

LANDLADY. I tell you, Madam, it will do you good; I think I know by   40

this time what's good for the north road. It's a raw night, Madam.—
Sir—

LEONT. Not a drop more, good Madam. I should now take it as a
greater favour, if you hasten the horses, for I am afraid to be seen
myself.

LANDLADY. That shall be done. Wha, Solomon! are you all dead there?
Wha, Solomon, I say.   [*Exit Bawling.*

OLIVIA. Well; I dread, lest an expedition begun in fear, should end in
repentance.—Every moment we stay increases our danger, and adds
to my apprehensions.   10

LEONT. There's no danger, trust me, my dear; there can be none: if
Honeywood has acted with honour, and kept my father, as he promised, in employment till we are out of danger, nothing can interrupt
our journey.

OLIVIA. I have no doubt of Mr. Honeywood's sincerity, and even his
desires to serve us. My fears are from your father's suspicions. A
mind so disposed to be alarmed without a cause, will be but too
ready when there's a reason.

LEONT. Why, let him, when we are out of his power. But, believe me,
Olivia, you have no great reason to dread his resentment. His repin-   20
ing temper, as it does no manner of injury to himself, so will it never
do harm to others. He only frets to keep himself employed, and
scolds for his private amusement.

OLIVIA. I don't know that; but, I'm sure, on some occasions, it makes
him look most shockingly.

CROAKER. (*Discovering himself*) How does he look now?—How does he
look now?

OLIVIA. Ah!

LEONT. Undone.

CROAKER. How do I look now? Sir, I am your very humble servant.   30
Madam, I am your's. What, you are going off, are you? Then, first,
if you please, take a word or two from me with you before you go.
Tell me first where you are going? and when you have told me that,
perhaps, I shall know as little as I did before.

LEONT. If that be so, our answer might but increase your displeasure,
without adding to your information.

CROAKER. I want no information from you, puppy: and you too, good
Madam, what answer have you got? Eh (*a cry without, stop him*). I
think I heard a noise. My friend, Honeywood, without—has he
seized the incendiary? Ah, no, for now I hear no more on't.   40

LEONT. Honeywood, without! Then, Sir, it was Mr. Honeywood that
directed you hither?

CROAKER. No, Sir, it was Mr. Honeywood conducted me hither.

LEONT. Is it possible?

CROAKER. Possible! Why, he's in the house now, Sir. More anxious about me, than my own son, Sir.

LEONT. Then, Sir, he's a villian.

CROAKER. How, sirrah! a villian, because he takes most care of your father? I'll not bear it. I tell you I'll not bear it. Honeywood is a friend to the family, and I'll have him treated as such.

LEONT. I shall study to repay his friendship as it deserves.

CROAKER. Ah, rogue, If you knew how earnestly he entered into my 10 griefs, and pointed out the means to detect them, you would love him as I do. (*A cry without, stop him*) Fire and fury! they have seized the incendiary: they have the villian, the incendiary in view. Stop him, stop an incendiary, a murderer; stop him.   [*Exit.*

OLIVIA. Oh, my terrors! What can this new tumult mean?

LEONT. Some new mark, I suppose, of Mr. Honeywood's sincerity. But we shall have satisfaction: he shall give me instant satisfaction.

OLIVIA. It must not be, my Leontine, if you value my esteem, or my happiness. Whatever be our fate, let us not add guilt to our misfortunes—Consider that our innocence will shortly be all we have left 20 us. You must forgive him.

LEONT. Forgive him! Has he not in every instance betrayed us? Forced me to borrow money from him, which appears a mere trick to delay us: promised to keep my father engaged till we were out of danger, and here brought him to the very scene of our escape?

OLIVIA. Don't be precipitate. We may yet be mistaken.

Enter POSTBOY, *dragging in* JARVIS:
HONEYWOOD *entering soon after*

POSTBOY. Ay, master, we have him fast enough. Here is the incendiary dog. I'm entitled to the reward; I'll take my oath I saw him ask for 30 the money at the bar, and then run for it.

HONEYW. Come, bring him along. Let us see him. Let him learn to blush for his crimes. (*Discovering his mistake*) Death! what's here! Jarvis, Leontine, Olivia! What can all this mean?

JARVIS. Why, I'll tell you what it means: that I was an old fool, and that you are my master—that's all.

HONEYW. Confusion!

LEONT. Yes, Sir, I find you have kept your word with me. After such baseness, I wonder how you can venture to see the man you have injured.   40

HONEYW. My dear Leontine, by my life, my honour—

LEONT. Peace, peace, for shame; and do not continue to aggravate
baseness by hypocrisy. I know you Sir, I know you.

HONEYW. Why, wont you hear me! By all that's just, I knew not—

LEONT. Hear you, Sir! to what purpose? I now see through all your
low arts; your ever complying with every opinion; your never
refusing any request; your friendship as common as a prostitute's
favours, and as fallacious; all these, Sir, have long been contemptible to the world, and are now perfectly so to me.

HONEYW. Ha! contemptible to the world! That reaches me. (*Aside*)

LEONT. All the seeming sincerity of your professions I now find were   10
only allurements to betray; and all your seeming regret for their
consequences, only calculated to cover the cowardice of your heart.
Draw, villain!

Enter CROAKER *out of Breath*

CROAKER. Where is the villain? Where is the incendiary? (*seizing the
post-boy*) Hold him fast, the dog; he has the gallows in his face. Come,
you dog, confess; confess all, and hang yourself.

POST-BOY. Zounds! Master, what do you throttle me for?

CROAKER. (*Beating him*) Dog, do you resist; do you resist?

POST-BOY. Zounds! Master, I'm not he; there's the man that we   20
thought was the rogue, and turns out to be one of the company.

CROAKER. How!

HONEYW. Mr. Croaker, we have all been under a strange mistake here;
I find there is nobody guilty; it was all an error; entirely an error of
our own.

CROAKER. And I say, Sir, that you're in an error; for there's guilt and
double guilt, a plot, a damn'd jesuitical pestilential plot, and I must
have proof of it.

HONEYW. Do but hear me.

CROAKER. What, you intend to bring 'em off, I suppose; I'll hear   30
nothing.

HONEYW. Madam, you seem at least calm enough to hear reason.

OLIVIA. Excuse me.

HONEYW. Good Jarvis, let me then explain it to you.

JARVIS. What signifies explanations, when the thing is done?

HONEYW. Will nobody hear me? Was there ever such a set, so blinded
by passion and prejudice! (*To the* POST-BOY) My good friend, I
believe you'll be surprized when I assure you——

POST-BOY. Sure me nothing—I'm sure of nothing but a good beating.

CROAKER. Come then, you, Madam, if you ever hope for any favour   40
or forgiveness, tell me sincerely all you know of this affair.

OLIVIA. Unhappily, Sir, I'm but too much the cause of your suspicions: you see before you, Sir, one that with false pretences has stept into your family to betray it: not your daughter—

CROAKER. Not my daughter!

OLIVIA. Not your daughter—but a mean deceiver—who—support me, I cannot—

HONEYW. Help, she's going, give her air.

CROAKER. Ay, ay; take the young woman to the air, I would not hurt a hair of her head, whose ever daughter she may be—not so bad as that neither.   [*Exeunt all but* CROAKER. 10

CROAKER. Yes, yes, all's out; I now see the whole affair: my son is either married, or going to be so, to this lady, whom he imposed upon me as his sister. Ay, certainly so; and yet I don't find it afflicts me so much as one might think. There's the advantage of fretting away our misfortunes beforehand, we never feel them when they come.

Enter MISS RICHLAND *and* SIR WILLIAM

SIR WILL. But how do you know, Madam, that my nephew intends setting off from this place?

MISS RICH. My maid assured me he was come to this inn, and my own knowledge of his intending to leave the kingdom, suggested the 20 rest. But what do I see, my guardian here before us! Who, my dear Sir, could have expected meeting you here; to what accident do we owe this pleasure?

CROAKER. To a fool, I believe.

MISS RICH. But to what purpose did you come?

CROAKER. To play the fool.

MISS RICH. But with whom?

CROAKER. With greater fools than myself.

MISS RICH. Explain.

CROAKER. Why, Mr. Honeywood brought me here, to do nothing now 30 I am here; and my son is going to be married to I don't know who that is here; so now you are as wise as I am.

MISS RICH. Married! to whom, Sir?

CROAKER. To Olivia; my daughter, as I took her to be; but who the devil she is, or whose daughter she is, I know no more than the man in the moon.

SIR WILL. Then, Sir, I can inform you; and, tho' a stranger, yet you shall find me a friend to your family: it will be enough at present, to assure you, that, both in point of birth and fortune, the young lady is at least your son's equal. Being left by her father, Sir James 40 Woodville—

CROAKER. Sir James Woodville! What, of the West?

SIR WILL. Being left by him, I say, to the care of a mercenary wretch, whose only aim was to secure her fortune to himself, she was sent into France, under pretence of education; and there every art was tried to fix her for life in a convent, contrary to her inclinations. Of this I was informed upon my arrival at Paris; and, as I had been once her father's friend, I did all in my power to frustrate her guardian's base intentions. I had even meditated to rescue her from his authority, when your son stept in with more pleasing violence, gave her liberty, and you a daughter.   10

CROAKER. But I intend to have a daughter of my own chusing, Sir. A young lady, Sir, whose fortune, by my interest with those that have interest, will be double what my son has a right to expect. Do you know Mr. Lofty, Sir?

SIR WILL. Yes, Sir; and know that you are deceived in him. But step this way, and I'll convince you.

[CROAKER *and* SIR WILLIAM *seem to confer*

Enter HONEYWOOD

HONEYW. Obstinate man, still to persist in his outrage! Insulted by him, despis'd by all, I now begin to grow contemptible, even to   20 myself. How have I sunk by too great an assiduity to please! How have I overtax'd all my abilities, lest the approbation of a single fool should escape me! But all is now over; I have survived my reputation, my fortune, my friendships, and nothing remains henceforward for me but solitude and repentance.

MISS RICH. Is it true, Mr. Honeywood, that you are setting off, without taking leave of your friends? The report is, that you are quitting England. Can it be?

HONEYW. Yes, Madam; and tho' I am so unhappy as to have fallen under your displeasure, yet, thank Heaven, I leave you to happiness; to one   30 who loves you, and deserves your love; to one who has power to procure you affluence, and generosity to improve your enjoyment of it.

MISS RICH. And are you sure, Sir, that the gentleman you mean is what you describe him?

HONEYW. I have the best assurances of it, his serving me. He does indeed deserve the highest happiness, and that is in your power to confer. As for me! weak and wavering as I have been, obliged by all, and incapable of serving any, what happiness can I find but in solitude? What hope but in being forgotten?

MISS RICH. A thousand! to live among friends that esteem you, whose   40 happiness it will be to be permitted to oblige you.

HONEYW. No, Madam; my resolution is fix'd. Inferiority among
strangers is easy; but among those that once were equals, insupportable. Nay, to shew you how far my resolution can go, I can
now speak with calmness of my former follies, my vanity, my dissipation, my weakness. I will even confess, that, among the number
of my other presumptions, I had the insolence to think of loving
you. Yes, Madam, while I was pleading the passion of another, my
heart was tortur'd with its own. But it is over, it was unworthy our
friendship, and let it be forgotten.

MISS RICH. You amaze me!   10

HONEYW. But you'll forgive it, I know you will; since the confession
should not have come from me even now, but to convince you of
the sincerity of my intention of—never mentioning it more. [Going

MISS RICH. Stay, Sir, one moment—Ha! he here—

Enter LOFTY

LOFTY. Is the coast clear? None but friends. I have followed you here
with a trifling piece of intelligence: but it goes no farther, things are
not yet ripe for a discovery. I have spirits working at a certain board;
Your affair at the treasury will be done in less than—a thousand years.
Mum!   20

MISS RICH. Sooner, Sir, I should hope.

LOFTY. Why, yes, I believe it may, if it falls into proper hands, that
know where to push and where to parry; that know how the land
lies—eh, Honeywood?

MISS RICH. It is fallen into yours.

LOFTY. Well, to keep you no longer in suspense, your thing is done. It
is done, I say—that's all. I have just had assurances from Lord Never-
out, that the claim has been examined, and found admissible. *Quietus*
is the word, Madam.

HONEYW. But how! his Lordship has been at Newmarket these ten 30
days.

LOFTY. Indeed! Then Sir Gilbert Goose must have been most damnably mistaken. I had it of him.

MISS RICH. He! why Sir Gilbert and his family have been in the country
this month.

LOFTY. This month! It must certainly be so—Sir Gilbert's Letter did
come to me from Newmarket, so that he must have met his Lordship
there; and so it came about. I have his letter about me, I'll read it to
you. (*Taking out a large bundle*) That's from Paoli of Corsica, that
from the Marquis of Squilachi.—Have you a mind to see a letter 40
from Count Poniatowski, now King of Poland—Honest Pon——
[*Searching.*

O, Sir, what are you here too? I'll tell you what, honest friend, if you have not absolutely delivered my letter to Sir William Honeywood, you may return it. The thing will do without him.

SIR WIL. Sir, I have delivered it, and must inform you, it was received with the most mortifying contempt.

CROAKER. Contempt! Mr. Lofty, what can that mean?

LOFTY. Let him go on, let him go on, I say. You'll find it come to something presently.

SIR WILL. Yes, Sir, I believe you'll be amazed, if, after waiting some time in the anti-chamber, after being surveyed with insolent curiosity 10 by the passing servants, I was at last assured, that Sir William Honeywood knew no such person, and I must certainly have been imposed upon.

LOFTY. Good; let me die, very good. Ha! ha! ha!

CROAKER. Now, for my life, I can't find out half the goodness of it.

LOFTY. You can't. Ha! ha!

CROAKER. No, for the soul of me; I think it was as confounded a bad answer, as ever was sent from one private gentleman to another.

LOFTY. And so you can't find out the force of the message? Why I was in the house at that very time. Ha! ha! It was I that sent that very 20 answer to my own letter. Ha! ha!

CROAKER. Indeed! How! why!

LOFTY. In one word, things between Sir William and me must be behind the curtain. A party has many eyes. He sides with Lord Buzzard, I side with Sir Gilbert Goose. So that unriddles the mystery.

CROAKER. And so it does indeed, and all my suspicions are over.

LOFTY. Your suspicions! What then you have been suspecting, you have been suspecting, have you? Mr. Croaker, you and I were friends, we are friends no longer. Never talk to me. It's over; I say, it's over. 30

CROAKER. As I hope for your favour, I did not mean to offend. It escaped me. Don't be discomposed.

LOFTY. Zounds, Sir, but I am discomposed, and will be discomposed. To be treated thus! Who am I! Was it for this I have been dreaded both by ins and outs! Have I been libelled in the Gazetteer, and praised in the St. James's; have I been chaired at Wildman's, and a speaker at Merchant Taylor's Hall; have I had my hand to addresses, and my head in the print-shops, and talk to me of suspects!

CROAKER. My dear Sir, be pacified. What can you have but asking pardon? 40

LOFTY. Sir, I will not be pacified—Suspects! Who am I! To be used thus, have I paid court to men in favour to serve my friends, the

Lords of the Treasury, Sir William Honeywood, and the rest of the gang, and talk to me of suspects! Who am I, I say, who am I!

SIR WILL. Since, Sir, you're so pressing for an answer, I'll tell you who you are. A gentleman, as well acquainted with politics, as with men in power: as well acquainted with persons of fashion, as with modesty; with Lords of the Treasury, as with truth; and with all, as you are with Sir William Honeywood. I am Sir William Honeywood.

[Discovering his ensigns of the Bath

CROAKER. Sir William Honeywood!

HONEYW. Astonishment! my uncle!   *[Aside* 10

LOFTY. So then my confounded genius has been all this time only leading me up to the garret, in order to fling me out of the window.

CROAKER. What, Mr. Importance, and are these your works? Suspect you! You who have been dreaded by the ins and outs: you who have had your hand to addresses, and your head stuck up in print-shops. If you were served right, you should have your head stuck up in the pillory.

LOFTY. Ay, stick it where you will, for, by the Lord, it cuts but a very poor figure where it sticks at present.

SIR WILL. Well, Mr. Croaker, I hope you now see how incapable this 20 gentleman is of serving you, and how little Miss Richland has to expect from his influence.

CROAKER. Ay, Sir, too well I see it, and I can't but say I had some boding of it these ten days. So I'm resolved, since my son has placed his affections on a lady of moderate fortune, to be satisfied with his choice, and not run the hazard of another Mr. Lofty, in helping him to a better.

SIR WILL. I approve your resolution, and here they come, to receive a confirmation of your pardon and consent.

Enter MRS. CROAKER, JARVIS, LEONTINE, OLIVIA   30

MRS. CROAKER. Where's my husband! Come, come, lovey, you must forgive them. Jarvis here has been to tell me the whole affair; and, I say, you must forgive them. Our own was a stolen match, you know, my dear; and we never had any reason to repent of it.

CROAKER. I wish we could both say so: however, this gentleman, Sir William Honeywood, has been beforehand with you, in obtaining their pardon. So, if the two poor fools have a mind to marry, I think, we can tack them together without crossing the Tweed for it.

[Joining their hands

LEONT. How blest, and unexpected! What, what can we say to such 40 goodness! But our future obedience shall be the best reply. And, as for this gentleman, to whom we owe——

SIR WILL. Excuse me, Sir, if I interrupt your thanks, as I have here an interest that calls me. (*Turning to* HONEYWOOD) Yes, Sir, you are surprised to see me; and I own that a desire of correcting your follies led me hither. I saw, with indignation, the errors of a mind that only sought applause from others; that easiness of disposition, which, tho' inclin'd to the right, had not courage to condemn the wrong. I saw with regret those splendid errors, that still took name from some neighbouring duty. Your charity, that was but injustice; your benevolence, that was but weakness; and your friendship but credulity. I saw, with regret, great talents and extensive learning, only employed to add sprightliness to error, and encrease your perplexities. I saw your mind with a thousand natural charms: but the greatness of its beauty served only to heighten my pity for its prostitution.

HONEY. Cease to upbraid me, Sir; I have for some time but too strongly felt the justice of your reproaches. But there is one way still left me. Yes, Sir, I have determined, this very hour, to quit for ever a place where I have made myself the voluntary slave of all; and to seek among strangers that fortitude which may give strength to the mind, and marshal all its dissipated virtues. Yet, ere I depart, permit me to solicit favour for this gentleman; who, notwithstanding what has happened, has laid me under the most signal obligations. Mr. Lofty—

LOFTY. Mr. Honeywood, I'm resolv'd upon a reformation, as well as you. I now begin to find, that the man who first invented the art of speaking truth was a much cunninger fellow than I thought him. And to prove that I design to speak truth for the future, I must now assure you, that you owe your late enlargement to another; as, upon my soul, I had no hand in the matter. So now, if any of the company has a mind for preferment, he may take my place. I'm determined to resign.   [*Exit.*

HONEYW. How have I been deceived!

SIR WILL. No, Sir, you have been obliged to a kinder, fairer friend for that favour. To Miss Richland. Would she complete our joy, and make the man she has honoured by her friendship happy in her love, I should then forget all, and be as blest as the welfare of my dearest kinsman can make me.

MISS RICH. After what is past, it would be but affectation to pretend to indifference. Yes, I will own an attachment, which, I find, was more than friendship. And if my intreaties cannot alter his resolution to quit the country; I will even try, if my hand has not power to detain him.   [*Giving her hand*

HONEYW. Heavens! how can I have deserved all this? How express my happiness, my gratitude! A moment, like this, over-pays an age of apprehension.

CROAKER. Well, now I see content in every face; but Heaven send we be all better this day three months.

SIR WILL. Henceforth, nephew, learn to respect yourself. He who seeks only for applause from without, has all his happiness in another's keeping.

HONEYW. Yes, Sir, I now too plainly perceive my errors. My vanity, in attempting to please all, by fearing to offend any. My meanness in approving folly, lest fools should disapprove. Henceforth, therefore, 10 it shall be my study to reserve my pity for real distress; my friendship for true merit, and my love for her, who first taught me what it is to be happy.

EPILOGUE *

SPOKEN BY

MRS. BULKLEY

As puffing quacks some caitiff wretch procure
To swear the pill, or drop, has wrought a cure;
Thus on the stage, our play-wrights still depend
For Epilogues and Prologues on some friend,
Who knows each art of coaxing up the town,
And make full many a bitter pill go down.
Conscious of this, our bard has gone about,   10
And teaz'd each rhyming friend to help him out.
An Epilogue, things can't go on without it;
It cou'd not fail, wou'd you but set about it.
Young man, cries one (a bard laid up in clover)
Alas, young man, my writing days are over;
Let boys play tricks, and kick the straw, not I;
Your brother Doctor there, perhaps, may try.
What I! dear Sir, the Doctor interposes
What, plant my thistle, Sir, among his roses!
No, no, I've other contests to maintain;   20
To-night I head our troops at Warwick-Lane.
Go, ask your manager—Who, me? your pardon;
Those things are not our sort at Covent-Garden.
Our author's friends, thus plac'd at happy distance,
Give him good words indeed, but no assistance.
As some unhappy wight, at some new play,
At the Pit door stands elbowing away,

---

* The Author, in expectation of an Epilogue from a Friend at Oxford, deferred writing one himself till the very last hour. What is here offered, owes all its success to the graceful manner of the Actress who spoke it.

While oft, with many a smile, and many a shrug,
He eyes the centre, where his friends sit snug,
His simpering friends, with pleasure in their eyes,
Sink as he sinks, and as he rises rise:
He nods, they nod; he cringes, they grimace;
But not a soul will budge to give him place.
Since then, unhelp'd, our bard must now conform
To 'bide the pelting of this pittiless storm,
Blame where you must, be candid where you can,
And be each critick, the Good-natur'd Man.   10

FINIS

She Stoops to Conquer:

O R,

The Mistakes of a Night.

A

C O M E D Y.

AS IT IS ACTED AT THE

THEATRE-ROYAL

IN

COVENT-GARDEN.

WRITTEN BY

Doctor GOLDSMITH.

LONDON:

Printed for F. NEWBERY, in St. Paul's Church-Yard.
MDCCLXXIII.

DRAMATIS PERSONAE

MEN

Mr. Honeywood,	Mr. Powell
Croaker,	Mr. Shuter
Lofty,	Mr. Woodward
Sir William Honeywood,	Mr. Clarke
Leontine,	Mr. Bensley
Jarvis,	Mr. Dunstall
Butler,	Mr. Cushing
Bailiff,	Mr. R. Smith
Dubardieu,	Mr. Holtom
Postboy,	Mr. Quick

WOMEN

Miss Richland,	Mrs. Bulkley
Olivia,	Mrs. Mattocks
Mrs. Croaker,	Mrs. Pitt
Garnet,	Mrs. Green
Landlady,	Mrs. White

Scene LONDON

TO SAMUEL JOHNSON, L.L.D.

Dear Sir,

By inscribing this slight performance to you, I do not mean so much to compliment you as myself. It may do me some honour to inform the public, that I have lived many years in intimacy with you. It may serve the interests of mankind also to inform them, that the greatest wit may be found in a character, without impairing the most unaffected piety.

I have, particularly, reason to thank you for your partiality to this performance. The undertaking a comedy, not merely sentimental, was 10 very dangerous; and Mr. Colman, who saw this piece in its various stages, always thought it so. However I ventured to trust it to the public; and though it was necessarily delayed till late in the season, I have every reason to be grateful.

> I am, Dear Sir,
> Your most sincere friend,
> And admirer,
> OLIVER GOLDSMITH.

PROLOGUE

BY DAVID GARRICK, ESQ.

Enter MR. WOODWARD,
Dressed in Black, and holding a Handkerchief to his Eyes

Excuse me, Sirs, I pray—I can't yet speak—
I'm crying now—and have been all the week!
'Tis not alone this mourning suit, *good masters;*
I've that within—*for which there are no plaisters!*
Pray wou'd you know the reason why I'm crying?
The Comic muse, long sick, is now a dying!   10
And if she goes, my tears will never stop;
For as a play'r, I can't squeeze out one drop:
I am undone, that's all—shall lose my bread—
I'd rather, but that's nothing—lose my head.
When the sweet maid is laid upon the bier,
Shuter and I shall be chief mourners here.
To her a mawkish drab of spurious breed,
Who deals in sentimentals will succeed!
Poor Ned and I are dead to all intents,
We can as soon speak Greek as sentiments!   20
Both nervous grown, to keep our spirits up,
We now and then take down a hearty cup.
What shall we do?—If Comedy forsake us!
They'll turn us out, and no one else will take us,
But why can't I be moral?—Let me try—
My heart thus pressing—fix'd my face and eye—
With a sententious look, that nothing means,
(Faces are blocks, in sentimental scenes)
Thus I begin—All is not gold that glitters,
Pleasure seems sweet, but proves a glass of bitters.   30

When ign'rance enters, folly is at hand;
Learning is better far than house and land:
Let not your virtue trip, who trips may stumble,
And virtue is not virtue, if she tumble.
   I give it up—morals won't do for me;
To make you laugh I must play tragedy.
One hope remains—hearing the maid was ill,
A doctor *comes this night to shew his skill.*
To cheer her heart, and give your muscles motion,
He in five draughts *prepar'd, presents a potion:*   10
A kind of magic charm—for be assur'd,
If you will swallow it, *the maid is cur'd:*
But desp'rate the Doctor, and her case is,
If you reject the dose, and make wry faces!
This truth he boasts, will boast it while he lives,
No pois'nous drugs *are mix'd in what he gives;*
Should he succeed, you'll give him his degree;
If not, within he will receive no fee!
The college you, *must his pretensions back,*
Pronounce him regular, *or dub him* quack.   20

SHE STOOPS TO CONQUER:
OR,
THE MISTAKES OF A NIGHT

ACT I

SCENE, *A Chamber in an old fashioned House*

Enter MRS. HARDCASTLE *and* MR. HARDCASTLE

MRS. HARDCASTLE. I vow, Mr. Hardcastle, you're very particular. Is there
a creature in the whole country, but ourselves, that does not take a
trip to town now and then, to rub off the rust a little? There's the
two Miss Hoggs, and our neighbour, Mrs. Grigsby, go to take a 10
month's polishing every winter.

HARDCASTLE. Ay, and bring back vanity and affectation to last them
the whole year. I wonder why London cannot keep its own fools at
home. In my time, the follies of the town crept slowly among us,
but now they travel faster than a stage-coach. Its fopperies come
down, not only as inside passengers, but in the very basket.

MRS. HARDCASTLE. Ay, *your* times were fine times, indeed; you have
been telling us of *them* for many a long year. Here we live in an old
rumbling mansion, that looks for all the world like an inn, but that
we never see company. Our best visitors are old Mrs. Oddfish, the 20
curate's wife, and little Cripplegate, the lame dancing-master: And
all our entertainment your old stories of Prince Eugene and the
Duke of Marlborough. I hate such old-fashioned trumpery.

HARDCASTLE. And I love it. I love every thing that's old: old friends,
old times, old manners, old books, old wine; and, I believe, Dorothy,
(*taking her hand*) you'll own I have been pretty fond of an old wife.

MRS. HARDCASTLE. Lord, Mr. Hardcastle, you're for ever at your
Dorothy's and your old wife's. You may be a Darby, but I'll be no

69

Joan, I promise you. I'm not so old as you'd make me, by more than one good year. Add twenty to twenty, and make money of that.

HARDCASTLE. Let me see; twenty added to twenty, makes just fifty and seven.

MRS. HARDCASTLE. It's false, Mr. Hardcastle: I was but twenty when I was brought to bed of Tony, that I had by Mr. Lumpkin, my first husband; and he's not come to years of discretion yet.

HARDCASTLE. Nor ever will, I dare answer for him. Ay, you have taught *him* finely.

MRS. HARDCASTLE. No matter, Tony Lumpkin has a good fortune. My son is not to live by his learning. I don't think a boy wants much learning to spend fifteen hundred a year.

HARDCASTLE. Learning, quotha! A mere composition of tricks and mischief.

MRS. HARDCASTLE. Humour, my dear: nothing but humour. Come, Mr. Hardcastle, you must allow the boy a little humour.

HARDCASTLE. I'd sooner allow him an horse-pond. If burning the footmen's shoes, frighting the maids, and worrying the kittens, be humour, he has it. It was but yesterday he fastened my wig to the back of my chair, and when I went to make a bow, I popt my bald head in Mrs. Frizzle's face.

MRS. HARDCASTLE. And am I to blame? The poor boy was always too sickly to do any good. A school would be his death. When he comes to be a little stronger, who knows what a year or two's Latin may do for him?

HARDCASTLE. Latin for him! A cat and fiddle. No, no, the ale-house and the stable are the only schools he'll ever go to.

MRS. HARDCASTLE. Well, we must not snub the poor boy now, for I believe we shan't have him long among us. Any body that looks in his face may see he's consumptive.

HARDCASTLE. Ay, if growing too fat be one of the symptoms.

MRS. HARDCASTLE. He coughs sometimes.

HARDCASTLE. Yes, when his liquor goes the wrong way.

MRS. HARDCASTLE. I'm actually afraid of his lungs.

HARDCASTLE. And truly so am I; for he sometimes whoops like a speaking trumpet—(TONY *hallooing behind the Scenes*)—O there he goes—A very consumptive figure, truly.

Enter TONY, *crossing the Stage*

MRS. HARDCASTLE. Tony, where are you going, my charmer? Won't you give papa and I a little of your company, lovee?

TONY. I'm in haste, mother, I cannot stay.

MRS. HARDCASTLE. You shan't venture out this raw evening, my dear:
You look most shockingly.

TONY. I can't stay, I tell you. The Three Pigeons expects me down
every moment. There's some fun going forward.

HARDCASTLE. Ay; the ale-house, the old place: I thought so.

MRS. HARDCASTLE. A low, paltry set of fellows.

TONY. Not so low neither. There's Dick Muggins the exciseman, Jack
Slang the horse doctor, Little Aminadab that grinds the music box,
and Tom Twist that spins the pewter platter.

MRS. HARDCASTLE. Pray, my dear, disappoint them for one night at least. 10

TONY. As for disappointing *them*, I should not so much mind; but I
can't abide to disappoint *myself*.

MRS. HARDCASTLE. (*Detaining him*) You shan't go.

TONY. I will, I tell you.

MRS. HARDCASTLE. I say you shan't.

TONY. We'll see which is strongest, you or I.   [*Exit, bawling her out.*

HARDCASTLE. *Solus*

HARDCASTLE. Ay, there goes a pair that only spoil each other. But is
not the whole age in a combination to drive sense and discretion
out of doors? There's my pretty darling Kate; the fashions of the 20
times have almost infected her too. By living a year or two in town,
she is as fond of gauze, and French frippery, as the best of them.

Enter MISS HARDCASTLE

HARDCASTLE. Blessings on my pretty innocence! Drest out as usual
my Kate. Goodness! What a quantity of superfluous silk hast thou
got about thee, girl! I could never teach the fools of this age, that the
indigent world could be cloathed out of the trimmings of the vain.

MISS HARDCASTLE. You know our agreement, Sir. You allow me the
morning to receive and pay visits, and to dress in my own manner;
and in the evening, I put on my housewife's dress to please you.   30

HARDCASTLE. Well, remember I insist on the terms of our agreement;
and, by the bye, I believe I shall have occasion to try your obedience
this very evening.

MISS HARDCASTLE. I protest, Sir, I don't comprehend your meaning.

HARDCASTLE. Then, to be plain with you, Kate, I expect the young
gentleman I have chosen to be your husband from town this very
day. I have his father's letter, in which he informs me his son is set
out, and that he intends to follow himself shortly after.

MISS HARDCASTLE. Indeed! I wish I had known something of this
before. Bless me, how shall I behave? It's a thousand to one I shan't 40

like him; our meeting will be so formal, and so like a thing of business, that I shall find no room for friendship or esteem.

HARDCASTLE. Depend upon it, child, I'll never controul your choice;
but Mr. Marlow, whom I have pitched upon, is the son of my old
friend, Sir Charles Marlow, of whom you have heard me talk so
often. The young gentleman has been bred a scholar, and is designed
for an employment in the service of his country. I am told he's a
man of an excellent understanding.

MISS HARDCASTLE. Is he?

HARDCASTLE. Very generous.   10

MISS HARDCASTLE. I believe I shall like him.

HARDCASTLE. Young and brave.

MISS HARDCASTLE. I'm sure I shall like him.

HARDCASTLE. And very handsome.

MISS HARDCASTLE. My dear Papa, say no more (*kissing his hand*) he's
mine, I'll have him.

HARDCASTLE. And to crown all, Kate, he's one of the most bashful and
reserved young fellows in all the world.

MISS HARDCASTLE. Eh! you have frozen me to death again. That word
reserved, has undone all the rest of his accomplishments. A reserved   20
lover, it is said, always makes a suspicious husband.

HARDCASTLE. On the contrary, modesty seldom resides in a breast that
is not enriched with nobler virtues. It was the very feature in his
character that first struck me.

MISS HARDCASTLE. He must have more striking features to catch me, I
promise you. However, if he be so young, so handsome, and so
every thing, as you mention, I believe he'll do still. I think I'll have
him.

HARDCASTLE. Ay, Kate, but there is still an obstacle. Its more than an
even wager, he may not have *you*.   30

MISS HARDCASTLE. My dear Papa, why will you mortify one so?—Well,
if he refuses, instead of breaking my heart at his indifference, I'll
only break my glass for its flattery. Set my cap to some newer fashion,
and look out for some less difficult admirer.

HARDCASTLE. Bravely resolved! In the mean time I'll go prepare the
servants for his reception; as we seldom see company they want as
much training as a company of recruits, the first day's muster. [*Exit.*

MISS HARDCASTLE, *Sola*

MISS HARDCASTLE. Lud, this news of Papa's, puts me all in a flutter.
Young, handsome; these he put last; but I put them foremost.   40
Sensible, good-natured; I like all that. But then reserved, and

sheepish, that's much against him. Yet can't he be cured of his timidity, by being taught to be proud of his wife? Yes, and can't I—But I vow I'm disposing of the husband, before I have secured the lover.

Enter MISS NEVILLE

MISS HARDCASTLE. I'm glad you're come, Neville, my dear. Tell me, Constance, how do I look this evening? Is there any thing whimsical about me? Is it one of my well looking days, child? Am I in face to day?

MISS NEVILLE. Perfectly, my dear. Yet now I look again—bless me!— 10 sure no accident has happened among the canary birds or the gold fishes. Has your brother or the cat been meddling? Or has the last novel been too moving?

MISS HARDCASTLE. No; nothing of all this. I have been threatened—I can scarce get it out—I have been threatened with a lover.

MISS NEVILLE. And his name——

MISS HARDCASTLE. Is Marlow.

MISS NEVILLE. Indeed!

MISS HARDCASTLE. The son of Sir Charles Marlow.

MISS NEVILLE. As I live, the most intimate friend of Mr. Hastings, *my* 20 admirer. They are never asunder. I believe you must have seen him when we lived in town.

MISS HARDCASTLE. Never.

MISS NEVILLE. He's a very singular character, I assure you. Among women of reputation and virtue, he is the modestest man alive; but his acquaintance give him a very different character among creatures of another stamp: you understand me.

MISS HARDCASTLE. An odd character, indeed. I shall never be able to manage him. What shall I do? Pshaw, think no more of him, but trust to occurrences for success. But how goes on your own affair 30 my dear, has my mother been courting you for my brother Tony, as usual?

MISS NEVILLE. I have just come from one of our agreeable tête-à-têtes. She has been saying a hundred tender things, and setting off her pretty monster as the very pink of perfection.

MISS HARDCASTLE. And her partiality is such, that she actually thinks him so. A fortune like your's is no small temptation. Besides, as she has the sole management of it, I'm not surprized to see her unwilling to let it go out of the family.

MISS NEVILLE. A fortune like mine, which chiefly consists in jewels, is 40 no such mighty temptation. But at any rate if my dear Hastings be

but constant, I make no doubt to be too hard for her at last. However, I let her suppose that I am in love with her son, and she never
once dreams that my affections are fixed upon another.

MISS HARDCASTLE. My good brother holds out stoutly. I could almost
love him for hating you so.

MISS NEVILLE. It is a good natured creature at bottom, and I'm sure
would wish to see me married to any body but himself. But my
aunt's bell rings for our afternoon's walk round the improvements.
Allons. Courage is necessary as our affairs are critical.

MISS HARDCASTLE. Would it were bed time and all were well. [*Exeunt.* 10

SCENE, *An Alehouse Room. Several shabby fellows, with Punch and Tobacco.*
TONY *at the head of the Table, a little higher than the rest: A mallet in his hand.*

OMNES. Hurrea, hurrea, hurrea, bravo.

FIRST FELLOW. Now, gentlemen, silence for a song. The 'Squire is
going to knock himself down for a song.

OMNES. Ay, a song, a song.

TONY. Then I'll sing you, gentlemen, a song I made upon this ale-house,
the Three Pigeons.

SONG

> *Let school-masters puzzle their brain,* 　　　　　　　　　20
> 　　*With grammar, and nonsense, and learning;*
> *Good liquor, I stoutly maintain,*
> 　　*Gives* genus *a better discerning.*
> *Let them brag of their Heathenish Gods,*
> 　　*Their Lethes, their Styxes, and Stygians;*
> *Their Quis, and their Quæs, and their Quods,*
> 　　*They're all but a parcel of Pigeons.*
> 　　　　*Toroddle, toroddle, toroll.*
>
> *When Methodist preachers came down,*
> 　　*A preaching that drinking is sinful,* 　　　　　　　　30
> *I'll wager the rascals a crown,*
> 　　*They always preach best with a skinful.*
> *But when you come down with your pence,*
> 　　*For a slice of their scurvy religion,*
> *I'll leave it to all men of sense,*
> 　　*But you my good friend are the pigeon.*
> 　　　　*Toroddle, toroddle, toroll.*
>
> *Then come, put the jorum about,*
> 　　*And let us be merry and clever,*

Our hearts and our liquors are stout,
  Here's the Three Jolly Pigeons for ever.
Let some cry up woodcock or hare,
  Your bustards, your ducks, and your widgeons;
But of all the birds in the air,
  Here's a health to the Three Jolly Pigeons.
      Toroddle, toroddle, toroll.

OMNES. Bravo, bravo.

FIRST FELLOW. The 'Squire has got spunk in him.

SECOND FELLOW. I love to hear him sing, bekeays he never gives us   10
nothing that's *low*.

THIRD FELLOW. O damn any thing that's *low*, I cannot bear it.

FOURTH FELLOW. The genteel thing is the genteel thing at any time. If
so be that a gentleman bees in a concatenation accordingly.

THIRD FELLOW. I like the maxum of it, Master Muggins. What, tho' I
am obliged to dance a bear, a man may be a gentleman for all that.
May this be my poison if my bear ever dances but to the very genteel-
est of tunes. Water Parted, or the minuet in Ariadne.

SECOND FELLOW. What a pity it is the 'Squire is not come to his own. It
would be well for all the publicans within ten miles round of him.   20

TONY. Ecod and so it would Master Slang. I'd then shew what it was
to keep choice of company.

SECOND FELLOW. O he takes after his own father for that. To be sure
old 'Squire Lumpkin was the finest gentleman I ever set my eyes on.
For winding the streight horn, or beating a thicket for a hare, or a
wench, he never had his fellow. It was a saying in the place, that he
kept the best horses, dogs and girls in the whole county.

TONY. Ecod, and when I'm of age I'll be no bastard I promise you. I
have been thinking of Bett Bouncer and the miller's grey mare to
begin with. But come, my boys, drink about and be merry, for you   30
pay no reckoning. Well Stingo, what's the matter?

Enter LANDLORD

LANDLORD. There be two gentlemen in a post-chaise at the door. They
have lost their way upo' the forest; and they are talking something
about Mr. Hardcastle.

TONY. As sure as can be one of them must be the gentleman that's coming down to court my sister. Do they seem to be Londoners?

LANDLORD. I believe they may. They look woundily like Frenchmen.

TONY. Then desire them to step this way, and I'll set them right in a
twinkling. (*Exit* LANDLORD.) Gentlemen, as they mayn't be good   40

enough company for you, step down for a moment, and I'll be with
you in the squeezing of a lemon.   [*Exeunt Mob.*

TONY *solus*

TONY. Father-in-law has been calling me whelp, and hound, this half
year. Now if I pleased, I could be so revenged upon the old grumbletonian. But then I'm afraid—afraid of what! I shall soon be worth
fifteen hundred a year, and let him frighten me out of *that* if he can.

Enter LANDLORD, *conducting* MARLOW *and* HASTINGS

MARLOW. What a tedious uncomfortable day have we had of it! We
were told it was but forty miles across the country, and we have 10
come above threescore.

HASTINGS. And all Marlow, from that unaccountable reserve of yours,
that would not let us enquire more frequently on the way.

MARLOW. I own, Hastings, I am unwilling to lay myself under an obligation to every one I meet; and often, stand the chance of an un-
mannerly answer.

HASTINGS. At present, however, we are not likely to receive any answer.

TONY. No offence, gentlemen. But I'm told you have been enquiring
for one Mr. Hardcastle, in these parts. Do you know what part of
of the country you are in?   20

HASTINGS. Not in the least Sir, but should thank you for information.

TONY. Nor the way you came?

HASTINGS. No, Sir; but if you can inform us——

TONY. Why, gentlemen, if you know neither the road you are going,
nor where you are, nor the road you came, the first thing I have to
inform you is, that—You have lost your way.

MARLOW. We wanted no ghost to tell us that.

TONY. Pray, gentlemen, may I be so bold as to ask the place from
whence you came?

MARLOW. That's not necessary towards directing us where we are to 30
go.

TONY. No offence; but question for question is all fair, you know.
Pray, gentlemen, is not this same Hardcastle a cross-grain'd, old-
fashion'd, whimsical fellow, with an ugly face; a daughter, and a
pretty son?

HASTINGS. We have not seen the gentleman, but he has the family you
mention.

TONY. The daughter, a tall trapesing, trolloping, talkative maypole—
The son, a pretty, well-bred, agreeable youth, that every body is
fond of.   40

MARLOW. Our information differs in this. The daughter is said to be
well-bred and beautiful; the son, an aukward booby, reared up, and
spoiled at his mother's apron-string.

TONY. He-he-hem—Then, gentlemen, all I have to tell you is, that you
won't reach Mr. Hardcastle's house this night, I believe.

HASTINGS. Unfortunate!

TONY. It's a damn'd long, dark, boggy, dirty, dangerous way. Stingo,
tell the gentlemen the way to Mr. Hardcastle's; (*winking upon the*
LANDLORD) Mr. Hardcastle's, of Quagmire Marsh, you understand
me.   10

LANDLORD. Master Hardcastle's! Lock-a-daisy, my masters, you're
come a deadly deal wrong! When you came to the bottom of the
hill, you should have cross'd down Squash-lane.

MARLOW. Cross down Squash-lane!

LANDLORD. Then you were to keep streight forward, 'till you came to
four roads.

MARLOW. Come to where four roads meet!

TONY. Ay; but you must be sure to take only one of them.

MARLOW. O Sir, you're facetious.

TONY. Then keeping to the right, you are to go side-ways till you come 20
upon Crack-skull common: there you must look sharp for the track
of the wheel, and go forward, 'till you come to farmer Murrain's
barn. Coming to the farmer's barn, you are to turn to the right, and
then to the left, and then to the right about again, till you find out
the old mill——

MARLOW. Zounds, man! we could as soon find out the longitude!

HASTINGS. What's to be done, Marlow?

MARLOW. This house promises but a poor reception; though perhaps
the Landlord can accommodate us.

LANDLORD. Alack, master, we have but one spare bed in the whole   30
house.

TONY. And to my knowledge, that's taken up by three lodgers already.
(*after a pause, in which the rest seem disconcerted*) I have hit it. Don't you
think, Stingo, our landlady could accommodate the gentlemen by
the fire-side, with—three chairs and a bolster?

HASTINGS. I hate sleeping by the fire-side.

MARLOW. And I detest your three chairs and a bolster.

TONY. You do, do you?—then let me see—what if you go on a mile
further, to the Buck's Head; the old Buck's Head on the hill, one
of the best inns in the whole county?   40

HASTINGS. O ho! so we have escaped an adventure for this night, however.

LANDLORD. (*Apart to* TONY) Sure, you ben't sending them to your father's as an inn, be you?

TONY. Mum, you fool you. Let *them* find that out. (*to them*) You have only to keep on streight forward, till you come to a large old house by the road side. You'll see a pair of large horns over the door. That's the sign. Drive up the yard, and call stoutly about you.

HASTINGS. Sir, we are obliged to you. The servants can't miss the way?

TONY. No, no: But I tell you though, the landlord is rich, and going to leave off business; so he wants to be thought a Gentleman, saving your presence, he! he! he! He'll be for giving you his company, and 10 ecod if you mind him, he'll persuade you that his mother was an alderman, and his aunt a justice of peace.

LANDLORD. A troublesome old blade to be sure; but a keeps as good wines and beds as any in the whole country.

MARLOW. Well, if he supplies us with these, we shall want no further connexion. We are to turn to the right, did you say?

TONY. No, no; streight forward. I'll just step myself, and shew you a piece of the way. (*to the* LANDLORD) Mum.

LANDLORD. Ah, bless your heart, for a sweet, pleasant——damn'd mischievous son of a whore. [*Exeunt.* 20

END OF THE FIRST ACT

ACT II

Scene, *An old-fashioned House*

Enter HARDCASTLE, *followed by three or four aukward* SERVANTS

HARDCASTLE. Well, I hope you're perfect in the table exercise I have been teaching you these three days. You all know your posts and your places, and can shew that you have been used to good company, without ever stirring from home.

OMNES. Ay, ay.

HARDCASTLE. When company comes, you are not to pop out and stare, and then run in again, like frighted rabbits in a warren.   10

OMNES. No, no.

HARDCASTLE. You, Diggory, whom I have taken from the barn, are to make a shew at the side-table; and you, Roger, whom I have advanced from the plough, are to place yourself behind *my* chair. But you're not to stand so, with your hands in your pockets. Take your hands from your pockets, Roger; and from your head, you blockhead you. See how Diggory carries his hands. They're a little too stiff, indeed, but that's no great matter.

DIGGORY. Ay, mind how I hold them. I learned to hold my hands this way, when I was upon drill for the militia. And so being upon   20 drill——

HARDCASTLE. You must not be so talkative, Diggory. You must be all attention to the guests. You must hear us talk, and not think of talking; you must see us drink, and not think of drinking; you must see us eat, and not think of eating.

DIGGORY. By the laws, your worship, that's parfectly unpossible. Whenever Diggory sees yeating going forward, ecod he's always wishing for a mouthful himself.

HARDCASTLE. Blockhead! Is not a belly-full in the kitchen as good as a belly-full in the parlour? Stay your stomach with that reflection.   30

DIGGORY. Ecod I thank your worship, I'll make a shift to stay my
stomach with a slice of cold beef in the pantry.

HARDCASTLE. Diggory, you are too talkative. Then if I happen to say a
good thing, or tell a good story at table, you must not all burst out
a-laughing, as if you made part of the company.

DIGGORY. Then ecod your worship must not tell the story of Ould
Grouse in the gun-room: I can't help laughing at that—he! he! he!
—for the soul of me. We have laughed at that these twenty years—
ha! ha! ha!

HARDCASTLE. Ha! ha! ha! The story is a good one. Well, honest 10
Diggory, you may laugh at that—but still remember to be attentive.
Suppose one of the company should call for a glass of wine, how
will you behave? A glass of wine, Sir, if you please (*to* DIGGORY)—
Eh, why don't you move?

DIGGORY. Ecod, your worship, I never have courage till I see the eatables and drinkables brought upo' the table, and then I'm as bauld
as a lion.

HARDCASTLE. What, will no body move?

FIRST SERVANT. I'm not to leave this pleace.

SECOND SERVANT. I'm sure it's no pleace of mine.   20

THIRD SERVANT. Nor mine, for sartain.

DIGGORY. Wauns, and I'm sure it canna be mine.

HARDCASTLE. You numbskulls! and so while, like your betters, you are
quarrelling for places, the guests must be starved. O you dunces! I
find I must begin all over again.——But don't I hear a coach drive
into the yard? To your posts, you blockheads. I'll go in the mean
time and give my old friend's son a hearty reception at the gate.

[*Exit* HARDCASTLE.

DIGGORY. By the elevens, my pleace is gone quite out of my head.

ROGER. I know that my pleace is to be every where.   30

FIRST SERVANT. Where the devil is mine?

SECOND SERVANT. My pleace is to be no where at all; and so Ize go
about my business.

[*Exeunt* SERVANTS, *running about as if frighted, different ways.*

Enter SERVANT *with Candles, shewing in* MARLOW *and* HASTINGS

SERVANT. Welcome, gentlemen, very welcome. This way.

HASTINGS. After the disappointments of the day, welcome once more,
Charles, to the comforts of a clean room and a good fire. Upon my
word, a very well-looking house; antique, but creditable.

MARLOW. The usual fate of a large mansion. Having first ruined the 40 master by good housekeeping, it at last comes to levy contributions as an inn.

HASTINGS. As you say, we passengers are to be taxed to pay all these fineries. I have often seen a good sideboard, or a marble chimney-piece, tho' not actually put in the bill, enflame a reckoning confoundedly.

MARLOW. Travellers, George, must pay in all places. The only difference is, that in good inns, you pay dearly for luxuries; in bad ones, you are fleeced and starved.

HASTINGS. You have lived pretty much among them. In truth, I have been often surprized, that you who have seen so much of the world, with your natural good sense, and your many opportunities, could never yet acquire a requisite share of assurance.

MARLOW. The Englishman's malady. But tell me, George, where could I have learned that assurance you talk of? My life has been chiefly spent in a college, or an inn, in seclusion from that lovely part of the creation that chiefly teach men confidence. I don't know that I was ever familiarly acquainted with a single modest woman—except my mother—But among females of another class you know—

HASTINGS. Ay, among them you are impudent enough of all conscience.

MARLOW. They are of *us* you know.

HASTINGS. But in the company of women of reputation I never saw such an ideot, such a trembler; you look for all the world as if you wanted an opportunity of stealing out of the room.

MARLOW. Why man that's because I *do* want to steal out of the room. Faith, I have often formed a resolution to break the ice, and rattle away at any rate. But I don't know how, a single glance from a pair of fine eyes has totally overset my resolution. An impudent fellow may counterfeit modesty, but I'll be hanged if a modest man can ever counterfeit impudence.

HASTINGS. If you could but say half the fine things to them that I have heard you lavish upon the bar-maid of an inn, or even a college bed maker—

MARLOW. Why, George, I can't say fine things to them. They freeze, they petrify me. They may talk of a comet, or a burning mountain, or some such bagatelle. But to me, a modest woman, drest out in all her finery, is the most tremendous object of the whole creation.

HASTINGS. Ha! ha! ha! At this rate, man, how can you ever expect to marry!

MARLOW. Never, unless as among kings and princes, my bride were to be courted by proxy. If, indeed, like an Eastern bridegroom, one were to be introduced to a wife he never saw before, it might be endured. But to go through all the terrors of a formal courtship, together with the episode of aunts, grandmothers and cousins, and at last to blurt out the broad staring question, of, *madam will you marry me?* No, no, that's a strain much above me I assure you.

HASTINGS. I pity you. But how do you intend behaving to the lady you are come down to visit at the request of your father?

MARLOW. As I behave to all other ladies. Bow very low. Answer yes, or no, to all her demands—But for the rest, I don't think I shall venture to look in her face, till I see my father's again.

HASTINGS. I'm surprized that one who is so warm a friend can be so 10 cool a lover.

MARLOW. To be explicit, my dear Hastings, my chief inducement down was to be instrumental in forwarding your happiness, not my own. Miss Neville loves you, the family don't know you, as my friend you are sure of a reception, and let honour do the rest.

HASTINGS. My dear Marlow! But I'll suppress the emotion. Were I a wretch, meanly seeking to carry off a fortune, you should be the last man in the world I would apply to for assistance. But Miss Neville's person is all I ask, and that is mine, both from her deceased father's consent, and her own inclination. 20

MARLOW. Happy man! You have talents and art to captivate any woman. I'm doom'd to adore the sex, and yet to converse with the only part of it I despise. This stammer in my address, and this aukward prepossessing visage of mine, can never permit me to soar above the reach of a milliner's 'prentice, or one of the dutchesses of Drury-lane. Pshaw! this fellow here to interrupt us.

Enter HARDCASTLE

HARDCASTLE. Gentlemen, once more you are heartily welcome. Which is Mr. Marlow? Sir, you're heartily welcome. It's not my way, you see, to receive my friends with my back to the fire. I like to give them 30 a hearty reception in the old stile at my gate. I like to see their horses and trunks taken care of.

MARLOW. *(aside)* He has got our names from the servants already. (*To Him*) We approve your caution and hospitality, Sir. (*To* HASTINGS) I have been thinking, George, of changing our travelling dresses in the morning. I am grown confoundedly ashamed of mine.

HARDCASTLE. I beg, Mr. Marlow, you'll use no ceremony in this house.

HASTINGS. I fancy, Charles, you're right: the first blow is half the battle. I intend opening the campaign with the white and gold. 40

HARDCASTLE. Mr. Marlow—Mr. Hastings—gentlemen—pray be under

no constraint in this house. This is Liberty-hall, gentlemen. You may
do just as you please here.

MARLOW. Yet, George, if we open the campaign too fiercely at first, we
may want ammunition before it is over. I think to reserve the embroidery to secure a retreat.

HARDCASTLE. Your talking of a retreat, Mr. Marlow, puts me in mind
of the Duke of Marlborough, when we went to besiege Denain. He
first summoned the garrison.

MARLOW. Don't you think the *ventre dor* waistcoat will do with the plain
brown?   10

HARDCASTLE. He first summoned the garrison, which might consist of
about five thousand men——

HASTINGS. I think not: Brown and yellow mix but very poorly.

HARDCASTLE. I say, gentlemen, as I was telling you, he summoned the
garrison, which might consist of about five thousand men——

MARLOW. The girls like finery.

HARDCASTLE. Which might consist of about five thousand men, well
appointed with stores, ammunition, and other implements of war.
Now, says the Duke of Marlborough, to George Brooks, that stood
next to him—You must have heard of George Brooks; I'll pawn my   20
Dukedom, says he, but I take that garrison without spilling a drop
of blood. So——

MARLOW. What, my good friend, if you gave us a glass of punch in the
mean time, it would help us to carry on the siege with vigour.

HARDCASTLE. Punch, Sir! (*aside*) This is the most unaccountable kind
of modesty I ever met with.

MARLOW. Yes, Sir, Punch. A glass of warm punch, after our journey,
will be comfortable. This is Liberty-Hall, you know.

HARDCASTLE. Here's Cup, Sir.

MARLOW. (*Aside*) So this fellow, in his Liberty-hall, will only let us have   30
just what he pleases.

HARDCASTLE. (*Taking the Cup*) I hope you'll find it to your mind. I have
prepared it with my own hands, and I believe you'll own the ingredients are tolerable. Will you, be so good as to pledge me, Sir? Here,
Mr. Marlow, here is to our better acquaintance. (*drinks*)

MARLOW. (*Aside*) A very impudent fellow this! but he's a character,
and I'll humour him a little. Sir, my service to you. (*drinks*)

HASTINGS. (*Aside*) I see this fellow wants to give us his company, and
forgets that he's an innkeeper, before he has learned to be a gentleman.

MARLOW. From the excellence of your cup, my old friend, I suppose   40
you have a good deal of business in this part of the country. Warm
work, now and then, at elections, I suppose.

HARDCASTLE. No, Sir, I have long given that work over. Since our betters have hit upon the expedient of electing each other, there's no business *for us that sell ale*.

HASTINGS. So, then you have no turn for politics I find.

HARDCASTLE. Not in the least. There was a time, indeed, I fretted myself about the mistakes of government, like other people; but finding myself every day grow more angry, and the government growing no better, I left it to mend itself. Since that, I no more trouble my head about *Heyder Ally*, or *Ally Cawn*, than about *Ally Croaker*. Sir, my service to you.   10

HASTINGS. So that with eating above stairs, and drinking below, with receiving your friends without, and amusing them within, you lead a good pleasant bustling life of it.

HARDCASTLE. I do stir about a great deal, that's certain. Half the differences of the parish are adjusted in this very parlour.

MARLOW. (*After drinking*) And you have an argument in your cup, old gentleman, better than any in Westminster-hall.

HARDCASTLE. Ay, young gentleman, that, and a little philosophy.

MARLOW. (*Aside*) Well, this is the first time I ever heard of an inn-keeper's philosophy.   20

HASTINGS. So then, like an experienced general, you attack them on every quarter. If you find their reason manageable, you attack it with your philosophy; if you find they have no reason, you attack them with this. Here's your health, my philosopher. (*drinks*)

HARDCASTLE. Good, very good, thank you; ha, ha. Your Generalship puts me in mind of Prince Eugene, when he fought the Turks at the battle of Belgrade. You shall hear.

MARLOW. Instead of the battle of Belgrade, I believe it's almost time to talk about supper. What has your philosophy got in the house for supper?   30

HARDCASTLE. For Supper, Sir! (*aside*) Was ever such a request to a man in his own house!

MARLOW. Yes, Sir, supper Sir; I begin to feel an appetite. I shall make devilish work to-night in the larder, I promise you.

HARDCASTLE. (*Aside*) Such a brazen dog sure never my eyes beheld. (*to him*) Why really, Sir, as for supper I can't well tell. My Dorothy, and the cook maid, settle these things between them. I leave these kind of things entirely to them.

MARLOW. You do, do you?

HARDCASTLE. Entirely. By-the-bye, I believe they are in actual consul- 40
tation upon what's for supper this moment in the kitchen.

MARLOW. Then I beg they'll admit *me* as one of their privy council. It's a way I have got. When I travel, I always chuse to regulate my own supper. Let the cook be called. No offence I hope, Sir.

HARDCASTLE. O no, Sir, none in the least; yet I don't know how: our Bridget, the cook maid, is not very communicative upon these occasions. Should we send for her, she might scold us all out of the house.

HASTINGS. Let's see your list of the larder then. I ask it as a favour. I always match my appetite to my bill of fare.

MARLOW. (*To* HARDCASTLE, *who looks at them with surprize*) Sir, he's very right, and it's my way too.   10

HARDCASTLE. Sir, you have a right to command here. Here, Roger, bring us the bill of fare for to night's supper. I believe it's drawn out. Your manner, Mr. Hastings, puts me in mind of my uncle, Colonel Wallop. It was a saying of his, that no man was sure of his supper till he had eaten it.

Enter ROGER, *who gives a Bill of Fare.*

HASTINGS. (*Aside*) All upon the high ropes! His uncle a Colonel! We shall soon hear of his mother being a justice of peace. But let's hear the bill of fare.

MARLOW. (*Perusing*) What's here? For the first course; for the second 20 course; for the desert. The devil, Sir, do you think we have brought down the whole Joiners Company, or the Corporation of Bedford, to eat up such a supper? Two or three little things, clean and comfortable, will do.

HASTINGS. But, let's hear it.

MARLOW. (*Reading*) For the first course at the top, a pig, and pruin sauce.

HASTINGS. Damn your pig, I say.

MARLOW. And damn your pruin sauce, say I.

HARDCASTLE. And yet, gentlemen, to men that are hungry, pig, with 30 pruin sauce, is very good eating.

MARLOW. At the bottom, a calve's tongue and brains.

HASTINGS. Let your brains be knock'd out, my good Sir; I don't like them.

MARLOW. Or you may clap them on a plate by themselves. I do.

HARDCASTLE. (*Aside*) Their impudence confounds me. (*to them*) Gentlemen, you are my guests, make what alterations you please. Is there any thing else you wish to retrench or alter, gentlemen?

MARLOW. Item. A pork pie, a boiled rabbet and sausages, a florentine, a shaking pudding, and a dish of tiff—taff—taffety cream!   40

HASTINGS. Confound your made dishes, I shall be as much at a loss in this house as at a green and yellow dinner at the French ambassador's table. I'm for plain eating.

HARDCASTLE. I'm sorry, gentlemen, that I have nothing you like, but if there be any thing you have a particular fancy to——

MARLOW. Why, really, Sir, your bill of fare is so exquisite, that any one part of it is full as good as another. Send us what you please. So much for supper. And now to see that our beds are air'd, and properly taken care of.

HARDCASTLE. I entreat you'll leave all that to me. You shall not stir a step. 10

MARLOW. Leave that to you! I protest, Sir, you must excuse me, I always look to these things myself.

HARDCASTLE. I must insist, Sir, you'll make yourself easy on that head.

MARLOW. You see I'm resolved on it. (*aside*) A very troublesome fellow this, as ever I met with.

HARDCASTLE. Well, Sir, I'm resolved at least to attend you. (*aside*) This may be modern modesty, but I never saw any thing look so like old-fashioned impudence.   [*Exeunt* MARLOW *and* HARDCASTLE.

HASTINGS *solus*

HASTINGS. So I find this fellow's civilities begin to grow troublesome. 20 But who can be angry at those assiduities which are meant to please him? Ha! what do I see? Miss Neville, by all that's happy!

Enter MISS NEVILLE

MISS NEVILLE. My dear Hastings! To what unexpected good fortune? to what accident am I to ascribe this happy meeting?

HASTINGS. Rather let me ask the same question, as I could never have hoped to meet my dearest Constance at an inn.

MISS NEVILLE. An inn! sure you mistake! my aunt, my guardian, lives here. What could induce you to think this house an inn?

HASTINGS. My friend Mr. Marlow, with whom I came down, and I, 30 have been sent here as to an inn, I assure you. A young fellow whom we accidentally met at a house hard by directed us hither.

MISS NEVILLE. Certainly it must be one of my hopeful cousin's tricks, of whom you have heard me talk so often, ha! ha! ha! ha!

HASTINGS. He whom your aunt intends for you? He of whom I have such just apprehensions?

MISS NEVILLE. You have nothing to fear from him, I assure you. You'd adore him if you knew how heartily he despises me. My aunt knows it too, and has undertaken to court me for him, and actually begins to think she has made a conquest. 40

HASTINGS. Thou dear dissembler! You must know, my Constance, I have just seized this happy opportunity of my friend's visit here to get admittance into the family. The horses that carried us down are now fatigued with their journey, but they'll soon be refreshed; and then if my dearest girl will trust in her faithful Hastings, we shall soon be landed in France, where even among slaves the laws of marriage are respected.

MISS NEVILLE. I have often told you, that though ready to obey you, I yet should leave my little fortune behind with reluctance. The greatest part of it was left me by my uncle, the India Director, and chiefly 10 consists in jewels. I have been for some time persuading my aunt to let me wear them. I fancy I'm very near succeeding. The instant they are put into my possession you shall find me ready to make them and myself yours.

HASTINGS. Perish the baubles! Your person is all I desire. In the meantime, my friend Marlow must not be let into his mistake. I know the strange reserve of his temper is such, that if abruptly informed of it, he would instantly quit the house before our plan was ripe for execution.

MISS NEVILLE. But how shall we keep him in the deception? Miss 20 Hardcastle is just returned from walking; what if we still continue to deceive him?——This, this way——

[*They confer*]

Enter MARLOW

MARLOW. The assiduities of these good people teize me beyond bearing. My host seems to think it ill manners to leave me alone, and so he claps not only himself but his old-fashioned wife on my back. They talk of coming to sup with us too; and then, I suppose, we are to run the gauntlet thro' all the rest of the family.—What have we got here!— 30

HASTINGS. My dear Charles! Let me congratulate you!—The most fortunate accident!—Who do you think is just alighted?

MARLOW. Cannot guess.

HASTINGS. Our mistresses my boy, Miss Hardcastle and Miss Neville. Give me leave to introduce Miss Constance Neville to your acquaintance. Happening to dine in the neighbourhood, they called on their return to take fresh horses here. Miss Hardcastle has just stept into the next room, and will be back in an instant. Wasn't it lucky? eh!

MARLOW. (*Aside*) I have just been mortified enough of all conscience, 40 and here comes something to complete my embarrassment.

HASTINGS. Well! but wasn't it the most fortunate thing in the world?

MARLOW. Oh! yes. Very fortunate—a most joyful encounter——But our dresses, George, you know, are in disorder——What if we should postpone the happiness 'till to-morrow?——To-morrow at her own house——It will be every bit as convenient—And rather more respectful——To-morrow let it be.   [*offering to go*

MISS NEVILLE. By no means, Sir. Your ceremony will displease her. The disorder of your dress will shew the ardour of your impatience. Besides, she knows you are in the house, and will permit you to see her.   10

MARLOW. O! the devil! how shall I support it? Hem! hem! Hastings, you must not go. You are to assist me, you know. I shall be confoundedly ridiculous.

HASTINGS. Pshaw man! it's but the first plunge, and all's over. She's but a woman, you know.

MARLOW. And of all women, she that I dread most to encounter! Yet, hang it! I'll take courage. Hem!

Enter MISS HARDCASTLE *as returned from walking, a Bonnet, &c.*

HASTINGS. (*introducing them*) Miss Hardcastle, Mr. Marlow, I'm proud of bringing two persons of such merit together, that only want to   20 know, to esteem each other.

MISS HARDCASTLE. (*aside*) Now, for meeting my modest gentleman with a demure face, and quite in his own manner. (*After a pause, in which he appears very uneasy and disconcerted*) I'm glad of your safe arrival, Sir——I'm told you had some accidents by the way.

MARLOW. Only a few madam. Yet, we had some. Yes, Madam, a good many accidents, but should be sorry—Madam—or rather glad of any accidents—that are so agreeably concluded. Hem!

HASTINGS. (*To him*) You never spoke better in your whole life. Keep it up, and I'll insure you the victory.   30

MISS HARDCASTLE. I'm afraid you flatter, Sir. You that have seen so much of the finest company can find little entertainment in an obscure corner of the country.

MARLOW. (*Gathering courage*) I have lived, indeed, in the world, Madam; but I have kept very little company. I have been but an observer upon life, Madam, while others were enjoying it.

MISS NEVILLE. But that, I am told, is the way to enjoy it at last.

HASTINGS. (*To him*) Cicero never spoke better. Once more, and you are confirm'd in assurance for ever.

MARLOW. (*To him*) Hem! Stand by me then, and when I'm down, throw   40 in a word or two to set me up again.

MISS HARDCASTLE. An observer, like you, upon life, were, I fear, dis-
agreeably employed, since you must have had much more to censure
than to approve.

MARLOW. Pardon me, Madam. I was always willing to be amused. The
folly of most people is rather an object of mirth than uneasiness.

HASTINGS. (*To him*) Bravo, Bravo. Never spoke so well in your whole
life. Well! Miss Hardcastle, I see that you and Mr. Marlow are going
to be very good company. I believe our being here will but em-
barrass the interview.

MARLOW. Not in the least, Mr. Hastings. We like your company of all 10
things. (*To him*) Zounds! George, sure you won't go? How can
you leave us?

HASTINGS. Our presence will but spoil conversation, so we'll retire to
the next room. (*To him*) You don't consider, man, that we are to
manage a little tête-à-tête of our own.   [*Exeunt.*

MISS HARDCASTLE. (*After a pause*) But you have not been wholly an
observer, I presume, Sir: The ladies I should hope have employed
some part of your addresses.

MARLOW. (*Relapsing into timidity*) Pardon me, Madam, I—I—I—as yet
have studied—only—to—deserve them.   20

MISS HARDCASTLE. And that some say is the very worst way to obtain
them.

MARLOW. Perhaps so, madam. But I love to converse only with the
more grave and sensible part of the sex.——But I'm afraid I grow
tiresome.

MISS HARDCASTLE. Not at all, Sir; there is nothing I like so much as
grave conversation myself; I could hear it for ever. Indeed I have
often been surprized how a man of *sentiment* could ever admire those
light airy pleasures, where nothing reaches the heart.

MARLOW. It's——a disease——of the mind, madam. In the variety of 30
tastes there must be some who wanting a relish——for——um-a-um.

MISS HARDCASTLE. I understand you, Sir. There must be some, who
wanting a relish for refined pleasures, pretend to despise what they
are incapable of tasting.

MARLOW. My meaning, madam, but infinitely better expressed. And I
can't help observing——a——

MISS HARDCASTLE. (*Aside*) Who could ever suppose this fellow
impudent upon some occasions. (*To him*) You were going to observe,
Sir——

MARLOW. I was observing, madam——I protest, madam, I forget what 40
I was going to observe.

MISS HARDCASTLE. (*Aside*) I vow and so do I. (*To him*) You were observing, Sir, that in this age of hypocrisy—something about hypocrisy, Sir.

MARLOW. Yes, madam. In this age of hypocrisy there are few who upon strict enquiry do not—a—a—a——

MISS HARDCASTLE. I understand you perfectly, Sir.

MARLOW. (*Aside*) Egad! and that's more than I do myself.

MISS HARDCASTLE. You mean that in this hypocritical age there are few that do not condemn in public what they practise in private, and think they pay every debt to virtue when they praise it.

MARLOW. True, madam; those who have most virtue in their mouths, 10 have least of it in their bosoms. But I'm sure I tire you, madam.

MISS HARDCASTLE. Not in the least, Sir; there's something so agreeable and spirited in your manner, such life and force—pray, Sir, go on.

MARLOW. Yes, madam. I was saying——that there are some occasions ——when a total want of courage, madam, destroys all the——and puts us——upon a——a——a——

MISS HARDCASTLE. I agree with you entirely, a want of courage upon some occasions assumes the appearance of ignorance, and betrays us when we most want to excel. I beg you'll proceed.   20

MARLOW. Yes, Madam. Morally speaking, madam—But I see Miss Neville expecting us in the next room. I would not intrude for the world.

MISS HARDCASTLE. I protest, Sir, I never was more agreeably entertained in all my life. Pray go on.

MARLOW. Yes, madam. I was——But she beckons us to join her. Madam, shall I do myself the honour to attend you?

MISS HARDCASTLE. Well then, I'll follow.

MARLOW. (*aside*) This pretty smooth dialogue has done for me.   [*Exit.*

MISS HARDCASTLE *sola*   30

MISS HARDCASTLE. Ha! ha! ha! Was there ever such a sober sentimental interview? I'm certain he scarce look'd in my face the whole time. Yet the fellow, but for his unaccountable bashfulness, is pretty well too. He has good sense, but then so buried in his fears, that it fatigues one more than ignorance. If I could teach him a little confidence, it would be doing somebody that I know of a piece of service. But who is that somebody?—that, faith, is a question I can scarce answer.   [*Exit.*

Enter TONY *and* MISS NEVILLE, *followed by* MRS. HARDCASTLE
and HASTINGS   40

TONY. What do you follow me for, cousin Con? I wonder you're not
ashamed to be so very engaging.

MISS NEVILLE. I hope, cousin, one may speak to one's own relations,
and not be to blame.

TONY. Ay, but I know what sort of a relation you want to make me
though; but it won't do. I tell you, cousin Con, it won't do, so I beg
you'll keep your distance, I want no nearer relationship.

[*She follows coqueting him to the back scene*

MRS. HARDCASTLE. Well! I vow, Mr. Hastings, you are very enter-
taining. There's nothing in the world I love to talk of so much as 10
London, and the fashions, though I was never there myself.

HASTINGS. Never there! You amaze me! From your air and manner, I
concluded you had been bred all your life either at Ranelagh, St.
James's, or Tower Wharf.

MRS. HARDCASTLE. O! Sir, you're only pleased to say so. We Country
persons can have no manner at all. I'm in love with the town, and
that serves to raise me above some of our neighbouring rustics; but
who can have a manner, that has never seen the Pantheon, the
Grotto Gardens, the Borough, and such places where the Nobility
chiefly resort? All I can do, is to enjoy London at second-hand. I 20
take care to know every tête-à-tête from the Scandalous Magazine,
and have all the fashions, as they come out, in a letter from the two
Miss Rickets of Crooked-lane. Pray how do you like this head, Mr.
Hastings?

HASTINGS. Extremely elegant and degagée, upon my word, Madam.
Your Friseur is a Frenchman, I suppose?

MRS. HARDCASTLE. I protest I dressed it myself from a print in the
Ladies Memorandum-book for the last year.

HASTINGS. Indeed. Such a head in a side-box, at the Playhouse, would
draw as many gazers as my Lady May'ress at a City Ball.   30

MRS. HARDCASTLE. I vow, since inoculation began, there is no such
thing to be seen as a plain woman; so one must dress a little particular or one may escape in the crowd.

HASTINGS. But that can never be your case, Madam, in any dress.
                                                    (*bowing*)

MRS. HARDCASTLE. Yet, what signifies *my* dressing when I have such a
piece of antiquity by my side as Mr. Hardcastle: all I can say will
never argue down a single button from his cloaths. I have often
wanted him to throw off his great flaxen wig, and where he was bald,
to plaister it over like my Lord Pately, with powder.   40

HASTINGS. You are right, Madam; for, as among the ladies, there are
none ugly, so among the men there are none old.

MRS. HARDCASTLE. But what do you think his answer was? Why, with his usual Gothic vivacity, he said I only wanted him to throw off his wig to convert it into a tête for my own wearing.

HASTINGS. Intolerable! At your age you may wear what you please, and it must become you.

MRS. HARDCASTLE. Pray, Mr. Hastings, what do you take to be the most fashionable age about town?

HASTINGS. Some time ago, forty was all the mode; but I'm told the ladies intend to bring up fifty for the ensuing winter.

MRS. HARDCASTLE. Seriously? Then I shall be too young for the fashion.   10

HASTINGS. No lady begins now to put on jewels 'till she's past forty. For instance, Miss there, in a polite circle, would be considered as a child, as a mere maker of samplers.

MRS. HARDCASTLE. And yet Mrs. Niece thinks herself as much a woman, and is as fond of jewels as the oldest of us all.

HASTINGS. Your niece, is she? And that young gentleman, a brother of yours, I should presume?

MRS. HARDCASTLE. My son, Sir. They are contracted to each other. Observe their little sports. They fall in and out ten times a day, as if they were man and wife already. (*To them*) Well Tony, child, what   20 soft things are you saying to your cousin Constance this evening?

TONY. I have been saying no soft things; but that it's very hard to be followed about so. Ecod! I've not a place in the house now that's left to myself but the stable.

MRS. HARDCASTLE. Never mind him, Con. my dear. He's in another story behind your back.

MISS NEVILLE. There's something generous in my cousin's manner. He falls out before faces to be forgiven in private.

TONY. That's a damned confounded——crack.

MRS. HARDCASTLE. Ah! he's a sly one. Don't you think they're like each   30 other about the mouth, Mr. Hastings? The Blenkinsop mouth to a T. They're of a size too. Back to back, my pretties, that Mr. Hastings may see you. Come Tony.

TONY. You had as good not make me, I tell you.   (*measuring*)

MISS NEVILLE. O lud! he has almost cracked my head.

MRS. HARDCASTLE. O the monster! For shame, Tony. You a man, and behave so!

TONY. If I'm a man, let me have my fortin. Ecod! I'll not be made a fool of no longer.

MRS. HARDCASTLE. Is this, ungrateful boy, all that I'm to get for the   40 pains I have taken in your education? I that have rock'd you in your cradle, and fed that pretty mouth with a spoon! Did not I work that waistcoat to make you genteel? Did not I prescribe for you every day, and weep while the receipt was operating?

TONY. Ecod! you had reason to weep, for you have been dosing me ever since I was born. I have gone through every receipt in the complete huswife ten times over; and you have thoughts of coursing me through *Quincy* next spring. But, Ecod! I tell you, I'll not be made a fool of no longer.

MRS. HARDCASTLE. Wasn't it all for your good, viper? Wasn't it all for your good?

TONY. I wish you'd let me and my good alone then. Snubbing this way 10 when I'm in spirits. If I'm to have any good, let it come of itself; not to keep dinging it, dinging it into one so.

MRS. HARDCASTLE. That's false; I never see you when you're in spirits. No, Tony, you then go to the alehouse or the kennel. I'm never to be delighted with your agreeable, wild notes, unfeeling monster!

TONY. Ecod! Mamma, your own notes are the wildest of the two.

MRS. HARDCASTLE. Was ever the like? But I see he wants to break my heart, I see he does.

HASTINGS. Dear Madam, permit me to lecture the young gentleman a little. I'm certain I can persuade him to his duty.   20

MRS. HARDCASTLE. Well! I must retire. Come, Constance, my love. You see Mr. Hastings, the wretchedness of my situation: Was ever poor woman so plagued with a dear, sweet, pretty, provoking, undutiful boy.   [*Exeunt* MRS. HARDCASTLE *and* MISS NEVILLE.

HASTINGS, TONY

TONY (*singing*). *There was a young man riding by, and fain would have his will. Rang do didlo dee.* Don't mind her. Let her cry. It's the comfort of her heart. I have seen her and sister cry over a book for an hour together, and they said, they liked the book the better the more it made them cry.   30

HASTINGS. Then you're no friend to the ladies, I find, my pretty young gentleman?

TONY. That's as I find 'um.

HASTINGS. Not to her of your mother's chusing, I dare answer? And yet she appears to me a pretty well-tempered girl.

TONY. That's because you don't know her as well as I. Ecod! I know every inch about her; and there's not a more bitter cantanckerous toad in all Christendom.

HASTINGS. (*Aside*) Pretty encouragement this for a lover!

TONY. I have seen her since the height of that. She has as many tricks 40 as a hare in a thicket, or a colt the first day's breaking.

HASTINGS. To me she appears sensible and silent!

TONY. Ay, before company. But when she's with her play-mates she's as loud as a hog in a gate.

HASTINGS. But there is a meek modesty about her that charms me.

TONY. Yes, but curb her never so little, she kicks up, and you're flung in a ditch.

HASTINGS. Well, but you must allow her a little beauty.—Yes, you must allow her some beauty.

TONY. Bandbox! She's all a made up thing, mun. Ah! could you but see Bet Bouncer of these parts, you might then talk of beauty. Ecod, she has two eyes as black as sloes, and cheeks as broad and red as a pulpit cushion. She'd make two of she.

HASTINGS. Well, what say you to a friend that would take this bitter bargain off your hands?

TONY. Anon?

HASTINGS. Would you thank him that would take Miss Neville and leave you to happiness and your dear Betsy?

TONY. Ay; but where is there such a friend, for who would take *her*?

HASTINGS. I am he. If you but assist me, I'll engage to whip her off to France, and you shall never hear more of her.

TONY. Assist you! Ecod I will, to the last drop of my blood. I'll clap a pair of horses to your chaise that shall trundle you off in a twinkling, and may be get you a part of her fortin beside, in jewels, that you little dream of.

HASTINGS. My dear squire, this looks like a lad of spirit.

TONY. Come along then, and you shall see more of my spirit before you have done with me (*singing*). *We are the boys that fears no noise where the thundering cannons roar.* [*Exeunt.*

END OF SECOND ACT

ACT III

Enter HARDCASTLE *solus*

HARDCASTLE. What could my old friend Sir Charles mean by recommending his son as the modestest young man in town? To me he appears the most impudent piece of brass that ever spoke with a tongue. He has taken possession of the easy chair by the fire-side already. He took off his boots in the parlour, and desired me to see them taken care of. I'm desirous to know how his impudence affects my daughter.—She will certainly be shocked at it.

Enter MISS HARDCASTLE, *plainly dress'd*   10

HARDCASTLE. Well, my Kate, I see you have changed your dress as I bid you; and yet, I believe, there was no great occasion.

MISS HARDCASTLE. I find such a pleasure, Sir, in obeying your commands, that I take care to observe them without ever debating their propriety.

HARDCASTLE. And yet, Kate, I sometimes give you some cause, particularly when I recommended my *modest* gentleman to you as a lover to-day.

MISS HARDCASTLE. You taught me to expect something extraordinary, and I find the original exceeds the description.   20

HARDCASTLE. I was never so surprized in my life! He has quite confounded all my faculties!

MISS HARDCASTLE. I never saw any thing like it: And a man of the world too!

HARDCASTLE. Ay, he learned it all abroad,—what a fool was I, to think a young man could learn modesty by travelling. He might as soon learn wit at a masquerade.

MISS HARDCASTLE. It seems all natural to him.

HARDCASTLE. A good deal assisted by bad company and a French dancing-master.   30

MISS HARDCASTLE. Sure you mistake, papa! a French dancing-master could never have taught him that timid look,—that aukward address,—that bashful manner——

HARDCASTLE. Whose look? whose manner? child!

MISS HARDCASTLE. Mr. Marlow's: his meauvaise honte, his timidity struck me at the first sight.

HARDCASTLE. Then your first sight deceived you; for I think him one of the most brazen first sights that ever astonished my senses.

MISS HARDCASTLE. Sure, Sir, you rally! I never saw any one so modest.

HARDCASTLE. And can you be serious! I never saw such a bouncing swaggering puppy since I was born. Bully Dawson was but a fool to him.

MISS HARDCASTLE. Surprizing! He met me with a respectful bow, a stammering voice, and a look fixed on the ground.

HARDCASTLE. He met me with loud voice, a lordly air, and a familiarity that made my blood freeze again.

MISS HARDCASTLE. He treated me with diffidence and respect; censured the manners of the age; admired the prudence of girls that never laughed; tired me with apologies for being tiresome; then left the room with a bow, and, madam, I would not for the world detain you.

HARDCASTLE. He spoke to me as if he knew me all his life before. Asked twenty questions, and never waited for an answer. Interrupted my best remarks with some silly pun, and when I was in my best story of the Duke of Marlborough and Prince Eugene, he asked if I had not a good hand at making punch. Yes, Kate, he ask'd your father if he was a maker of punch!

MISS HARDCASTLE. One of us must certainly be mistaken.

HARDCASTLE. If he be what he has shewn himself, I'm determined he shall never have my consent.

MISS HARDCASTLE. And if he be the sullen thing I take him, he shall never have mine.

HARDCASTLE. In one thing then we are agreed—to reject him.

MISS HARDCASTLE. Yes. But upon conditions. For if you should find him less impudent, and I more presuming; if you find him more respectful, and I more importunate——I don't know——the fellow is well enough for a man—Certainly we don't meet many such at a horse race in the country.

HARDCASTLE. If we should find him so——But that's impossible. The first appearance has done my business. I'm seldom deceived in that.

MISS HARDCASTLE. And yet there may be many good qualities under that first appearance.

HARDCASTLE. Ay, when a girl finds a fellow's outside to her taste, she
then sets about guessing the rest of his furniture. With her, a smooth
face stands for good sense, and a genteel figure for every virtue.

MISS HARDCASTLE. I hope, Sir, a conversation begun with a compliment to my good sense won't end with a sneer at my understanding?

HARDCASTLE. Pardon me, Kate. But if young Mr. Brazen can find the
art of reconciling contradictions, he may please us both, perhaps.

MISS HARDCASTLE. And as one of us must be mistaken, what if we go to
make further discoveries?

HARDCASTLE. Agreed. But depend on't I'm in the right.   10

MISS HARDCASTLE. And depend on't I'm not much in the wrong.

[*Exeunt.*

Enter TONY *running in with a Casket*

TONY. Ecod! I have got them. Here they are. My Cousin Con's neck-
laces, bobs and all. My mother shan't cheat the poor souls out of
their fortune neither. O! my genus, is that you?

Enter HASTINGS

HASTINGS. My dear friend, how have you managed with your mother?
I hope you have amused her with pretending love for your cousin,
and that you are willing to be reconciled at last? Our horses will be   20
refreshed in a short time, and we shall soon be ready to set off.

TONY. And here's something to bear your charges by the way, (*giving
the casket.*) Your sweetheart's jewels. Keep them, and hang those, I
say, that would rob you of one of them.

HASTINGS. But how have you procured them from your mother?

TONY. Ask me no questions, and I'll tell you no fibs. I procured them
by the rule of thumb. If I had not a key to every drawer in mother's
bureau, how could I go to the alehouse so often as I do? An honest
man may rob himself of his own at any time.

HASTINGS. Thousands do it every day. But to be plain with you; Miss   30
Neville is endeavouring to procure them from her aunt this very
instant. If she succeeds, it will be the most delicate way at least of
obtaining them.

TONY. Well, keep them, till you know how it will be. But I know how
it will be well enough, she'd as soon part with the only sound tooth
in her head.

HASTINGS. But I dread the effects of her resentment, when she finds
she has lost them.

TONY. Never you mind her resentment, leave *me* to manage that. I don't

value her resentment the bounce of a cracker. Zounds! here they are.
Morrice. Prance.   [*Exit* HASTINGS.

TONY, MRS. HARDCASTLE, MISS NEVILLE

MRS. HARDCASTLE. Indeed, Constance, you amaze me. Such a girl as you
want jewels? It will be time enough for jewels, my dear, twenty years
hence, when your beauty begins to want repairs.

MISS NEVILLE. But what will repair beauty at forty, will certainly
improve it at twenty, Madam.

MRS. HARDCASTLE. Yours, my dear, can admit of none. That natural
blush is beyond a thousand ornaments. Besides, child, jewels are   10
quite out at present. Don't you see half the ladies of our acquaintance,
my Lady Kill-day-light, and Mrs. Crump, and the rest of them, carry
their jewels to town, and bring nothing but Paste and Marcasites
back.

MISS NEVILLE. But who knows, Madam, but somebody that shall be
nameless would like me best with all my little finery about me?

MRS. HARDCASTLE. Consult your glass, my dear, and then see, if with
such a pair of eyes, you want any better sparklers. What do you think,
Tony, my dear, does your cousin Con. want any jewels, in your eyes,
to set off her beauty.   20

TONY. That's as thereafter may be.

MISS NEVILLE. My dear aunt, if you knew how it would oblige me.

MRS. HARDCASTLE. A parcel of old-fashioned rose and table-cut things.
They would make you look like the court of king Solomon at a
puppet-shew. Besides, I believe I can't readily come at them. They
may be missing for aught I know to the contrary.

TONY. (*Apart to* MRS. HARDCASTLE) Then why don't you tell her so at
once, as she's so longing for them. Tell her they're lost. It's the only
way to quiet her. Say they're lost, and call me to bear witness.

MRS. HARDCASTLE. (*Apart to* TONY) You know, my dear, I'm only keep-   30
ing them for you. So if I say they're gone, you'll bear me witness,
will you? He! he! he!

TONY. Never fear me. Ecod! I'll say I saw them taken out with my own
eyes.

MISS NEVILLE. I desire them but for a day, Madam. Just to be permitted
to shew them as relicks, and then they may be lock'd up again.

MRS. HARDCASTLE. To be plain with you, my dear Constance; if I could
find them, you should have them. They're missing, I assure you.
Lost, for aught I know; but we must have patience wherever they
are.   40

MISS NEVILLE. I'll not believe it; this is but a shallow pretence to deny me. I know they're too valuable to be so slightly kept, and as you are to answer for the loss.

MRS. HARDCASTLE. Don't be alarm'd, Constance. If they be lost, I must restore an equivalent. But my son knows they are missing, and not to be found.

TONY. That I can bear witness to. They are missing, and not to be found, I'll take my oath on't.

MRS. HARDCASTLE. You must learn resignation, my dear; for tho' we lose our fortune, yet we should not lose our patience. See me, how calm I am.   10

MISS NEVILLE. Ay, people are generally calm at the misfortunes of others.

MRS. HARDCASTLE. Now, I wonder a girl of your good sense should waste a thought upon such trumpery. We shall soon find them; and, in the mean time, you shall make use of my garnets till your jewels be found.

MISS NEVILLE. I detest garnets.

MRS. HARDCASTLE. The most becoming things in the world to set off a clear complexion. You have often seen how well they look upon me. You *shall* have them.   [*Exit.* 20

MISS NEVILLE. I dislike them of all things. You shan't stir.—Was ever any thing so provoking to mislay my own jewels, and force me to wear her trumpery.

TONY. Don't be a fool. If she gives you the garnets, take what you can get. The jewels are your own already. I have stolen them out of her bureau, and she does not know it. Fly to your spark, he'll tell you more of the matter. Leave me to manage *her.*

MISS NEVILLE. My dear cousin.

TONY. Vanish. She's here, and has missed them already. Zounds! how she fidgets and spits about like a Catharine wheel.   30

Enter MRS. HARDCASTLE

MRS. HARDCASTLE. Confusion! thieves! robbers! We are cheated, plundered, broke open, undone.

TONY. What's the matter, what's the matter, mamma? I hope nothing has happened to any of the good family!

MRS. HARDCASTLE. We are robbed. My bureau has been broke open, the jewels taken out, and I'm undone.

TONY. Oh! is that all? Ha, ha, ha. By the laws, I never saw it better acted in my life. Ecod, I thought you was ruin'd in earnest, ha, ha, ha.

MRS. HARDCASTLE. Why boy, I *am* ruin'd in earnest. My bureau has been 40 broke open, and all taken away.

TONY. Stick to that; ha, ha, ha; stick to that. I'll bear witness, you
know, call me to bear witness.

MRS. HARDCASTLE. I tell you, Tony, by all that's precious, the jewels are
gone, and I shall be ruin'd for ever.

TONY. Sure I know they're gone, and I am to say so.

MRS. HARDCASTLE. My dearest Tony, but hear me. They're gone, I say.

TONY. By the laws, mamma, you make me for to laugh, ha, ha. I know
who took them well enough, ha, ha.

MRS. HARDCASTLE. Was there ever such a blockhead, that can't tell the
difference between jest and earnest. I tell you I'm not in jest, booby. 10

TONY. That's right, that's right: You must be in a bitter passion, and
then nobody will suspect either of us. I'll bear witness that they are
gone.

MRS. HARDCASTLE. Was there ever such a cross-grain'd brute, that won't
hear me! Can you bear witness that you're no better than a fool!
Was ever poor woman so beset with fools on one hand, and thieves
on the other.

TONY. I can bear witness to that.

MRS. HARDCASTLE. Bear witness again, you blockhead you, and I'll turn
you out of the room directly. My poor niece, what will become of 20
her! Do you laugh, you unfeeling brute, as if you enjoy'd my
distress?

TONY. I can bear witness to that.

MRS. HARDCASTLE. Do you insult me, monster? I'll teach you to vex
your mother, I will.

TONY. I can bear witness to that.   [*He runs off, she follows him*

Enter MISS HARDCASTLE *and* MAID

MISS HARDCASTLE. What an unaccountable creature is that brother of
mine, to send them to the house as an inn, ha, ha. I don't wonder at
his impudence.   30

MAID. But what is more, madam, the young gentleman as you passed
by in your present dress, ask'd me if you were the bar maid? He
mistook you for the bar maid, madam.

MISS HARDCASTLE. Did he? Then as I live I'm resolved to keep up the
delusion. Tell me, Pimple, how do you like my present dress. Don't
you think I look something like Cherry in the Beaux Stratagem?

MAID. It's the dress, madam, that every lady wears in the country, but
when she visits or receives company.

MISS HARDCASTLE. And are you sure he does not remember my face or
person?   40

MAID. Certain of it.

MISS HARDCASTLE. I vow I thought so; for though we spoke for some
time together, yet his fears were such, that he never once looked up
during the interview. Indeed, if he had, my bonnet would have kept
him from seeing me.

MAID. But what do you hope from keeping him in his mistake?

MISS HARDCASTLE. In the first place, I shall be *seen*, and that is no small
advantage to a girl who brings her face to market. Then I shall perhaps make an acquaintance and that's no small victory gained over
one who never addresses any but the wildest of her sex. But my
chief aim is to take my gentleman off his guard, and like an invisible   10
champion of romance examine the giant's force before I offer to
combat.

MAID. But are you sure you can act your part, and disguise your voice,
so that he may mistake that, as he has already mistaken your person?

MISS HARDCASTLE. Never fear me. I think I have got the true bar cant.—
Did your honour call?——Attend the Lion there.——Pipes and
tobacco for the Angel.—The Lamb has been outrageous this half
hour.

MAID. It will do, madam. But he's here.   [*Exit* MAID.

Enter MARLOW   20

MARLOW. What a bawling in every part of the house; I have scarce a
moment's repose. If I go to the best room, there I find my host and
his story. If I fly to the gallery, there we have my hostess with her
curtesy down to the ground. I have at last got a moment to myself,
and now for recollection.   [*Walks and muses*

MISS HARDCASTLE. Did you call, Sir? did your honour call?

MARLOW. (*Musing*) As for Miss Hardcastle, she's too grave and sentimental for me.

MISS HARDCASTLE. Did your honour call?

[*She still places herself before him, he turning away* 30

MARLOW. No, child (*musing*). Besides from the glimpse I had of her, I
think she squints.

MISS HARDCASTLE. I'm sure, Sir, I heard the bell ring.

MARLOW. No, No. (*musing*) I have pleased my father, however, by
coming down, and I'll to-morrow please myself by returning.

[*Taking out his tablets, and perusing*

MISS HARDCASTLE. Perhaps the other gentleman called, Sir.

MARLOW. I tell you, no.

MISS HARDCASTLE. I should be glad to know, Sir. We have such a
parcel of servants.   40

MARLOW. No, no, I tell you. (*Looks full in her face*) Yes, child, I think I did call. I wanted——I wanted——I vow, child, you are vastly handsome.

MISS HARDCASTLE. O la, Sir, you'll make one asham'd.

MARLOW. Never saw a more sprightly malicious eye. Yes, yes, my dear, I did call. Have you got any of your—a—what d'ye call it in the house?

MISS HARDCASTLE. No, Sir, we have been out of that these ten days.

MARLOW. One may call in this house, I find, to very little purpose. Suppose I should call for a taste, just by way of trial, of the nectar of your lips; perhaps I might be disappointed in that too.   10

MISS HARDCASTLE. Nectar! nectar! that's a liquor there's no call for in these parts. French, I suppose. We keep no French wines here, Sir.

MARLOW. Of true English growth, I assure you.

MISS HARDCASTLE. Then it's odd I should not know it. We brew all sorts of wines in this house, and I have lived here these eighteen years.

MARLOW. Eighteen years! Why one would think, child, you kept the bar before you were born. How old are you?

MISS HARDCASTLE. O! Sir, I must not tell my age. They say women and music should never be dated.   20

MARLOW. To guess at this distance, you can't be much above forty (*approaching.*) Yet nearer I don't think so much (*approaching.*) By coming close to some women they look younger still; but when we come very close indeed (*attempting to kiss her.*)

MISS HARDCASTLE. Pray, Sir, keep your distance. One would think you wanted to know one's age as they do horses, by mark of mouth.

MARLOW. I protest, child, you use me extremely ill. If you keep me at this distance, how is it possible you and I can be ever acquainted?

MISS HARDCASTLE. And who wants to be acquainted with you? I want no such acquaintance, not I. I'm sure you did not treat Miss Hard-   30 castle that was here awhile ago in this obstropalous manner. I'll warrant me, before her you look'd dash'd, and kept bowing to the ground, and talk'd, for all the world, as if you was before a justice of peace.

MARLOW. (*Aside*) Egad! she has hit it, sure enough. (*To her*) In awe of her, child? Ha! ha! ha! A mere, aukward, squinting thing, no, no. I find you don't know me. I laugh'd, and rallied her a little; but I was unwilling to be too severe. No, I could not be too severe, *curse me!*

MISS HARDCASTLE. O! then, Sir, you are a favourite, I find, among the ladies?   40

MARLOW. Yes, my dear, a great favourite. And yet, hang me, I don't see what they find in me to follow. At the Ladies Club in town, I'm called their agreeable Rattle. Rattle, child, is not my real name, but one I'm known by. My name is Solomons. Mr. Solomons, my dear, at your service. (*Offering to salute her*)

MISS HARDCASTLE. Hold, Sir; you were introducing me to your club, not to yourself. And you're so great a favourite there you say?

MARLOW. Yes, my dear. There's Mrs. Mantrap, Lady Betty Blackleg, the Countess of Sligo, Mrs. Langhorns, old Miss Biddy Buckskin, and your humble servant, keep up the spirit of the place.

MISS HARDCASTLE. Then it's a very merry place, I suppose.

MARLOW. Yes, as merry as cards, suppers, wine, and old women can 10 make us.

MISS HARDCASTLE. And their agreeable Rattle, ha ! ha ! ha !

MARLOW. (*Aside*) Egad ! I don't quite like this chit. She looks knowing, methinks. You laugh, child !

MISS HARDCASTLE. I can't but laugh to think what time they all have for minding their work or their family.

MARLOW. (*Aside*) All's well, she don't laugh at me. (*To her*) Do *you* ever work, child?

MISS HARDCASTLE. Ay, sure. There's not a screen or a quilt in the whole house but what can bear witness to that. 20

MARLOW. Odso ! Then you must shew me your embroidery. I embroider and draw patterns myself a little. If you want a judge of your work you must apply to me. [*Seizing her hand*

MISS HARDCASTLE. Ay, but the colours don't look well by candle light. You shall see all in the morning. [*Struggling*

MARLOW. And why not now, my angel? Such beauty fires beyond the power of resistance.———Pshaw ! the father here ! My old luck: I never nick'd seven that I did not throw ames ace three times following. [*Exit* MARLOW.

Enter HARDCASTLE, *who stands in surprize* 30

HARDCASTLE. So, madam ! So I find *this* is your *modest* lover. This is your humble admirer that kept his eyes fixed on the ground, and only ador'd at humble distance. Kate, Kate, art thou not asham'd to deceive your father so?

MISS HARDCASTLE. Never trust me, dear papa, but he's still the modest man I first took him for, you'll be convinced of it as well as I.

HARDCASTLE. By the hand of my body I believe his impudence is infectious ! Didn't I see him seize your hand? Didn't I see him hawl you about like a milk maid? and now you talk of his respect and his modesty, forsooth ! 40

MISS HARDCASTLE. But if I shortly convince you of his modesty, that he has only the faults that will pass off with time, and the virtues that will improve with age, I hope you'll forgive him.

HARDCASTLE. The girl would actually make one run mad! I tell you I'll not be convinced. I am convinced. He has scarcely been three hours in the house, and he has already encroached on all my prerogatives. You may like his impudence, and call it modesty. But my son-in-law, madam, must have very different qualifications.

MISS HARDCASTLE. Sir, I ask but this night to convince you.

HARDCASTLE. You shall not have half the time, for I have thoughts of turning him out this very hour.   10

MISS HARDCASTLE. Give me that hour then, and I hope to satisfy you.

HARDCASTLE. Well, an hour let it be then. But I'll have no trifling with your father. All fair and open, do you mind me?

MISS HARDCASTLE. I hope, Sir, you have ever found that I considered your commands as my pride; for your kindness is such, that my duty as yet has been inclination.   [*Exeunt.*

END OF THIRD ACT

ACT IV

Enter HASTINGS *and* MISS NEVILLE

HASTINGS. You surprise me! Sir Charles Marlow expected here this night? Where have you had your information?

MISS NEVILLE. You may depend upon it. I just saw his letter to Mr. Hardcastle, in which he tells him he intends setting out a few hours after his son.

HASTINGS. Then, my Constance, all must be completed before he arrives. He knows me; and should he find me here, would discover my name, and perhaps my designs, to the rest of the family. 10

MISS NEVILLE. The jewels, I hope, are safe.

HASTINGS. Yes, yes. I have sent them to Marlow, who keeps the keys of our baggage. In the meantime, I'll go to prepare matters for our elopement. I have had the Squire's promise of a fresh pair of horses; and, if I should not see him again, will write him further directions.
[*Exit.*

MISS NEVILLE. Well! success attend you. In the meantime, I'll go amuse my aunt with the old pretence of a violent passion for my cousin.
[*Exit.*

Enter MARLOW, *followed by a* SERVANT 20

MARLOW. I wonder what Hastings could mean by sending me so valuable a thing as a casket to keep for him, when he knows the only place I have is the seat of a post-coach at an Inn-door. Have you deposited the casket with the landlady, as I ordered you? Have you put it into her own hands?

SERVANT. Yes, your honour.

MARLOW. She said she'd keep it safe, did she?

SERVANT. Yes, she said she'd keep it safe enough; she ask'd me how I came by it? and she said she had a great mind to make me give an account of myself. [*Exit* SERVANT. 30

MARLOW. Ha! ha! ha! They're safe however. What an unaccountable set of beings have we got amongst! This little bar-maid though runs in my head most strangely, and drives out the absurdities of all the rest of the family. She's mine, she must be mine, or I'm greatly mistaken.

Enter HASTINGS

HASTINGS. Bless me! I quite forgot to tell her that I intended to prepare at the bottom of the garden. Marlow here, and in spirits too!

MARLOW. Give me joy, George! Crown me, shadow me with laurels! Well, George, after all, we modest fellows don't want for success among the women.

HASTINGS. Some women you mean. But what success has your honour's modesty been crowned with now, that it grows so insolent upon us?

MARLOW. Didn't you see the tempting, brisk, lovely, little thing that runs about the house with a bunch of keys to its girdle?

HASTINGS. Well! and what then?

MARLOW. She's mine, you rogue you. Such fire, such motion, such eyes, such lips——but, egad! she would not let me kiss them though.

HASTINGS. But are you so sure, so very sure of her?

MARLOW. Why man, she talk'd of shewing me her work above-stairs, and I am to improve the pattern.

HASTINGS. But how can *you*, Charles, go about to rob a woman of her honour?

MARLOW. Pshaw! pshaw! we all know the honour of the bar-maid of an inn. I don't intend to *rob* her, take my word for it, there's nothing in this house, I shan't honestly *pay* for.

HASTINGS. I believe the girl has virtue.

MARLOW. And if she has, I should be the last man in the world that would attempt to corrupt it.

HASTINGS. You have taken care, I hope, of the casket I sent you to lock up? It's in safety?

MARLOW. Yes, yes. It's safe enough. I have taken care of it. But how could you think the seat of a post-coach at an Inn-door a place of safety? Ah! numbskull! I have taken better precautions for you than you did for yourself.——I have——

HASTINGS. What!

MARLOW. I have sent it to the landlady to keep for you.

HASTINGS. To the landlady!

MARLOW. The landlady.

HASTINGS. You did.

MARLOW. I did. She's to be answerable for its forth-coming, you know.

HASTINGS. Yes, she'll bring it forth, with a witness.

MARLOW. Wasn't I right? I believe you'll allow that I acted prudently upon this occasion?

HASTINGS. (*Aside*) He must not see my uneasiness.

MARLOW. You seem a little disconcerted though, methinks. Sure nothing has happened?

HASTINGS. No, nothing. Never was in better spirits in all my life. And so you left it with the landlady, who, no doubt, very readily undertook the charge?

MARLOW. Rather too readily. For she not only kept the casket; but, thro' her great precaution, was going to keep the messenger too. Ha! ha! ha!

HASTINGS. He! he! he! They're safe however.

MARLOW. As a guinea in a miser's purse.

HASTINGS. (*Aside*) So now all hopes of fortune are at an end, and we must set off without it. (*To him*) Well, Charles, I'll leave you to your meditations on the pretty bar-maid, and, he! he! he! may you be as successful for yourself as you have been for me.   [*Exit*.

MARLOW. Thank ye, George! I ask no more. Ha! ha! ha!

Enter HARDCASTLE

HARDCASTLE. I no longer know my own house. It's turned all topsey-turvey. His servants have got drunk already. I'll bear it no longer, and yet, from my respect for his father, I'll be calm. (*To him*) Mr. Marlow, your servant. I'm your very humble servant. [*bowing low*

MARLOW. Sir, your humble servant. (*Aside*) What's to be the wonder now?

HARDCASTLE. I believe, Sir, you must be sensible, Sir, that no man alive ought to be more welcome than your father's son, Sir. I hope you think so?

MARLOW. I do from my soul, Sir. I don't want much intreaty. I generally make my father's son welcome wherever he goes.

HARDCASTLE. I believe you do, from my soul, Sir. But tho' I say nothing to your own conduct, that of your Servants is insufferable. Their manner of drinking is setting a very bad example in this house, I assure you.

MARLOW. I protest, my very good Sir, that's no fault of mine. If they don't drink as they ought *they* are to blame. I ordered them not to spare the cellar. I did, I assure you. (*To the side scene*) Here, let one of my servants come up. (*To him*) My positive directions were, that as I did not drink myself, they should make up for my deficiencies below.

HARDCASTLE. Then they had your orders for what they do! I'm satisfied!

MARLOW. They had, I assure you. You shall hear from one of themselves.

Enter SERVANT *drunk*

MARLOW. You, Jeremy! Come forward, sirrah! What were my orders? Were you not told to drink freely, and call for what you thought fit, for the good of the house?

HARDCASTLE. (*Aside*) I begin to lose my patience.

JEREMY. Please your honour, liberty and Fleet-street for ever! Tho' 10 I'm but a servant, I'm as good as another man. I'll drink for no man before supper, Sir, dammy! Good liquor will sit upon a good supper, but a good supper will not sit upon——hiccup——upon my conscience, Sir.

MARLOW. You see, my old friend, the fellow is as drunk as he can possibly be. I don't know what you'd have more, unless you'd have the poor devil soused in a beer-barrel.

HARDCASTLE. Zounds! He'll drive me distracted if I contain myself any longer. Mr. Marlow. Sir; I have submitted to your insolence for more than four hours, and I see no likelihood of its coming to an 20 end. I'm now resolved to be master here, Sir, and I desire that you and your drunken pack may leave my house directly.

MARLOW. Leave your house!——Sure you jest, my good friend? What, when I'm doing what I can to please you.

HARDCASTLE. I tell you, Sir, you don't please me; so I desire you'll leave my house.

MARLOW. Sure you cannot be serious? At this time o'night, and such a night. You only mean to banter me?

HARDCASTLE. I tell you, Sir, I'm serious; and, now that my passions are rouzed, I say this house is mine, Sir; this house is mine, and I 30 command you to leave it directly.

MARLOW. Ha! ha! ha! A puddle in a storm. I shan't stir a step, I assure you. (*In a serious tone*) This, your house, fellow! It's my house. This is my house. Mine, while I chuse to stay. What right have you to bid me leave this house, Sir? I never met with such impudence, curse me, never in my whole life before.

HARDCASTLE. Nor I, confound me if ever I did. To come to my house, to call for what he likes, to turn me out of my own chair, to insult the family, to order his servants to get drunk, and then to tell me *This house is mine, Sir*. By all that's impudent it makes me laugh. Ha! 40 ha! ha! Pray, Sir, (*bantering*) as you take the house, what think you of taking the rest of the furniture? There's a pair of silver candlesticks, and there's a fire-screen, and here's a pair of brazen nosed bellows, perhaps you may take a fancy to them?

MARLOW. Bring me your bill, Sir, bring me your bill, and let's make no more words about it.

HARDCASTLE. There are a set of prints too. What think you of the rake's progress for your own apartment?

MARLOW. Bring me your bill, I say; and I'll leave you and your infernal house directly.

HARDCASTLE. Then there's a mahogony table, that you may see your 10 own face in.

MARLOW. My bill, I say.

HARDCASTLE. I had forgot the great chair, for your own particular slumbers, after a hearty meal.

MARLOW. Zounds! bring me my bill, I say, and let's hear no more on't.

HARDCASTLE. Young man, young man, from your father's letter to me, I was taught to expect a well-bred modest man, as a visitor here, but now I find him no better than a coxcomb and a bully; but he will be down here presently, and shall hear more of it.   [Exit. 20

MARLOW. How's this! Sure I have not mistaken the house! Every thing looks like an inn. The servants cry, *Coming*. The attendance is aukward; the bar-maid too to attend us. But she's here, and will further inform me. Whither so fast, child. A word with you.

Enter MISS HARDCASTLE

MISS HARDCASTLE. Let it be short then. I'm in a hurry. (*Aside*) (I believe he begins to find out his mistake, but its too soon quite to undeceive him.)

MARLOW. Pray, child, answer me one question. What are you, and what may your business in this house be?   30

MISS HARDCASTLE. A relation of the family, Sir.

MARLOW. What. A poor relation?

MISS HARDCASTLE. Yes, Sir. A poor relation appointed to keep the keys, and to see that the guests want nothing in my power to give them.

MARLOW. That is, you act as the bar-maid of this inn.

MISS HARDCASTLE. Inn. O law—What brought that in your head. One of the best families in the county keep an inn. Ha, ha, ha, old Mr. Hardcastle's house an inn.

MARLOW. Mr. Hardcastle's house! Is this house Mr. Hardcastle's house, 40 child!

MISS HARDCASTLE. Ay, sure. Whose else should it be.

MARLOW. So then all's out, and I have been damnably imposed on. O, confound my stupid head, I shall be laugh'd at over the whole town. I shall be stuck up in caricatura in all the print-shops. The Dullissimo Maccaroni. To mistake this house of all others for an inn, and my father's old friend for an inn-keeper. What a swaggering puppy must he take me for. What a silly puppy do I find myself. There again, may I be hang'd, my dear, but I mistook you for the bar-maid.

MISS HARDCASTLE. Dear me! dear me! I'm sure there's nothing in my *behaviour* to put me upon a level with one of that stamp. 10

MARLOW. Nothing, my dear, nothing. But I was in for a list of blunders, and could not help making you a subscriber. My stupidity saw every thing the wrong way. I mistook your assiduity for assurance, and your simplicity for allurement. But its over—This house I no more shew *my* face in.

MISS HARDCASTLE. I hope, Sir, I have done nothing to disoblige you. I'm sure I should be sorry to affront any gentleman who has been so polite, and said so many civil things to me. I'm sure I should be sorry (*pretending to cry*) if he left the family upon my account. I'm sure I should be sorry people said any thing amiss, since I have no 20 fortune but my character.

MARLOW. (*Aside*) By heaven, she weeps. This is the first mark of tenderness I ever had from a modest woman, and it touches me; (*to her*) Excuse me, my lovely girl, you are the only part of the family I leave with reluctance. But to be plain with you, the difference of our birth, fortune and education, make an honourable connexion impossible; and I can never harbour a thought of seducing simplicity that trusted in my honour, or bringing ruin upon one, whose only fault was being too lovely.

MISS HARDCASTLE. (*Aside*) Generous man! I now begin to admire him. 30 (*to him*) But I'm sure my family is as good as miss Hardcastle's, and though I'm poor, that's no great misfortune to a contented mind, and, until this moment, I never thought that it was bad to want fortune.

MARLOW. And why now, my pretty simplicity?

MISS HARDCASTLE. Because it puts me at a distance from one, that if I had a thousand pound I would give it all to.

MARLOW. (*Aside*) This simplicity bewitches me, so that if I stay I'm undone. I must make one bold effort, and leave her. (*to her*) Your partiality in my favour, my dear, touches me most sensibly, and were 40 I to live for myself alone, I could easily fix my choice. But I owe too much to the opinion of the world, too much to the authority of a

father, so that—I can scarcely speak it—it affects me. Farewell.
                                                      [*Exit.*

MISS HARDCASTLE. I never knew half his merit till now. He shall not go,
if I have power or art to detain him. I'll still preserve the character
in which I stoop'd to conquer, but will undeceive my papa, who,
perhaps, may laugh him out of his resolution.   [*Exit.*

Enter TONY, MISS NEVILLE

TONY. Ay, you may steal for yourselves the next time. I have done my
duty. She has got the jewels again, that's a sure thing; but she
believes it was all a mistake of the servants.   10

MISS NEVILLE. But, my dear cousin, sure you won't forsake us in this
distress. If she in the least suspects that I am going off, I shall certainly be locked up, or sent to my aunt Pedigree's, which is ten times
worse.

TONY. To be sure, aunts of all kinds are damn'd bad things. But what
can I do? I have got you a pair of horses that will fly like Whistlejacket, and I'm sure you can't say but I have courted you nicely
before her face. Here she comes, we must court a bit or two more,
for fear she should suspect us.   [*They retire, and seem to fondle*

Enter MRS. HARDCASTLE   20

MRS. HARDCASTLE. Well, I was greatly fluttered, to be sure. But my son
tells me it was all a mistake of the servants. I shan't be easy, however,
till they are fairly married, and then let her keep her own fortune. But
what do I see! Fondling together, as I'm alive.   I never saw Tony
so sprightly before. Ah! have I caught you, my pretty doves! What,
billing, exchanging stolen glances, and broken murmurs. Ah!

TONY. As for murmurs, mother, we grumble a little now and then, to
be sure. But there's no love lost between us.

MRS. HARDCASTLE. A mere sprinkling, Tony, upon the flame, only to
make it burn brighter.   30

MISS NEVILLE. Cousin Tony promises to give us more of his company
at home. Indeed, he shan't leave us any more. It won't leave us
cousin Tony, will it?

TONY. O! it's a pretty creature. No, I'd sooner leave my horse in a
pound, than leave you when you smile upon one so. Your laugh
makes you so becoming.

MISS NEVILLE. Agreeable cousin! Who can help admiring that natural
humour, that pleasant, broad, red, thoughtless, (*patting his cheek*) ah!
it's a bold face.

MRS. HARDCASTLE. Pretty innocence.   40

TONY. I'm sure I always lov'd cousin Con's hazle eyes, and her pretty
   long fingers, that she twists this way and that, over the haspicholls,
   like a parcel of bobbins.

MRS. HARDCASTLE. Ah, he would charm the bird from the tree. I was
   never so happy before. My boy takes after his father, poor Mr. Lumpkin, exactly. The jewels, my dear Con, shall be your's incontinently.
   You shall have them. Isn't he a sweet boy, my dear? You shall be
   married to-morrow, and we'll put off the rest of his education, like
   Dr. Drowsy's sermons, to a fitter opportunity.

Enter DIGGORY   10

DIGGORY. Where's the 'Squire? I have got a letter for your worship.

TONY. Give it to my mamma. She reads all my letters first.

DIGGORY. I had orders to deliver it into your own hands.

TONY. Who does it come from?

DIGGORY. Your worship mun ask that o' the letter itself.

TONY. I could wish to know, tho' (*turning the letter, and gazing on it*).

MISS NEVILLE. (*Aside*) Undone, undone. A letter to him from Hastings.
   I know the hand. If my aunt sees it, we are ruined for ever. I'll keep
   her employ'd a little if I can. (*To* MRS. HARDCASTLE) But I have not
   told you, Madam, of my cousin's smart answer just now to Mr.   20
   Marlow. We so laugh'd—You must know, Madam—this way a
   little, for he must not hear us.   [*They confer*

TONY. (*Still gazing*) A damn'd cramp piece of penmanship, as ever I
   saw in my life. I can read your print-hand very well. But here there
   are such handles, and shanks, and dashes, that one can scarce tell the
   head from the tail. *To Anthony Lumpkin, Esquire.* It's very odd, I can
   read the outside of my letters, where my own name is, well enough.
   But when I come to open it, it's all—buzz. That's hard, very hard;
   for the inside of the letter is always the cream of the correspondence.

MRS. HARDCASTLE. Ha, ha, ha. Very well, very well. And so my son was   30
   too hard for the philosopher.

MISS NEVILLE. Yes, Madam; but you must hear the rest, Madam. A
   little more this way, or he may hear us. You'll hear how he puzzled
   him again.

MRS. HARDCASTLE. He seems strangely puzzled now himself, methinks.

TONY. (*Still gazing*) A damn'd up and down hand, as if it was disguised
   in liquor. (*Reading*) *Dear Sir.* Ay, that's that. Then there's an *M*, and
   a *T*, and an *S*, but whether the next be an *izzard* or an *R*, confound
   me, I cannot tell.

MRS. HARDCASTLE. What's that, my dear. Can I give you any assistance?   40

MISS NEVILLE. Pray, aunt, let me read it. No body reads a cramp hand better than I. (*twitching the letter from her*) Do you know who it is from?

TONY. Can't tell, except from Dick Ginger the feeder.

MISS NEVILLE. Ay, so it is, (*pretending to read*) Dear 'Squire, Hoping that you're in health, as I am at this present. The gentlemen of the Shake bag club has cut the gentlemen of goose-green quite out of feather. The odds—um—odd battle—um—long fighting—um here, here, it's all about cocks, and fighting; it's of no consequence, here, put it up, put it up.   [*thrusting the crumpled letter upon him*

TONY. But I tell you, Miss, it's of all the consequence in the world. 10 I would not lose the rest of it for a guinea. Here, mother, do you make it out. Of no consequence! [*giving* MRS. HARDCASTLE *the letter*

MRS HARDCASTLE. How's this! (*reads*) Dear 'Squire, I'm now waiting for Miss Neville, with a post-chaise and pair, at the bottom of the garden, but I find my horses yet unable to perform the journey. I expect you'll assist us with a pair of fresh horses, as you promised. Dispatch is necessary, as the *hag* (ay the hag) your mother, will otherwise suspect us. Your's, Hastings. Grant me patience. I shall run distracted. My rage choaks me.

MISS NEVILLE. I hope, Madam, you'll suspend your resentment for a 20 few moments, and not impute to me any impertinence, or sinister design that belongs to another.

MRS. HARDCASTLE. (*Curtesying very low*) Fine spoken, Madam, you are most miraculously polite and engaging, and quite the very pink of curtesy and circumspection, Madam. (*Changing her tone*) And you, you great ill-fashioned oaf, with scarce sense enough to keep your mouth shut. Were you too join'd against me? But I'll defeat all your plots in a moment. As for you, Madam, since you have got a pair of fresh horses ready, it would be cruel to disappoint them. So, if you please, instead of running away with your spark, prepare, this very 30 moment, to run off with *me*. Your old aunt Pedigree will keep you secure, I'll warrant me. You too, Sir, may mount your horse, and guard us upon the way. Here, Thomas, Roger, Diggory, I'll shew you that I wish you better than you do yourselves.   [*Exit.*

MISS NEVILLE. So now I'm completely ruined.

TONY. Ay, that's a sure thing.

MISS NEVILLE. What better could be expected from being connected with such a stupid fool, and after all the nods and signs I made him.

TONY. By the laws, Miss, it was your own cleverness, and not my stupidity, that did your business. You were so nice and so busy with 40 your Shake-bags and Goose-greens, that I thought you could never be making believe.

Enter HASTINGS

HASTINGS. So, Sir, I find by my servant, that you have shewn my letter, and betray'd us. Was this well done, young gentleman?

TONY. Here's another. Ask Miss there who betray'd you. Ecod, it was her doing, not mine.

Enter MARLOW

MARLOW. So I have been finely used here among you. Rendered contemptible, driven into ill manners, despised, insulted, laugh'd at.

TONY. Here's another. We shall have old Bedlam broke loose presently.

MISS NEVILLE. And there, Sir, is the gentleman to whom we all owe every obligation.

MARLOW. What can I say to him, a mere boy, an ideot, whose ignorance and age are a protection.

HASTINGS. A poor contemptible booby, that would but disgrace correction.

MISS NEVILLE. Yet with cunning and malice enough to make himself merry with all our embarrassments.

HASTINGS. An insensible cub.

MARLOW. Replete with tricks and mischief.

TONY. Baw! damme, but I'll fight you both one after the other,—— with baskets.

MARLOW. As for him, he's below resentment. But your conduct, Mr. Hastings, requires an explanation. You knew of my mistakes, yet would not undeceive me.

HASTINGS. Tortured as I am with my own disappointments, is this a time for explanations! It is not friendly, Mr. Marlow.

MARLOW. But, Sir—

MISS NEVILLE. Mr. Marlow, we never kept on your mistake, till it was too late to undeceive you. Be pacified.

Enter SERVANT

SERVANT. My mistress desires you'll get ready immediately, Madam. The horses are putting to. Your hat and things are in the next room. We are to go thirty miles before morning.   [*Exit* SERVANT.

MISS NEVILLE. Well, well; I'll come presently.

MARLOW. [*To* HASTINGS] Was it well done, Sir, to assist in rendering me ridiculous? To hang me out for the scorn of all my acquaintance. Depend upon it, Sir, I shall expect an explanation.

HASTINGS. Was it well done, Sir, if you're upon that subject, to deliver what I entrusted to yourself, to the care of another, Sir?

MISS NEVILLE. Mr. Hastings. Mr. Marlow. Why will you increase my distress by this groundless dispute? I implore, I intreat you——

Enter SERVANT

SERVANT. Your cloak, Madam. My mistress is impatient.

MISS NEVILLE. I come. Pray be pacified. If I leave you thus, I shall die with apprehension.

SERVANT. Your fan, muff, and gloves, Madam. The horses are waiting.

MISS NEVILLE. O, Mr. Marlow! if you knew what a scene of constraint and ill-nature lies before me, I'm sure it would convert your resentment into pity.   10

MARLOW. I'm so distracted with a variety of passions, that I don't know what I do. Forgive me, Madam. George, forgive me. You know my hasty temper, and should not exasperate it.

HASTINGS. The torture of my situation is my only excuse.

MISS NEVILLE. Well, my dear Hastings, if you have that esteem for me that I think, that I am sure you have, your constancy for three years will but encrease the happiness of our future connexion. If—

MRS. HARDCASTLE. (*Within*) Miss Neville. Constance, why Constance, I say.

MISS NEVILLE. I'm coming. Well, constancy. Remember, constancy is   20 the word.   [*Exit.*

HASTINGS. My heart! How can I support this. To be so near happiness, and such happiness.

MARLOW. (*To* TONY) You see now, young gentleman, the effects of your folly. What might be amusement to you, is here disappointment, and even distress.

TONY. (*From a reverie*) Ecod, I have hit it. Its here. Your hands. Yours and yours, my poor Sulky. My boots there, ho. Meet me two hours hence at the bottom of the garden; and if you don't find Tony Lumpkin a more good-natur'd fellow than you thought for, I'll   30 give you leave to take my best horse, and Bet Bouncer into the bargain. Come along. My boots, ho.   [*Exeunt.*

END OF THE FOURTH ACT

ACT V

Scene *Continues*

Enter HASTINGS *and* SERVANT

HASTINGS. You saw the Old Lady and Miss Neville drive off, you say.

SERVANT. Yes, your honour. They went off in a post coach, and the young 'Squire went on horseback. They're thirty miles off by this time.

HASTINGS. Then all my hopes are over.

SERVANT. Yes, Sir. Old Sir Charles is arrived. He and the Old Gentleman of the house have been laughing at Mr. Marlow's mistake this half hour. They are coming this way. 10

HASTINGS. Then I must not be seen. So now to my fruitless appointment at the bottom of the garden. This is about the time.   [*Exit.*

Enter SIR CHARLES *and* HARDCASTLE

HARDCASTLE. Ha, ha, ha. The peremptory tone in which he sent forth his sublime commands.

SIR CHARLES. And the reserve with which I suppose he treated all your advances.

HARDCASTLE. And yet he might have seen something in me above a common inn-keeper, too.

SIR CHARLES. Yes, Dick, but he mistook you for an uncommon inn- 20 keeper, ha, ha, ha.

HARDCASTLE. Well, I'm in too good spirits to think of any thing but joy. Yes, my dear friend, this union of our families will make our personal friendship hereditary; and tho' my daughter's fortune is but small——

SIR CHARLES. Why, Dick, will you talk of fortune to *me*. My son is possessed of more than a competence already, and can want nothing but a good and virtuous girl to share his happiness and encrease it. If they like each other, as you say they do——

HARDCASTLE. *If*, man. I tell you they *do* like each other. My daughter as good as told me so.

SIR CHARLES. But girls are apt to flatter themselves, you know.

HARDCASTLE. I saw him grasp her hand in the warmest manner myself; and here he comes to put you out of your *iffs*, I warrant him.

Enter MARLOW

MARLOW. I come, Sir, once more, to ask pardon for my strange conduct. I can scarce reflect on my insolence without confusion.

HARDCASTLE. Tut, boy, a trifle. You take it too gravely. An hour or two's laughing with my daughter will set all to rights again. She'll 10 never like you the worse for it.

MARLOW. Sir, I shall be always proud of her approbation.

HARDCASTLE. Approbation is but a cold word, Mr. Marlow; if I am not deceived, you have something more than approbation thereabouts. You take me.

MARLOW. Really, Sir, I have not that happiness.

HARDCASTLE. Come, boy, I'm an old fellow, and know what's what, as well as you that are younger. I know what has past between you; but mum.

MARLOW. Sure, Sir, nothing has past between us but the most profound 20 respect on my side, and the most distant reserve on her's. You don't think, Sir, that my impudence has been past upon all the rest of the family.

HARDCASTLE. Impudence! No, I don't say that—Not quite impudence —Though girls like to be play'd with, and rumpled a little too sometimes. But she has told no tales, I assure you.

MARLOW. I never gave her the slightest cause.

HARDCASTLE. Well, well, I like modesty in its place well enough. But this is over-acting, young gentleman. You *may* be open. Your father and I will like you the better for it. 30

MARLOW. May I die, Sir, if I ever——

HARDCASTLE. I tell you, she don't dislike you; and as I'm sure you like her——

MARLOW. Dear Sir—I protest, Sir——

HARDCASTLE. I see no reason why you should not be joined as fast as the parson can tie you.

MARLOW. But hear me, Sir——

HARDCASTLE. Your father approves the match, I admire it, every moment's delay will be doing mischief, so——

MARLOW. But why won't you hear me? By all that's just and true, I 40 never gave miss Hardcastle the slightest mark of my attachment, or even the most distant hint to suspect me of affection. We had but one interview, and that was formal, modest and uninteresting.

HARDCASTLE. (*Aside*) This fellow's formal modest impudence is beyond bearing.

SIR CHARLES. And you never grasp'd her hand, or made any protestations!

MARLOW. As heaven is my witness, I came down in obedience to your commands. I saw the lady without emotion, and parted without reluctance. I hope you'll exact no further proofs of my duty, nor prevent me from leaving a house in which I suffer so many mortifications. [*Exit.*

SIR CHARLES. I'm astonish'd at the air of sincerity with which he parted.

HARDCASTLE. And I'm astonish'd at the deliberate intrepidity of his assurance.

SIR CHARLES. I dare pledge my life and honour upon his truth.

HARDCASTLE. Here comes my daughter, and I would stake my happiness upon her veracity.

Enter MISS HARDCASTLE

HARDCASTLE. Kate, come hither, child. Answer us sincerely, and without reserve; has Mr. Marlow made you any professions of love and affection?

MISS HARDCASTLE. The question is very abrupt, Sir! But since you require unreserved sincerity, I think he has.

HARDCASTLE. (*To* SIR CHARLES) You see.

SIR CHARLES. And pray, madam, have you and my son had more than one interview?

MISS HARDCASTLE. Yes, Sir, several.

HARDCASTLE. (*To* SIR CHARLES) You see.

SIR CHARLES. But did he profess any attachment?

MISS HARDCASTLE. A lasting one.

SIR CHALRES. Did he talk of love?

MISS HARDCASTLE. Much, Sir.

SIR CHARLES. Amazing! And all this formally?

MISS HARDCASTLE. Formally.

HARDCASTLE. Now, my friend, I hope you are satisfied.

SIR CHARLES. And how did he behave, madam?

MISS HARDCASTLE. As most profest admirers do. Said some civil things of my face, talked much of his want of merit, and the greatness of mine; mentioned his heart, gave a short tragedy speech, and ended with pretended rapture.

SIR CHARLES. Now I'm perfectly convinced, indeed. I know his conversation among women to be modest and submissive. This forward canting ranting manner by no means describes him, and I am
confident, he never sate for the picture.

MISS HARDCASTLE. Then what, Sir, if I should convince you to your
face of my sincerity? If you and my papa, in about half an hour, will
place yourselves behind that screen, you shall hear him declare his
passion to me in person.

SIR CHARLES. Agreed. And if I find him what you describe, all my
happiness in him must have an end.   [*Exit.* 10

MISS HARDCASTLE. And if you don't find him what I describe—I fear
my happiness must never have a beginning.   [*Exeunt.*

SCENE *changes to the Back of the Garden*

Enter HASTINGS

HASTINGS. What an ideot am I, to wait here for a fellow, who probably
takes a delight in mortifying me. He never intended to be punctual,
and I'll wait no longer. What do I see. It is he, and perhaps with
news of my Constance.

Enter TONY, *booted and spattered*

HASTINGS. My honest 'Squire! I now find you a man of your word. 20
This looks like friendship.

TONY. Ay, I'm your friend, and the best friend you have in the world,
if you knew but all. This riding by night, by the bye, is cursedly
tiresome. It has shook me worse than the basket of a stage-coach.

HASTINGS. But how? Where did you leave your fellow travellers? Are
they in safety? Are they housed?

TONY. Five and twenty miles in two hours and a half is no such bad
driving. The poor beasts have smoaked for it: Rabbet me, but I'd
rather ride forty miles after a fox, than ten with such *varment*.

HASTINGS. Well, but where have you left the ladies? I die with im- 30
patience.

TONY. Left them. Why where should I leave them, but where I found
them.

HASTINGS. This is a riddle.

TONY. Riddle me this then. What's that goes round the house, and
round the house, and never touches the house?

HASTINGS. I'm still astray.

TONY. Why that's it, mon. I have led them astray. By jingo, there's not a pond or slough within five miles of the place but they can tell the taste of.

HASTINGS. Ha, ha, ha, I understand; you took them in a round, while they supposed themselves going forward. And so you have at last brought them home again.

TONY. You shall hear. I first took them down Feather-bed-lane, where we stuck fast in the mud. I then rattled them crack over the stones of Up-and-down Hill—I then introduc'd them to the gibbet on Heavy-tree Heath, and from that, with a circumbendibus, I fairly lodged them in the horse-pond at the bottom of the garden.   10

HASTINGS. But no accident, I hope.

TONY. No, no. Only mother is confoundedly frightened. She thinks herself forty miles off. She's sick of the journey, and the cattle can scarce crawl. So if your own horses be ready, you may whip off with cousin, and I'll be bound that no soul here can budge a foot to follow you.

HASTINGS. My dear friend, how can I be grateful?

TONY. Ay, now its dear friend, noble 'Squire. Just now, it was all ideot, cub, and run me through the guts. Damn *your* way of fighting, I say. After we take a knock in this part of the country, we kiss and be 20 friends. But if you had run me through the guts, then I should be dead, and you might go kiss the hangman.

HASTINGS. The rebuke is just. But I must hasten to relieve miss Neville; if you keep the old lady employed, I promise to take care of the young one.   [*Exit* HASTINGS.

TONY. Never fear me. Here she comes. Vanish. She's got from the pond, and draggled up to the waist like a mermaid.

Enter MRS. HARDCASTLE

MRS. HARDCASTLE. Oh, Tony, I'm killed. Shook. Battered to death. I shall never survive it. That last jolt that laid us against the quickset 30 hedge has done my business.

TONY. Alack, mama, it was all your own fault. You would be for running away by night, without knowing one inch of the way.

MRS. HARDCASTLE. I wish we were at home again. I never met so many accidents in so short a journey. Drench'd in the mud, overturn'd in a ditch, stuck fast in a slough, jolted to a jelly, and at last to lose our way. Whereabouts do you think we are, Tony?

TONY. By my guess we should be upon Crackskull common, about forty miles from home.

MRS. HARDCASTLE. O lud! O lud! the most notorious spot in all the 40 country. We only want a robbery to make a complete night on't.

TONY. Don't be afraid, mama, don't be afraid. Two of the five that kept here are hanged, and the other three may not find us. Don't be afraid. Is that a man that's galloping behind us? No; its only a tree. Don't be afraid.

MRS. HARDCASTLE. The fright will certainly kill me.

TONY. Do you see any thing like a black hat moving behind the thicket?

MRS. HARDCASTLE. O death!

TONY. No, it's only a cow. Don't be afraid, mama; don't be afraid.

MRS. HARDCASTLE. As I'm alive, Tony, I see a man coming towards us. Ah! I'm sure on't. If he perceives us we are undone.   10

TONY. (*Aside*) Father-in-law, by all that's unlucky, come to take one of his night walks. (*To her*) Ah, it's a highwayman, with pistils as long as my arm. A damn'd ill-looking fellow.

MRS. HARDCASTLE. Good heaven defend us! He approaches.

TONY. Do you hide yourself in that thicket, and leave me to manage him. If there be any danger I'll cough and cry hem. When I cough be sure to keep close.

[MRS. HARDCASTLE *hides behind a tree in the back scene*

Enter HARDCASTLE

HARDCASTLE. I'm mistaken, or I heard voices of people in want of   20 help. Oh, Tony, is that you. I did not expect you so soon back. Are your mother and her charge in safety?

TONY. Very safe, Sir, at my aunt Pedigree's. Hem.

MRS. HARDCASTLE. (*From behind*) Ah death! I find there's danger.

HARDCASTLE. Forty miles in three hours; sure, that's too much, my youngster.

TONY. Stout horses and willing minds make short journies, as they say. Hem.

MRS. HARDCASTLE. (*From behind*) Sure he'll do the dear boy no harm.

HARDCASTLE. But I heard a voice here; I should be glad to know from   30 whence it came?

TONY. It was I, Sir, talking to myself, Sir. I was saying that forty miles in four hours was very good going. Hem. As to be sure it was. Hem. I have got a sort of cold by being out in the air. We'll go in, if you please. Hem.

HARDCASTLE. But if you talk'd to yourself, you did not answer yourself. I am certain I heard two voices, and am resolved (*raising his voice*) to find the other out.

MRS. HARDCASTLE. (*From behind*) Oh! he's coming to find me out. Oh!

TONY. What need you go, Sir, if I tell you. Hem. I'll lay down my life   40 for the truth—hem—I'll tell you all, Sir.   [*detaining him*

HARDCASTLE. I tell you, I will not be detained. I insist on seeing. It's in vain to expect I'll believe you.

MRS. HARDCASTLE. (*Running forward from behind*) O lud, he'll murder my poor boy, my darling. Here, good gentleman, whet your rage upon me. Take my money, my life, but spare that young gentleman, spare my child, if you have any mercy.

HARDCASTLE. My wife! as I'm a Christian. From whence can she come, or what does she mean!

MRS. HARDCASTLE. (*Kneeling*) Take compassion on us, good Mr. High-wayman. Take our money, our watches, all we have, but spare our 10 lives. We will never bring you to justice, indeed we won't, good Mr. Highwayman.

HARDCASTLE. I believe the woman's out of her senses. What, Dorothy, don't you know *me*?

MRS. HARDCASTLE. Mr. Hardcastle, as I'm alive. My fears blinded me. But who, my dear, could have expected to meet you here, in this frightful place, so far from home? What has brought you to follow us?

HARDCASTLE. Sure, Dorothy, you have not lost your wits? So far from home, when you are within forty yards of your own door. (*To him*) 20 This is one of your old tricks, you graceless rogue you. (*To her*) Don't you know the gate, and the mulberry-tree; and don't you remember the horsepond, my dear?

MRS. HARDCASTLE. Yes, I shall remember the horsepond as long as I live; I have caught my death in it. (*To* TONY) And is it to you, you graceless varlet, I owe all this. I'll teach you to abuse your mother, I will.

TONY. Ecod, mother, all the parish says you have spoil'd me, and so you may take the fruits on't.

MRS. HARDCASTLE. I'll spoil you, I will. 30

[*Follows him off the stage. Exit.*

HARDCASTLE. There's morality, however, in his reply. [*Exit.*

Enter HASTINGS *and* MISS NEVILLE

HASTINGS. My dear Constance, why will you deliberate thus? If we delay a moment, all is lost for ever. Pluck up a little resolution, and we shall soon be out of the reach of her malignity.

MISS NEVILLE. I find it impossible. My spirits are so sunk with the agitations I have suffered, that I am unable to face any new danger. Two or three years patience will at last crown us with happiness.

HASTINGS. Such a tedious delay is worse than inconstancy. Let us fly, 40 my charmer. Let us date our happiness from this very moment.

Perish fortune. Love and content will encrease what we possess beyond a monarch's revenue. Let me prevail.

MISS NEVILLE. No, Mr. Hastings; no. Prudence once more comes to my relief, and I will obey its dictates. In the moment of passion, fortune may be despised, but it ever produces a lasting repentance. I'm resolved to apply to Mr. Hardcastle's compassion and justice for redress.

HASTINGS. But tho' he had the will, he has not the power to relieve you.

MISS NEVILLE. But he has influence, and upon that I am resolved to rely.   10

HASTINGS. I have no hopes. But since you persist, I must reluctantly obey you.   [*Exeunt.*

SCENE *Changes*

Enter SIR CHARLES *and* MISS HARDCASTLE

SIR CHARLES. What a situation am I in. If what you say appears, I shall then find a guilty son. If what he says be true, I shall then lose one that, of all others, I most wish'd for a daughter.

MISS HARDCASTLE. I am proud of your approbation, and to shew I merit it, if you place yourselves as I directed, you shall hear his explicit declaration. But he comes.   20

SIR CHARLES. I'll to your father, and keep him to the appointment.
                                                        [*Exit Sir Charles.*

Enter MARLOW

MARLOW. Tho' prepar'd for setting out, I come once more to take leave, nor did I, till this moment, know the pain I feel in the separation.

MISS HARDCASTLE. (*In her own natural manner*) I believe those sufferings cannot be very great, Sir, which you can so easily remove. A day or two longer, perhaps, might lessen your uneasiness, by shewing the little value of what you now think proper to regret.

MARLOW. (*Aside*) This girl every moment improves upon me. (*To her*) 30 It must not be, Madam. I have already trifled too long with my heart. My very pride begins to submit to my passion. The disparity of education and fortune, the anger of a parent, and the contempt of my equals, begin to lose their weight; and nothing can restore me to myself, but this painful effort of resolution.

MISS HARDCASTLE. Then go, Sir. I'll urge nothing more to detain you. Tho' my family be as good as her's you came down to visit, and my education, I hope, not inferior, what are these advantages without equal affluence? I must remain contented with the slight approbation of imputed merit; I must have only the mockery of your addresses, while all your serious aims are fix'd on fortune.

Enter HARDCASTLE *and* SIR CHARLES *from behind*

SIR CHARLES. Here, behind this screen.

HARDCASTLE. Ay, Ay, make no noise. I'll engage my Kate covers him with confusion at last.

MARLOW. By heavens, Madam, fortune was ever my smallest consideration. Your beauty at first caught my eye; for who could see that without emotion. But every moment that I converse with you, steals in some new grace, heightens the picture, and gives it stronger 10 expression. What at first seem'd rustic plainness, now appears refin'd simplicity. What seem'd forward assurance, now strikes me as the result of courageous innocence, and conscious virtue.

SIR CHARLES. What can it mean! He amazes me!

HARDCASTLE. I told you how it would be. Hush!

MARLOW. I am now determined to stay, Madam, and I have too good an opinion of my father's discernment, when he sees you, to doubt his approbation.

MISS HARDCASTLE. No, Mr. Marlow, I will not, cannot detain you. Do you think I could suffer a connexion, in which there is the smallest 20 room for repentance? Do you think I would take the mean advantage of a transient passion, to load you with confusion? Do you think I could ever relish that happiness, which was acquired by lessening your's?

MARLOW. By all that's good, I can have no happiness but what's in your power to grant me. Nor shall I ever feel repentance, but in not having seen your merits before. I will stay, even contrary to your wishes; and tho' you should persist to shun me, I will make my respectful assiduities atone for the levity of my past conduct.   30

MISS HARDCASTLE. Sir, I must entreat you'll desist. As our acquaintance began, so let it end, in indifference. I might have given an hour or two to levity; but seriously, Mr. Marlow, do you think I could ever submit to a connexion, where *I* must appear mercenary, and *you* imprudent? Do you think I could ever catch at the confident addresses of a secure admirer?

MARLOW. (*Kneeling*) Does this look like security. Does this look like confidence. No, Madam, every moment that shews me your merit, only serves to encrease my diffidence and confusion. Here let me continue——   40

SIR CHARLES. I can hold it no longer. Charles, Charles, how hast thou deceived me! Is this your indifference, your uninteresting conversation!

HARDCASTLE. Your cold contempt; your formal interview. What have you to say now?

MARLOW. That I'm all amazement! What can it mean!

HARDCASTLE. It means that you can say and unsay things at pleasure. That you can address a lady in private, and deny it in public; that you have one story for us, and another for my daughter.

MARLOW. Daughter!—this lady your daughter!

HARDCASTLE. Yes, Sir, my only daughter. My Kate, whose else should   10
she be.

MARLOW. Oh, the devil.

MISS HARDCASTLE. Yes, Sir, that very identical tall squinting lady you were pleased to take me for, (*curtesying.*) She that you addressed as the mild, modest, sentimental man of gravity, and the bold forward agreeable rattle of the ladies club; ha, ha, ha.

MARLOW. Zounds, there's no bearing this; it's worse than death.

MISS HARDCASTLE. In which of your characters, Sir, will you give us leave to address you. As the faultering gentleman, with looks on the ground, that speaks just to be heard, and hates hypocrisy; or the   20
loud confident creature, that keeps it up with Mrs. Mantrap, and old Miss Biddy Buckskin, till three in the morning; ha, ha, ha.

MARLOW. O, curse on my noisy head. I never attempted to be impudent yet, that I was not taken down. I must be gone.

HARDCASTLE. By the hand of my body, but you shall not. I see it was all a mistake, and I am rejoiced to find it. You shall not stir, I tell you. I know she'll forgive you. Won't you forgive him, Kate. We'll all forgive you. Take courage, man.

[*They retire, she tormenting him to the back Scene*

Enter MRS. HARDCASTLE, TONY   30

MRS. HARDCASTLE. So, so, they're gone off. Let them go, I care not.

HARDCASTLE. Who gone?

MRS. HARDCASTLE. My dutiful niece and her gentleman, Mr. Hastings, from Town. He who came down with our modest visitor here.

SIR CHARLES. Who, my honest George Hastings? As worthy a fellow as lives, and the girl could not have made a more prudent choice.

HARDCASTLE. Then, by the hand of my body, I'm proud of the connexion.

MRS. HARDCASTLE. Well, if he has taken away the lady, he has not taken her fortune, that remains in this family to console us for her   40
loss.

HARDCASTLE. Sure Dorothy you would not be so mercenary?

MRS. HARDCASTLE. Ay, that's my affair, not your's.

HARDCASTLE. But you know if your son, when of age, refuses to marry
his cousin, her whole fortune is then at her own disposal.

MRS. HARDCASTLE. Ay, but he's not of age, and she has not thought
proper to wait for his refusal.

Enter HASTINGS *and* MISS NEVILLE

MRS. HARDCASTLE. (*Aside*) What returned so soon, I begin not to like it.

HASTINGS. (*To* HARDCASTLE) For my late attempt to fly off with your
niece, let my present confusion be my punishment. We are now come   10
back, to appeal from your justice to your humanity. By her father's
consent, I first paid her my addresses, and our passions were first
founded in duty.

MISS NEVILLE. Since his death, I have been obliged to stoop to dissimulation to avoid oppression. In an hour of levity, I was ready even to
give up my fortune to secure my choice. But I'm now recover'd
from the delusion, and hope from your tenderness what is denied
me from a nearer connexion.

MRS. HARDCASTLE. Pshaw, pshaw, this is all but the whining end of a
modern novel.   20

HARDCASTLE. Be it what it will, I'm glad they're come back to reclaim
their due. Come hither, Tony boy. Do you refuse this lady's hand
whom I now offer you?

TONY. What signifies my refusing. You know I can't refuse her till I'm
of age, father.

HARDCASTLE. While I thought concealing your age boy was likely to
conduce to your improvement, I concurred with your mother's
desire to keep it secret. But since I find she turns it to a wrong use,
I must now declare, you have been of age these three months.

TONY. Of age! Am I of age, father?   30

HARDCASTLE. Above three months.

TONY. Then you'll see the first use I'll make of my liberty. (*taking* MISS
NEVILLE'*s hand*) Witness all men by these presents, that I, Anthony
Lumpkin, Esquire, of BLANK place, refuse you, Constantia Neville,
spinster, of no place at all, for my true and lawful wife. So Constance
Neville may marry whom she pleases, and Tony Lumpkin is his own
man again.

SIR CHARLES. O brave 'Squire.

HASTINGS. My worthy friend.

MRS. HARDCASTLE. My undutiful offspring.   40

MARLOW. Joy, my dear George, I give you joy sincerely. And could I prevail upon my little tyrant here to be less arbitrary, I should be the happiest man alive, if you would return me the favour.

HASTINGS. (*To* MISS HARDCASTLE) Come, madam, you are now driven to the very last scene of all your contrivances. I know you like him, I'm sure he loves you, and you must and shall have him.

HARDCASTLE. (*Joining their hands*) And I say so too. And Mr. Marlow, if she makes as good a wife as she has a daughter, I don't believe you'll ever repent your bargain. So now to supper, to-morrow we shall gather all the poor of the parish about us, and the Mistakes of the Night shall be crowned with a merry morning; so boy take her; and as you have been mistaken in the mistress, my wish is, that you may never be mistaken in the wife.

FINIS

EPILOGUE
BY DR. GOLDSMITH

WELL, *having stoop'd to conquer with success,*
And gain'd a husband without aid from dress,
Still as a Bar-maid, I could wish it too,
As I have conquer'd him to conquer you:
And let me say, for all your resolution,
That pretty Bar-maids have done execution.
Our life is all a play, compos'd to please,
"We have our exits and our entrances." 10
The first act shews the simple country maid,
Harmless and young, of ev'ry thing afraid;
Blushes when hir'd, and with unmeaning action,
I hopes as how to give you satisfaction.
Her second act displays a livelier scene,—
Th' unblushing Bar-maid of a country inn.
Who whisks about the house, at market caters,
Talks loud, coquets the guests, and scolds the waiters.
Next the scene shifts to town, and there she soars,
The chop house toast of ogling connoisseurs. 20
On 'Squires and Cits she there displays her arts,
And on the gridiron broils her lover's hearts—
And as she smiles, her triumphs to compleat,
Even Common Councilmen forget to eat.
The fourth act shews her wedded to the 'Squire,
And Madam now begins to hold it higher;
Pretends to taste, at Operas cries caro,
And quits her Nancy Dawson, for Che Faro.
Doats upon dancing, and in all her pride,
Swims round the room, the Heinel *of Cheapside:* 30
Ogles and leers with artificial skill,
Till having lost in age the power to kill,

She sits all night at cards, and ogles at spadille.
Such, thro' our lives, the eventful history—
The fifth and last act still remains for me.
The Bar-maid now for your protection prays,
Turns Female Barrister, and pleads for Bayes.

POEMS

POEMS

[PROLOGUE OF LABERIUS]

Necessitas cujus cursus transversi impetum, &c.

What! no way left to shun th' inglorious stage,
And save from infamy my sinking age.
Scarce half alive, opress'd with many a year,
What in the name of dotage drives me here?
A time there was, when glory was my guide,   5
Nor force nor fraud could turn my steps aside,
Unaw'd by pow'r and unappal'd by fear,
With honest thrift I held my honour dear,
But this vile hour disperses all my store,
And all my hoard of honour is no more.   10
For ah! too partial to my life's decline,
Caesar persuades, submission must be mine,
Him I obey, whom heaven itself obeys,
Hopeless of pleasing, yet inclin'd to please.
Here then at once, I welcome every shame,   15
And cancel at threescore a life of fame;
No more my titles shall my children tell,
The old buffoon will fit my name as well;
This day beyond its term my fate extends,
For life is ended when our honour ends.   20

ON A BEAUTIFUL YOUTH STRUCK
BLIND WITH LIGHTNING

Sure 'twas by Providence design'd,
Rather in pity, than in hate,
That he should be, like Cupid, blind,
To save him from Narcissus' fate.

133

THE GIFT
TO IRIS, IN BOW-STREET, COVENT-GARDEN

Say, cruel IRIS, pretty rake,
  Dear mercenary beauty,
What annual offering shall I make,
  Expressive of my duty.

My heart, a victim to thine eyes,   5
  Should I at once deliver,
Say, would the angry fair one prize
  The gift, who slights the giver.

A bill, a jewel, watch, or toy,
  My rivals give——and let 'em.   10
If gems, or gold, impart a joy,
  I'll give them——when I get 'em.

I'll give——but not the full-blown rose,
  Or rose-bud more in fashion;
Such short-liv'd offerings but disclose   15
  A transitory passion.

I'll give thee something yet unpaid,
  Not less sincere, than civil:
I'll give thee——Ah! too charming maid;
  I'll give thee——To the Devil.   20

A SONNET

Weeping, murmuring, complaining,
  Lost to every gay delight;
MYRA, too sincere for feigning,
  Fears th' approaching bridal night.

Yet, why this killing soft dejection?   5
  Why dim thy beauty with a tear?
Had MYRA followed my direction,
  She long had wanted cause to fear.

AN ELEGY
ON THAT GLORY OF HER SEX
MRS. MARY BLAIZE

Good people all, with one accord,
  Lament for Madam BLAIZE,
Who never wanted a good word——
  From those who spoke her praise.

The needy seldom pass'd her door,   5
  And always found her kind;
She freely lent to all the poor,——
  Who left a pledge behind.

She strove the neighbourhood to please,
  With manners wond'rous winning,   10
And never follow'd wicked ways,——
  Unless when she was sinning.

At church, in silks and sattins new,
  With hoop of monstrous size,
She never slumber'd in her pew,——   15
  But when she shut her eyes.

Her love was sought, I do aver,
  By twenty beaus and more;
The king himself has follow'd her,——
  When she has walk'd before.   20

But now her wealth and finery fled,
  Her hangers-on cut short all;
The doctors found, when she was dead,——
  Her last disorder mortal.

Let us lament, in sorrow sore,   25
  For Kent-Street well may say,
That had she liv'd a twelve-month more,——
  She had not dy'd to-day.

THE DOUBLE TRANSFORMATION: A TALE

Secluded from domestic strife
Jack Book-worm led a college life;
A fellowship at twenty five
Made him the happiest man alive,
He drank his glass, and crack'd his joke,   5
And Freshmen wonder'd as he spoke;
He rak'd and toasted, dived or shone:
And even was thought a knowing one.
Without politeness aim'd at breeding,
And laugh'd at pedantry and reading;   10
Thus sad or sober, gay or mellow,
Jack was a *college pretty fellow*.

    Such pleasures unallay'd with care,
Could any accident impair?
Could Cupid's shaft at length transfix,   15
Our swain arriv'd at thirty six?
O had the archer ne'er come down
To ravage in a country town!
Or Flavia been content to stop,
At triumphs in a Fleet-street shop.   20
O had her eyes forgot to blaze!
Or Jack had wanted eyes to gaze:
O—but let exclamation cease,
Her presence banish'd all his peace.

    Our altered Parson now began,   25
To be a perfect ladies man;
Made sonnets, lisp'd his sermons o'er,
And told the tales he told before,
Of bailiffs pump'd, and proctors bit,
At college how he shew'd his wit;   30
And as the fair one still approv'd,
He fell in love—or thought he lov'd.

    They laugh'd, they talk'd with giddy glee,
Miss had her jokes as well as he:
In short, their love was passing wonder,   35
They tallied as if torn assunder;
So with decorum all things carried,
Miss frown'd, and blush'd, and then was—married.

Need we expose to vulgar sight,
The raptures of the bridal night?   40
Need we intrude on hallow'd ground,
Or draw the curtains clos'd around:
Let it suffice, that each had charms,
He clasp'd a goddess in his arms;
And tho' she felt his usage rough,   45
Yet in a man 'twas well enough.

  And here discretion might prevail,
To interrupt the tedious tale;
Poetic justice bids it rest,
And leave 'em both completely blest: 50
Yet more importunate than they,
Truth bids me on, and I obey.

   The honey-moon like lightening flew,
The second brought its transports too.
A third, a fourth were not amiss,   55
The fifth was friendship mix'd with bliss:
But when a twelvemonth pass'd away
Jack found his goddess made of clay:
Found half the charms that deck'd her face,
Arose from powder, shreds or lace;   60
But still the worst remain'd behind,
That very face had rob'd her mind.

   Skill'd in no other arts was she,
But dressing, patching, repartee;
And just as humour rose or fell,   65
By turns a slattern or a belle:
'Tis true she dress'd with modern grace,
Half naked at a ball or race;
But when at home, at board or bed,
Five greasy nightcaps wrap'd her head: 70
Could so much beauty condescend,
To be a dull domestic friend?
Could any courtain lectures bring,
To decency so fine a thing?
In short by night 'twas fits or fretting,   75
By day 'twas gadding or coquetting.
Fond to be seen she k_pt a bevy,
Of powder'd coxcombs at her levy;
The squire and captain took their stations,
And twenty other near relations;   80

Jack suck'd his pipe and often broke
A sigh in suffocating smoke;
She in her turn became perplexing,
And found substantial bliss in vexing.
While all their hours were pass'd between   85
Insulting repartee or spleen:
    Thus as her faults each day were known,
He thinks her features coarser grown;
He fancies every vice she shews,
Or thins her lip, or points her nose: 90
Whenever rage or envy rise,
How wide her mouth, how wild her eyes!
He knows not how, but so it is,
Her face is grown a knowing phyz;
And tho' her fops are wondrous civil,   95
He thinks her ugly as the Devil.
    Now to perplex the ravell'd nooze,
As each a different way pursues,
While sullen or loquacious strife,
Promis'd to hold them on for life,   100
That dire disease whose ruthless power
Withers the beauty's transient flower:
Lo! the small pox with horrid glare,
Levell'd its terrors at the fair;
And rifling every youthful grace,   105
Left but the remnant of a face.
    The glass grown hateful to her sight,
Reflected now a perfect fright:
Each former art she vainly tries
To bring back lustre to her eyes.   110
In vain she tries her pastes and creams,
To smooth her skin, or hide its seams;
Her country beaux and city cousins,
Lovers no more; flew off by dozens:
The squire himself was seen to yield,   115
And even the captain quit the field.
    Poor Madam now condemn'd to hack
The rest of life with anxious Jack,
Perceiving others fairly flown
Attempted pleasing him alone.   120
Jack soon was dazzl'd to behold
Her present face surpass the old;

With modesty her cheeks are dy'd,
Humility displaces pride;
For tawdry finery is seen,   125
A person ever neatly clean:
No more presuming on her sway
She learns good nature every day,
Serenely gay, and strict in duty,
Jack finds his wife a perfect beauty.   130

[DESCRIPTION OF AN AUTHOR'S BED-CHAMBER]

Where the Red Lion flaring o'er the way,
Invites each passing stranger that can pay;
Where Calvert's butt, and Parson's black champaign,
Regale the drabs and bloods of Drury lane;
There in a lonely room, from bailiffs snug,   5
The muse found Scroggen stretch'd beneath a rug,
A window patch'd with paper lent a ray,
That dimly shew'd the state in which he lay;
The sanded floor that grits beneath the tread;
The humid wall with paltry pictures spread: 10
The royal game of goose was there in view,
And the twelve rules the royal martyr drew;
The seasons fram'd with listing found a place,
And brave prince William shew'd his lamp-black face:
The morn was cold, he views with keen desire   15
The rusty grate unconscious of a fire:
With beer and milk arrears the frieze was scor'd,
And five crack'd tea cups dress'd the chimney board.
A night-cap deck'd his brows instead of bay,
A cap by night—a stocking all the day!   20

ON SEEING MRS. ****, PERFORM IN THE
CHARACTER OF ****

To you bright fair the nine address their lays,
And tune my feeble voice to sing thy praise.
The heart-felt power of every charm divine,
Who can withstand their all-commanding shine?

See how she moves along with every grace
While soul-brought tears steal down each shining face.
She speaks, 'tis rapture all and nameless bliss,
Ye gods what transport e'er compar'd to this.
As when in Paphian groves the queen of love,
With fond complaint address'd the listening Jove,
'Twas joy, and endless blisses all around,
And rocks forgot their hardness at the sound.
Then first, at last even Jove was taken in,
And felt her charms, without disguise, within.

ON THE DEATH OF THE RIGHT HONOURABLE * * *

Ye muses, pour the pitying tear
For Pollio snatch'd away:
O had he liv'd another year!
——*He had not dy'd to-day.*

O, were he born to bless mankind,
In virtuous times of yore,
Heroes themselves had fallen behind!
——*Whene'er he went before.*

How sad the groves and plains appear,
And sympathetic sheep:
Even pitying hills would drop a tear!
——*If hills could learn to weep.*

His bounty in exalted strain
Each bard might well display:
Since none implor'd relief in vain!
——*That went reliev'd away.*

And hark! I hear the tuneful throng
His obsequies forbid.
He still shall live, shall live as long
——*As ever dead man did.*

[TRANSLATION OF A SOUTH AMERICAN ODE]

In all my Enna's beauties blest
Amidst profusion still I pine;
    For tho' she gives me up her breast
    It's panting tenant is not mine.

AN ELEGY ON THE DEATH OF A MAD DOG

Good people all, of every sort,
    Give ear unto my song;
And if you find it wond'rous short,
    It cannot hold you long.

In Isling town there was a man,   5
    Of whom the world might say,
That still a godly race he ran,
    Whene'er he went to pray.

A kind and gentle heart he had,
    To comfort friends and foes;   10
The naked every day he clad,
    When he put on his cloaths.

And in that town a dog was found,
    As many dogs there be,
Both mungrel, puppy, whelp, and hound,   15
    And curs of low degree.

This dog and man at first were friends;
    But when a pique began,
The dog, to gain some private ends,
    Went mad and bit the man.   20

Around from all the neighbouring streets,
    The wondering neighbours ran,
And swore the dog had lost his wits,
    To bite so good a man.

The wound it seem'd both sore and sad,   25
   To every christian eye;
And while they swore the dog was mad,
   They swore the man would die.

But soon a wonder came to light,
   That shew'd the rogues they lied,   30
The man recovered of the bite,
   The dog it was that dy'd.

[SONG FROM *THE VICAR OF WAKEFIELD*]

When lovely woman stoops to folly,
   And finds too late that men betray,
What charm can sooth her melancholy,
   What art can wash her guilt away?

The only art her guilt to cover,   5
   To hide her shame from every eye,
To give repentance to her lover,
   And wring his bosom——is to die.

A BALLAD

Turn, gentle hermit of the dale,
   And guide my lonely way,
To where yon taper cheers the vale,
   With hospitable ray.

For here forlorn and lost I tread,   5
   With fainting steps and slow;
Where wilds immeasurably spread,
   Seem lengthening as I go.

'Forbear, my son,' the hermit cries,
   'To tempt the dangerous gloom;   10
For yonder faithless phantom flies
   To lure thee to thy doom.

Here to the houseless child of want,
  My door is open still;
And tho' my portion is but scant,
  I give it with good will. 15

Then turn to-night, and freely share
  Whate'er my cell bestows;
My rushy couch, and frugal fare,
  My blessing and repose. 20

No flocks that range the valley free,
  To slaughter I condemn:
Taught by that power that pities me,
  I learn to pity them.

But from the mountain's grassy side, 25
  A guiltless feast I bring;
A scrip with herbs and fruits supply'd,
  And water from the spring.

Then, pilgrim, turn, thy cares forego;
  All earth-born cares are wrong: 30
'Man wants but little here below,
  Nor wants that little long.'

Soft as the dew from heav'n descends,
  His gentle accents fell:
The modest stranger lowly bends, 35
  And follows to the cell.

Far in a wilderness obscure
  The lonely mansion lay;
A refuge to the neighbouring poor,
  And strangers led astray. 40

No stores beneath its humble thatch
  Requir'd a master's care;
The wicket opening with a latch,
  Receiv'd the harmless pair.

And now when busy crowds retire 45
  To take their evening rest,

A Ballad

The hermit trimm'd his little fire,
   And cheer'd his pensive guest:

And spread his vegetable store,
   And gayly prest, and smil'd;   50
And skill'd in legendary lore,
   The lingering hours beguil'd.

Around in sympathetic mirth
   Its tricks the kitten tries,
The cricket chirrups in the hearth;   55
   The crackling faggot flies.

But nothing could a charm import
   To sooth the stranger's woe;
For grief was heavy at his heart,
   And tears began to flow.   60

His rising cares the hermit spy'd,
   With answering care opprest:
'And whence, unhappy youth,' he cry'd,
   'The sorrows of thy breast?

From better habitations spurn'd,   65
   Reluctant dost thou rove;
Or grieve for friendship unreturn'd,
   Or unregarded love?

Alas! the joys that fortune brings,
   Are trifling and decay;   70
And those who prize the paltry things,
   More trifling still than they.

And what is friendship but a name,
   A charm that lulls to sleep;
A shade that follows wealth or fame,   75
   But leaves the wretch to weep?

And love has still an emptier sound,
   The modern fair one's jest:
On earth unseen, or only found
   To warm the turtle's nest.   80

A Ballad

For shame fond youth thy sorrows hush,
  And spurn the sex,' he said:
But while he spoke a rising blush
  His love-lorn guest betray'd.

Surpriz'd he sees new beauties rise,　85
  Swift mantling to the view;
Like colours o'er the morning skies,
  As bright, as transient too.

The bashful look, the rising breast,
  Alternate spread alarms:　90
The lovely stranger stands confest
  A maid in all her charms.

'And, ah, forgive a stranger rude,
  A wretch forlorn,' she cry'd;
'Whose feet unhallowed thus intrude　95
  Where heaven and you reside.

But let a maid thy pity share,
  Whom love has taught to stray;
Who seeks for rest, but finds despair
  Companion of her way.　100

My father liv'd beside the Tyne,
  A wealthy Lord was he;
And all his wealth was mark'd as mine,
  He had but only me.

To win me from his tender arms,　105
  Unnumber'd suitors came;
Who prais'd me for imputed charms,
  And felt or feign'd a flame.

Each hour a mercenary crowd,
  With richest proffers strove:　110
Among the rest young Edwin bow'd,
  But never talk'd of love.

In humble simplest habit clad,
  No wealth nor power had he;

Wisdom and worth were all he had,   115
    But these were all to me.

The blossom opening to the day,
    The dews of heaven refin'd,
Could nought of purity display,
    To emulate his mind.   120

The dew, the blossom on the tree,
    With charms inconstant shine;
Their charms were his, but woe to me,
    Their constancy was mine.

For still I try'd each fickle art,   125
    Importunate and vain;
And while his passion touch'd my heart,
    I triumph'd in his pain.

Till quite dejected with my scorn,
    He left me to my pride;   130
And sought a solitude forlorn,
    In secret where he died.

But mine the sorrow, mine the fault,
    And well my life shall pay;
I'll seek the solitude he sought,   135
    And stretch me where he lay.

And there forlorn despairing hid,
    I'll lay me down and die:
'Twas so for me that Edwin did,
    And so for him will I.'   140

'Forbid it heaven!' the hermit cry'd,
    And clasp'd her to his breast:
The wondering fair one turn'd to chide,
    'Twas Edwin's self that prest.

'Turn, Angelina, ever dear,   145
    My charmer, turn to see,
Thy own, thy long-lost Edwin here,
    Restor'd to love and thee.

Thus let me hold thee to my heart,
   And ev'ry care resign: 150
And shall we never, never part,
   My life—my all that's mine.

No, never, from this hour to part,
   We'll live and love so true;
The sigh that rends thy constant heart, 155
   Shall break thy Edwin's too.'

THE CAPTIVITY

AN ORATORIO

Act I Scene I

Israelites sitting on the Banks of the Euphrates

1st Prophet

Recitativo

Ye Captive tribes that hourly work and weep
Where flows Euphrates murmuring to the deep,
Suspend a while the task, the tear suspend,
And turn to God your father and your friend:
Insulted, chaind, and all the world a foe, 5
Our God alone is all we boast below.

Chorus of Israelites

Our God is all we boast below:
To him we turn our eyes,
And every added weight of woe
Shall make our homage rise; 10

And tho' no temple richly drest
Nor sacrifice is here,
Wee'l make his temple in our breast
And offer up a tear.

2^d Prophet

Recitative

That strain once more, it bids remembrance rise,   15
And calls my long lost country to mine eyes.
Ye fields of Sharon, drest in flowery pride,
Ye Plains where Jordan rolls its glassy tide,
Ye hills of Lebanon with cedars crownd,
Ye Gilead groves that fling perfumes around: 20
These hills how sweet, those plains how wondrous fair,
But sweeter still when heaven was with us there.

Air

O memory thou fond deceiver,
Still importunate and vain,
To former joys recurring ever,   25
And turning all the past to pain:

Hence deceiver most distressing,
Seek the happy and the free,
They who want each other blessing
Ever want a friend in thee.   30

1st Prophet

Recitativo

Yet, why repine? What tho' by bonds confind,
Should bonds enslave the vigour of the mind?
Have we not cause for triumph when we see
Ourselves alone from idol worship free?
Are not this very day those rites begun   35
Where prostrate folly hails the rising sun?
Do not our tyrant Lords this day ordain
For superstition's rites and mirth profane?
And should we mourn? Should coward virtue fly
When impious folly rears her front on high?   40
No, rather let us triumph still the more
And as our fortune sinks our wishes soar.

Air

The triumphs that on vice attend
Shall ever in confusion end;
The good man suffers but to gain   45
And every virtue springs from pain;

As Aromatic plants bestow
No spicy fragrance while they grow,
But crush'd or trodden to the ground
Diffuse their balmy sweets around.   50

2^d Prophet

Recitative

But hush, my sons, our tyrant Lords are near;
The sound of barbarous mirth offends mine ear.
Triumphant music floats along the vale:
Near, nearer still, it gathers on the gale;
The growing note their near approach declares: 55
Desist my sons, nor mix the strain with theirs.

Enter Chaldean Priests attended

1st Priest

Air

Come on, my companions, the triumph display:
Let rapture the minutes employ,
The sun calls us out on this festival day,
And our monarch partakes of our Joy.   60

Like the sun our great monarch all pleasure supplies;
Both similar blessings bestow:
The sun with his splendour illumines the skies,
And our Monarch enlivens below.

Chaldean Woman

Air

Haste, ye sprightly sons of pleasure,   65
Love presents its brightest treasure,
Leave all other sports for me.

Chaldean Attendant

Or rather, loves delights despising,
Haste to raptures ever rising,
Wine shall bless the brave and free.   70

2ᵈ Priest

Wine and beauty thus inviting,
Each to different joys exciting,
Whither shall my choice encline?

1ˢᵗ Priest

I'll waste no longer thought in chusing,
But, neither love nor wine refusing,   75
I'll make them both together mine.

Recitative

But whence, when joy should brighten oer the land,
This sullen gloom in Judah's Captive band?
Ye sons of Judah, why the lute unstrung,
Or why those harps on yonder willows hung?   80
Come, leave your griefs, and Join our warbling Choir:
For who like you can wake the sleeping lyre?

2ᵈ Prophet

Bow'd down with Chains, the scorn of all mankind,
To Want, to toil, and every ill consign'd;
Is this a time to bid us raise the strain   85
And mix in rites that heaven regards with pain?

No, never; may this hand forget each art
That speeds the powers of music to the heart,
Ere I forget the land that gave me birth,
Or Join with sounds profane its sacred mirth.   90

1st Priest

Insulting slaves, if gentler methods fail,
The whips and angry tortures shall prevail.

Exeunt Chaldeans.

1st Prophet

Why, let them come, one good remains to cheer:
We fear the Lord, and know no other fear.

Chorus

Can whips or tortures hurt the mind   95
On God's supporting breast reclind?
Stand fast and let our tyrants see
That fortitude is Victory.

End of the first Act

Act II

Scene as Before

Chorus of Israelites

O Peace of mind, thou lovely guest,
Thou softest soother of the breast,   100
Dispense thy balmy store;
Wing all our thoughts to reach the skies,
Till earth, diminish'd to our eyes,
Shall vanish as we soar.

1st Priest

Recitative

No more, too long has justice been delay'd,   105
The king's commands must fully be obeyd;

Compliance with his will your peace secures:
Praise but our Gods, and every good is yours.
But if, rebellious to his high command,
You spurn the favours offer'd from his hand,   110
Think timely, think what ills remain behind:
Reflect, nor tempt to rage the royal mind.

2ᵈ Priest

Air

Fierce is the whirlwind howling
Oer Afric's sandy plain
And Fierce the tempest rolling   115
Along the furrow'd main.

But storms that fly
To rend the sky,
Every ill presaging,
Less dreadful shew   120
To worlds below
Than angry monarchs raging.

Israelitish Woman

Recitative

Ah me! what angry terrors round us grow,
How shrinks my soul to meet the threaten'd blow;
Ye Prophets, skilld in heaven's eternal truth,   125
Forgive my sexe's fears, forgive my youth,
If shrinking thus when frowning power appears
I wish for life, and yield me to my fears.
Let us one hour, one little hour, obey;
Tomorrows tears may wash our stains away.   130

Air

To the last moment of his breath
On hope the wretch relies,
And even the pang preceding death
Bids Expectation rise.

Hope like the gleaming taper's light
Adorns and cheers our way,
And still, as darker grows the night,
Emits a brighter ray.

2^d Priest

Recitative

Why this delay? at length for joy prepare;
I read your looks, and see compliance there.   140
Come raise the strain and grasp the full ton'd lyre:
The time, the theme, the place and all conspire.

Chaldean Woman

Air

See the ruddy morning smiling,
Hear the grove to bliss beguiling;
Zephyrs through the valley playing,   145
Streams along the meadow straying.

1st Priest

While these a constant revel keep,
Shall reason only bid me weep?
Hence, intruder! wee'l pursue
Nature, a better guide than you.   150

2^d Priest

Air

Every moment as it flows
Some peculiar pleasure owes:
Then let us, providently wise,
Sieze the Debtor as it flies.

Think not to morrow can repay   155
The pleasures that we lose to day;
To morrow's most unbounded store
Can but pay its proper score.

1st Priest

Recitative

But Hush, see, foremost of the Captive Choir,
The Master Prophet Grasps his full ton'd lyre.   160
Mark where he sits with executing art,
Feels for each tone, and speeds it to the heart.
See, inspiration fills his rising form,
Awful as clouds that nurse the growing storm,
And now his voice, accordant to the string,   165
Prepares our monarch's victories to sing.

1st Prophet

Air

From North, from South, from East, from West,
Conspiring foes shall come;
Tremble, thou vice polluted breast;
Blasphemers, all be dumb.   170

The tempest gathers all around,
On Babylon it lies;
Down with her, down, down to the ground,
She sinks, she groans, she dies.

2d Prophet

Down with her, Lord, to lick the dust,   175
Ere yonder setting sun;
Serve her as she hath servd the just.
'Tis fixt, it shall be done.

1st Priest

Recitative

Enough! when slaves thus insolent presume,
The king himself shall judge and fix their doom.   180
Short-sighted wretches, have not you, and all
Beheld our power in Zedekiah's fall?
To yonder gloomy dungeon turn your eyes;
See where dethron'd your captive monarch lies.

Deprived of sight, and rankling in his chain,   185
He calls on death to terminate his pain.
Yet know ye slaves, that still remain behind
More Pondrous chains and dungeons more confind.

Chorus

Arise, all potent ruler, rise
And vindicate the peoples cause;   190
Till every tongue in every land
Shall offer up unfeign'd applause.

End of the 2ᵈ Act

Act III

Scene as before

1ˢᵗ Priest

Recitative

Yes, my Companions, heaven's decrees are past,
And our fixt Empire shall for ever last;
In vain the madning prophet threatens woe,   195
In vain rebellion aims her secret blow;
Still shall our fame and growing power be spread,
And still our vengeance crush the guilty head.

Air

Coeval with man
Our Empire Began,   200
And never shall fall
Till ruin shakes all;
With the ruin of all
Shall Babylon fall.

2ᵈ Prophet

Recitative

Tis thus that pride triumphant rears the head: 205
A little while and all her power is fled.

But ha! what means yon sadly plaintive train,
That this way slowly bends along the plain?
And now, methinks, a pallid coarse they bear
To yonder bank, and rest the body there. 210
Alas, too well mine eyes observant trace
The last remains of Judah's royal race:
Our monarch falls and now our fears are ore:
The Wretched Zedekiah is no more.

Air

Ye wretches who, by fortune's hate, 215
In want and sorrow groan,
Come ponder his severer fate,
And learn to bless your own.

Ye sons, from fortune's lap supply'd,
A while the bliss suspend; 220
Like yours his life began in pride,
Like his your lives may end.

2ᵈ Prophet

Behold his squalid coarse with sorrow worn,
His wretched limbs with pondrous fetters torn;
Those eyeless orbs that shock with ghastly glare, 225
Those ill becoming robes and matted hair.
And shall not heaven for this its terrors shew,
And deal its angry vengeance on the foe?
How long, how long, Almighty lord of all,
Shall wrath vindictive threaten ere it fall? 230

Israelitish Woman

Air

As panting flies the hunted hind,
Where brooks refreshing stray,
And rivers through the valley wind,
That stop the hunters way:

Thus we, O Lord, alike distresst,   235
For streams of mercy Long;
Those streams which chear the sore opprest,
And overwhelm the strong.

1st Prophet

Recitative

But whence that shout? Good heavens! amazement all!
See yonder tower just nodding to the fall: 240
See where an army covers all the ground,
Saps the strong wall, and pours destruction round.
The ruin smokes, destruction pours along;
How low the great, how feeble are the strong!
The foe prevails, the lofty walls recline: 245
O God of hosts the victory is thine!

Chorus of Israelites

Down with her, Lord, to lick the dust;
Let vengeance be begun:
Serve her as she hath servd the just,
And let thy will be done.   250

1st Priest

All, All is lost. The Syrian army fails;
Cyrus, the conqueror of the world, prevails.
Save us, O Lord, to thee tho Late we pray,
And give repentance but an hour's delay.

2d Priest

Air

Thrice happy, who, in happy hour,   255
To heaven their praise bestow,
And own his all consuming power,
Before they feel the blow.

1st Prophet

Recitative

Now, Now's our time. Ye wretches bold and blind,
Brave but to God, and Cowards to Mankind;   260
Too late you seek that power unsought before:
Your wealth, your pride, your empire are no more.

Air

O Lucifer, thou son of morn,
Alike of heaven and man the foe,
Heaven, men, and all   265
Now press thy fall,
And sink thee lowest of the low.

2d Priest

O Babylon, how art thou fallen,
Thy fall more dreadful from delay!
Thy streets forelorn   270
To wilds shall turn,
Where toads shall pant and vultures prey.

1st Prophet

Recitative

Such be her fate. But listen, from afar
The Clarion's note proclaims the finish'd war!
Cyrus, our Great restorer, is at hand,   275
And this way leads his formidable band.
Now give your songs of Sion to the wind,
And hail the benefactor of mankind:
He comes pursuant to divine decree,
To Chain the strong and set the captive free.   280

Chorus of Youths

Rise to raptures past expressing,
Sweeter from remember'd woes;
Cyrus comes, our wrongs redressing,
Comes to give the world repose.

Chorus of Virgins

Cyrus Comes, the world redressing,   285
Love and pleasure in his train,
Comes to heighten every blessing,
Comes to soften every pain.

Chorus of Youths and Virgins

Hail to him with mercy reigning,
Skilld in every peaceful art,   290
Who from bonds our limbs unchaining,
Only binds the willing heart.

Last Chorus

But Chief to thee, our God, our father, friend,
Let praise be given to all eternity;
O thou, without beginning, without end,   295
Let us, and all, begin, and end in thee!

Finis

THE TRAVELLER
OR
A PROSPECT OF SOCIETY

TO THE
REV. HENRY GOLDSMITH   5

Dear Sir,

I am sensible that the friendship between us can acquire no new force
from the ceremonies of a Dedication; and perhaps it demands an
excuse thus to prefix your name to my attempts, which you decline
giving with your own. But as a part of this Poem was formerly written   10
to you from Switzerland, the whole can now, with propriety, be only
inscribed to you. It will also throw a light upon many parts of it, when
the reader understands that it is addressed to a man, who, despising
Fame and Fortune, has retired early to Happiness and Obscurity, with
an income of forty pounds a year.   15

I now perceive, my dear brother, the wisdom of your humble choice.
You have entered upon a sacred office, where the harvest is great, and
the labourers are but few; while you have left the field of Ambition,
where the labourers are many, and the harvest not worth carrying
away. But of all kinds of ambition, what from the refinement of the   20
times, from differing systems of criticism, and from the divisions of
party, that which pursues poetical fame, is the wildest.

Poetry makes a principal amusement among unpolished nations;
but in a country verging to the extremes of refinement, Painting and
Music come in for a share. As these offer the feeble mind a less labor- 25
ious entertainment, they at first rival Poetry, and at length supplant
her; they engross all that favour once shewn to her, and though but
younger sisters, seize upon the elder's birth-right.

Yet, however this art may be neglected by the powerful, it is still in
greater danger from the mistaken efforts of the learned to improve it.   30
What criticisms have we not heard of late in favour of blank verse,
and Pindaric odes, chorusses, anapests and iambics, alliterative care,

and happy negligence. Every absurdity has now a champion to defend
it, and as he is generally much in the wrong, so he has always much to
say; for error is ever talkative. —   35

But there is an enemy to this art still more dangerous, I mean party.
Party entirely distorts the judgement, and destroys the taste. When
the mind is once infected with this disease, it can only find pleasure in
what contributes to encrease the distemper. Like the tyger, that
seldom desists from pursuing man after having once preyed upon   40
human flesh, the reader, who has once gratified his appetite with
calumny, makes, ever after, the most agreeable feast upon murdered
reputation. Such readers generally admire some half-witted thing,
who wants to be thought a bold man, having lost the character of a
wise one. Him they dignify with the name of poet; his tawdry lampoons 45
are called satires, his turbulence is said to be force, and his phrenzy
fire.

What reception a Poem may find, which has neither abuse, party,
nor blank verse to support it, I cannot tell, nor am I solicitous to
know. My aims are right. Without espousing the cause of any party,   50
I have attempted to moderate the rage of all. I have endeavoured to
shew, that there may be equal happiness in states, that are differently
governed from our own; that every state has a particular principle
of happiness, and that this principle in each may be carried to a mischievous excess. There are few can judge, better than yourself, How 55
far these positions are illustrated in this Poem.

 I am, dear Sir,
  Your most affectionate Brother,
      OLIVER GOLDSMITH.

THE TRAVELLER

OR

A PROSPECT OF SOCIETY

Remote, unfriended, melancholy, slow,
Or by the lazy Scheld, or wandering Po;
Or onward, where the rude Carinthian boor
Against the houseless stranger shuts the door;
Or where Campania's plain forsaken lies,
A weary waste expanding to the skies:
Where'er I roam, whatever realms to see,
My heart untravell'd fondly turns to thee;
Still to my brother turns, with ceaseless pain,
And drags at each remove a lengthening chain.

Eternal blessings crown my earliest friend,
And round his dwelling guardian saints attend;
Blest be that spot, where chearful guests retire
To pause from toil, and trim their evening fire;
Blest that abode, where want and pain repair,
And every stranger finds a ready chair;
Blest be those feasts with simple plenty crown'd,
Where all the ruddy family around
Laugh at the jests or pranks that never fail,
Or sigh with pity at some mournful tale,
Or press the bashful stranger to his food,
And learn the luxury of doing good.

But me, not destin'd such delights to share,
My prime of life in wand'ring spent and care:
Impell'd, with steps unceasing, to pursue
Some fleeting good, that mocks me with the view;
That, like the circle bounding earth and skies,
Allures from far, yet, as I follow, flies;

My fortune leads to traverse realms alone,
And find no spot of all the world my own.   30

Even now, where Alpine solitudes ascend,
I sit me down a pensive hour to spend;
And, plac'd on high above the storm's career,
Look downward where an hundred realms appear;
Lakes, forests, cities, plains extending wide,   35
The pomp of kings, the shepherd's humbler pride.

When thus Creation's charms around combine,
Amidst the store, should thankless pride repine?
Say, should the philosophic mind disdain
That good, which makes each humbler bosome vain?   40
Let school-taught pride dissemble all it can,
These little things are great to little man;
And wiser he, whose sympathetic mind
Exults in all the good of all mankind.
Ye glittering towns, with wealth and splendour crown'd,   45
Ye fields, where summer spreads profusion round,
Ye lakes, whose vessels catch the busy gale,
Ye bending swains, that dress the flow'ry vale,
For me your tributary stores combine;
Creation's heir, the world, the world is mine.   50

As some lone miser visiting his store,
Bends at his treasure, counts, recounts it o'er;
Hoards after hoards his rising raptures fill,
Yet still he sighs, for hoards are wanting still:
Thus to my breast alternate passions rise,   55
Pleas'd with each good that heaven to man supplies:
Yet oft a sigh prevails, and sorrows fall,
To see the hoard of human bliss so small;
And oft I wish, amidst the scene, to find
Some spot to real happiness consign'd,   60
Where my worn soul, each wand'ring hope at rest,
May gather bliss to see my fellows blest.

But where to find that happiest spot below,
Who can direct, when all pretend to know?
The shudd'ring tenant of the frigid zone   65
Boldly proclaims that happiest spot his own,

Extols the treasures of his stormy seas,
And his long nights of revelry and ease;
The naked Negro, panting at the line,
Boasts of his golden sands and palmy wine,   70
Basks in the glare, or stems the tepid wave,
And thanks his Gods for all the good they gave.
Such is the patriot's boast, where'er we roam,
His first best country ever is at home.

    And yet, perhaps, if countries we compare,   75
And estimate the blessings which they share;
Though patriots flatter, still shall wisdom find
An equal portion dealt to all mankind,
As different good, by Art or Nature given,
To different nations makes their blessings even.   80

    Nature, a mother kind alike to all,
Still grants her bliss at Labour's earnest call;
With food as well the peasant is supply'd
On Idra's cliffs as Arno's shelvy side;
And though the rocky crested summits frown,   85
These rocks, by custom, turn to beds of down.
From Art more various are the blessings sent;
Wealth, commerce, honor, liberty, content:
Yet these each other's power so strong contest,
That either seems destructive of the rest.   90
Where wealth and freedom reign contentment fails,
And honour sinks where commerce long prevails.
Hence every state, to one lov'd blessing prone,
Conforms and models life to that alone.
Each to the favourite happiness attends,   95
And spurns the plan that aims at other ends;
'Till, carried to excess in each domain,
This favourite good begets peculiar pain.

    But let us try these truths with closer eyes,
And trace them through the prospect as it lies: 100
Here for a while my proper cares resign'd,
Here let me sit in sorrow for mankind,
Like yon neglected shrub, at random cast,
That shades the steep, and sighs at every blast.

Far to the right, where Appennine ascends, 105
Bright as the summer, Italy extends;
Its uplands sloping deck the mountain's side,
Woods over woods, in gay theatric pride;
While oft some temple's mould'ring top between,
With venerable grandeur marks the scene. 110

Could Nature's bounty satisfy the breast,
The sons of Italy were surely blest.
Whatever fruits in different climes are found,
That proudly rise or humbly court the ground,
Whatever blooms in torrid tracts appear, 115
Whose bright succession decks the varied year;
Whatever sweets salute the northern sky
With vernal lives that blossom but to die;
These here disporting, own the kindred soil,
Nor ask luxuriance from the planter's toil; 120
While sea-born gales their gelid wings expand
To winnow fragrance round the smiling land.

But small the bliss that sense alone bestows,
And sensual bliss is all the nation knows.
In florid beauty groves and fields appear, 125
Man seems the only growth that dwindles here.
Contrasted faults through all his manners reign,
Though poor, luxurious, though submissive, vain,
Though grave, yet trifling, zealous, yet untrue,
And even in penance planning sins anew. 130
All evils here contaminate the mind,
That opulence departed leaves behind;
For wealth was theirs, nor far remov'd the date,
When commerce proudly flourish'd through the state:
At her command the palace learnt to rise, 135
Again the long-fall'n column sought the skies;
The canvass glow'd beyond even Nature warm,
The pregnant quarry teem'd with human form.
Till, more unsteady than the southern gale,
Commerce on other shores display'd her sail; 140
While nought remain'd of all that riches gave,
But towns unman'd, and lords without a slave:
And late the nation found, with fruitless skill,
Its former strength was but plethoric ill.

Yet, still the loss of wealth is here supplied   145
By arts, the splendid wrecks of former pride;
From these the feeble heart and long fall'n mind
An easy compensation seem to find.
Here may be seen, in bloodless pomp array'd,
The paste-board triumph and the cavalcade;   150
Processions form'd for piety and love,
A mistress or a saint in every grove.
By sports like these are all their cares beguil'd,
The sports of children satisfy the child.
Each nobler aim represt by long controul,   155
Now sinks at last, or feebly mans the soul;
While low delights, succeeding fast behind,
In happier meanness occupy the mind:
As in those domes, where Caesars once bore sway,
Defac'd by time and tottering in decay,   160
There in the ruin, heedless of the dead,
The shelter-seeking peasant builds his shed,
And, wond'ring man could want the larger pile,
Exults, and owns his cottage with a smile.

My soul turn from them, turn we to survey   165
Where rougher climes a nobler race display,
Where the bleak Swiss their stormy mansions tread,
And force a churlish soil for scanty bread;
No product here the barren hills afford,
But man and steel, the soldier and his sword.   170
No vernal blooms their torpid rocks array,
But winter lingering chills the lap of May;
No Zephyr fondly sues the mountain's breast,
But meteors glare, and stormy glooms invest.
Yet still, even here, content can spread a charm,   175
Redress the clime, and all its rage disarm.
Though poor the peasant's hut, his feasts though small,
He sees his little lot, the lot of all;
Sees no contiguous palace rear its head
To shame the meanness of his humble shed;   180
No costly lord the sumptuous banquet deal
To make him loath his vegetable meal;
But calm, and bred in ignorance and toil,
Each wish contracting, fits him to the soil.

Chearful at morn he wakes from short repose,   185
Breasts the keen air, and carrols as he goes;
With patient angle trolls the finny deep,
Or drives his vent'rous plow-share to the steep;
Or seeks the den where snow tracks mark the way,
And drags the struggling savage into day.   190
At night returning, every labour sped,
He sits him down the monarch of a shed;
Smiles by his chearful fire, and round surveys
His childrens looks, that brighten at the blaze:
While his lov'd partner, boastful of her hoard,   195
Displays her cleanly platter on the board;
And haply too some pilgrim, thither led,
With many a tale repays the nightly bed.

      Thus every good his native wilds impart,
Imprints the patriot passion on his heart,   200
And even those ills, that round his mansion rise,
Enhance the bliss his scanty fund supplies.
Dear is that shed to which his soul conforms,
And dear that hill which lifts him to the storms;
And as a child, when scaring sounds molest,   205
Clings close and closer to the mother's breast;
So the loud torrent, and the whirlwind's roar,
But bind him to his native mountains more.

Such are the charms to barren states assign'd;
Their wants but few, their wishes all confin'd.   210
Yet let them only share the praises due,
If few their wants, their pleasures are but few;
For every want, that stimulates the breast,
Becomes a source of pleasure when redrest.
Whence from such lands each pleasing science flies,   215
That first excites desire, and then supplies;
Unknown to them, when sensual pleasures cloy,
To fill the languid pause with finer joy;
Unknown those powers that raise the soul to flame,
Catch every nerve, and vibrate through the frame.   220
Their level life is but a smould'ring fire,
Unquench'd by want, unfann'd by strong desire;
Unfit for raptures, or, if raptures cheer
On some high festival of once a year,

In wild excess the vulgar breast takes fire,   225
Till, buried in debauch, the bliss expire.

But not their joys alone thus coarsly flow:
Their morals, like their pleasures, are but low.
For, as refinement stops, from sire to son
Unalter'd, unimprov'd their manners run,   230
And love's and friendship's finely pointed dart
Fall blunted from each indurated heart.
Some sterner virtues o'er the mountain's breast
May sit, like falcons cow'ring on the nest;
But all the gentler morals, such as play   235
Through life's more cultur'd walks, and charm the way,
These far dispers'd, on timorous pinions fly,
To sport and flutter in a kinder sky.

To kinder skies, where gentler manners reign,
I turn; and France displays her bright domain.   240
Gay sprightly land of mirth and social ease,
Pleas'd with thyself, whom all the world can please,
How often have I led thy sportive choir,
With tuneless pipe, beside the murmuring Loire?
Where shading elms along the margin grew,   245
And freshen'd from the wave the Zephyr flew;
And haply, tho' my harsh touch faltering still,
But mock'd all tune, and marr'd the dancer's skill;
Yet would the village praise my wond'rous power,
And dance, forgetful of the noon-tide hour.   250
Alike all ages. Dames of ancient days
Have led their children through the mirthful maze,
And the gay grandsire, skill'd in gestic lore,
Has frisk'd beneath the burthen of threescore.

So blest a life these thoughtless realms display,   255
Thus idly busy rolls their world away:
Theirs are those arts that mind to mind endear,
For honour forms the social temper here.
Honour, that praise which real merit gains,
Or even imaginary worth obtains,   260
Here passes current; paid from hand to hand,
It shifts in splendid traffic round the land:

From courts, to camps, to cottages it strays,
And all are taught an avarice of praise;
They please, are pleas'd, they give to get esteem,   265
Till, seeming blest, they grow to what they seem.

But while this softer art their bliss supplies,
It gives their follies also room to rise;
For praise too dearly lov'd, or warmly sought,
Enfeebles all internal strength of thought,   270
And the weak soul, within itself unblest,
Leans for all pleasure on another's breast.
Hence ostentation here, with tawdry art,
Pants for the vulgar praise which fools impart;
Here vanity assumes her pert grimace,   275
And trims her robes of frize with copper lace,
Here beggar pride defrauds her daily cheer,
To boast one splendid banquet once a year;
The mind still turns where shifting fashion draws,
Nor weighs the solid worth of self applause.   280

To men of other minds my fancy flies,
Embosom'd in the deep where Holland lies,
Methinks her patient sons before me stand,
Where the broad ocean leans against the land,
And, sedulous to stop the coming tide,   285
Lift the tall rampire's artificial pride.
Onward methinks, and diligently slow
The firm connected bulwark seems to grow;
Spreads its long arms amidst the watry roar,
Scoops out an empire, and usurps the shore.   290
While the pent ocean rising o'er the pile,
Sees an amphibious world beneath him smile;
The slow canal, the yellow blossom'd vale,
The willow tufted bank, the gliding sail,
The crowded mart, the cultivated plain,   295
A new creation rescu'd from his reign.

Thus, while around, the wave-subjected soil
Impels the native to repeated toil,
Industrious habits in each bosom reign,
And industry begets a love of gain.   300

Hence all the good from opulence that springs,
With all those ills superfluous treasure brings,
Are here display'd. Their much-lov'd wealth imparts
Convenience, plenty, elegance, and arts;
But view them closer, craft and fraud appear,   30
Even liberty itself is barter'd here.
At gold's superior charms all freedom flies,
The needy sell it, and the rich man buys:
A land of tyrants, and a den of slaves,
Here wretches seek dishonourable graves,   31
And calmly bent, to servitude conform,
Dull as their lakes that slumber in the storm.

Heavens! how unlike their Belgic fires of old!
Rough, poor, content, ungovernably bold;
War in each breast, and freedom on each brow;   31
How much unlike the sons of Britain now!

Fir'd at the sound, my genius spreads her wing,
And flies where Britain courts the western spring;
Where lawns extend that scorn Arcadian pride,
And brighter streams than fam'd Hydaspis glide.   32
There all around the gentlest breezes stray,
There gentle music melts on every spray;
Creation's mildest charms are there combin'd,
Extremes are only in the master's mind;
Stern o'er each bosom reason holds her state.   32
With daring aims, irregularly great,
Pride in their port, defiance in their eye,
I see the lords of human kind pass by,
Intent on high designs, a thoughtful band,
By forms unfashion'd, fresh from Nature's hand;   33
Fierce in their native hardiness of soul,
True to imagin'd right, above controul,
While even the peasant boasts these rights to scan,
And learns to venerate himself as man.

Thine, Freedom, thine the blessings pictur'd here,   33
Thine are those charms that dazzle and endear;
Too blest indeed, were such without alloy,
But foster'd even by Freedom ills annoy:

That independence Britons prize too high,
Keeps man from man, and breaks the social tie;   340
The self-dependent lordlings stand alone,
All claims that bind and sweeten life unknown;
Here by the bonds of nature feebly held,
Minds combat minds, repelling and repell'd;
Ferments arise, imprison'd factions roar,   345
Represt ambition struggles round her shore,
Till over-wrought, the general system feels
Its motions stopt, or phrenzy fire the wheels.

    Nor this the worst. As nature's ties decay,
As duty, love, and honour fail to sway,   350
Fictitious bonds, the bonds of wealth and law,
Still gather strength, and force unwilling awe.
Hence all obedience bows to these alone,
And talent sinks, and merit weeps unknown;
Till Time may come, when, stript of all her charms,   355
The land of scholars, and the nurse of arms;
Where noble stems transmit the patriot flame,
Where kings have toil'd, and poets wrote for fame;
One sink of level avarice shall lie,
And scholars, soldiers, kings unhonor'd die.   360

    Yet think not, thus when Freedom's ills I state,
I mean to flatter kings, or court the great;
Ye powers of truth that bid my soul aspire,
Far from my bosom drive the low desire;
And thou fair freedom, taught alike to feel   365
The rabble's rage, and tyrant's angry steel;
Thou transitory flower, alike undone
By proud contempt, or favour's fostering sun,
Still may thy blooms the changeful clime endure,
I only would repress them to secure;   370
For just experience tells in every soil,
That those who think must govern those that toil,
And all that freedom's highest aims can reach,
Is but to lay proportion'd loads on each.
Hence, should one order disproportion'd grow,   375
Its double weight must ruin all below.
O then how blind to all that truth requires,
Who think it freedom when a part aspires!

Calm is my soul, nor apt to rise in arms,
Except when fast approaching danger warms: 3
But when contending chiefs blockade the throne,
Contracting regal power to stretch their own,
When I behold a factious band agree
To call it freedom, when themselves are free;
Each wanton judge new penal statutes draw,   3
Laws grind the poor, and rich men rule the law;
The wealth of climes, where savage nations roam,
Pillag'd from slaves, to purchase slaves at home;
Fear, pity, justice, indignation start,
Tear off reserve, and bare my swelling heart;   3
'Till half a patriot, half a coward grown,
I fly from petty tyrants to the throne.

Yes, brother, curse with me that baleful hour,
When first ambition struck at regal power;
And thus, polluting honour in its source,   3
Gave wealth to sway the mind with double force.
Have we not seen, round Britain's peopled shore,
Her useful sons exchang'd for useless ore?
Seen all her triumphs but destruction haste,
Like flaring tapers brightening as they waste;   4
Seen opulence, her grandeur to maintain,
Lead stern depopulation in her train,
And over fields, where scatter'd hamlets rose,
In barren solitary pomp repose?
Have we not seen, at pleasure's lordly call,
The smiling long-frequented village fall;
Beheld the duteous son, the sire decay'd,
The modest matron, and the blushing maid,
Forc'd from their homes, a melancholy train,
To traverse climes beyond the western main;   4
Where wild Oswego spreads her swamps around,
And Niagara stuns with thund'ring sound?

Even now, perhaps, as there some pilgrim strays
Through tangled forests, and through dangerous ways;
Where beasts with man divided empire claim,
And the brown Indian marks with murderous aim;
There, while above the giddy tempest flies,
And all around distressful yells arise,

The pensive exile, bending with his woe,
To stop too fearful, and too faint to go,   420
Casts a long look where England's glories shine,
And bids his bosom sympathize with mine.

   Vain, very vain, my weary search to find
That bliss which only centers in the mind:
Why have I stray'd, from pleasure and repose,   425
To seek a good each government bestows?
In every government, though terrors reign,
Though tyrant kings, or tyrant laws restrain,
How small, of all that human hearts endure,
That part which laws or kings can cause or cure.   430
Still to ourselves in every place consign'd,
Our own felicity we make or find:
With secret course, which no loud storms annoy,
Glides the smooth current of domestic joy.
The lifted ax, the agonizing wheel,   435
Luke's iron crown, and Damien's bed of steel,
To men remote from power but rarely known,
Leave reason, faith and conscience all our own.

THE END

A NEW SIMILE

IN THE MANNER OF SWIFT

Long had I sought in vain to find
A likeness for the scribbling kind;
The modern scribbling kind, who write,
In wit, and sense, and nature's spite:
'Till reading, I forget what day on,   5
A chapter out of Took's Pantheon;
I think I met with something there,
To suit my purpose to a hair;
But let us not proceed too furious,
First please to turn to God Mercurius;   10
You'll find him pictured at full length
In book the second, page the tenth:
The stress of all my proofs on him I lay,
And now proceed we to our simile.

   Imprimis, pray observe his hat   15
Wings upon either side——mark that.
Well! what is it from thence we gather?
Why these denote a brain of feather.
A brain of feather! very right,
With wit that's flighty, learning light;   20
Such as to modern bard's decreed:
A just comparison,—proceed.

   In the next place, his feet peruse,
Wings grow again from both his shoes;
Design'd no doubt, their part to bear,   25
And waft his godship through the air;
And here my simile unites,
For in a modern poet's flights,
I'm sure it may be justly said,
His feet are useful as his head.   30

Lastly, vouchsafe t' observe his hand,
Fill'd with a snake incircled wand;
By classic authors, term'd caducis,
And highly fam'd for several uses.
To wit—most wond'rously endu'd,   35
No poppy water half so good;
For let folks only get a touch,
It's soporific virtue's such,
Tho' ne'er so much awake before,
That quickly they begin to snore.   40
Add too, what certain writers tell,
With this he drives men's souls to hell.

Now to apply, begin we then;
His wand's a modern author's pen;
The serpents round about it twin'd,   45
Denote him of the reptile kind;
Denote the rage with which he writes,
His frothy slaver, venom'd bites;
An equal semblance still to keep,
Alike too, both conduce to sleep.   50
This diff'rence only, as the God,
Drove soul's to Tart'rus with his rod;
With his goosequill the scribing elf,
Instead of others, damns himself.

And here my simile almost tript,   55
Yet grant a word by way of postscript,
Moreover, Merc'ry had a failing:
Well! what of that? out with it—stealing;
In which all modern bards agree,
Being each as great a thief as he: 60
But ev'n this deities' existence,
Shall lend my simile assistance.
Our modern bards! why what a pox
Are they but senseless stones and blocks?

VERSES IN REPLY TO AN INVITATION TO DINNER AT DR. BAKER'S

Your mandate I got,
You may all go to pot;
Had your senses been right,
You'd have sent before night;
As I hope to be saved,
I put off being shaved;
For I could not make bold,
While the matter was cold,
To meddle in suds,
Or to put on my duds;
So tell Horneck and Nesbitt,
And Baker and his bit,
And Kauffman beside,
And the Jessamy bride,
With the rest of the crew,
The Reynoldses two,
Little Comedy's face,
And the Captain in lace.
(By the bye you may tell him,
I have something to sell him;
Of use I insist,
When he comes to enlist.
Your worships must know
That a few days ago,
An order went out,
For the foot guards so stout
To wear tails in high taste,
Twelve inches at least:
Now I've got him a scale
To measure each tail,
To lengthen a short tail,
And a long one to curtail.)—
    Yet how can I when vext,
Thus stray from my text?
Tell each other to rue
Your Devonshire crew,
For sending so late
To one of my state.

But 'tis Reynolds's way
From wisdom to stray,   40
And Angelica's whim
To be frolick like him,
But, alas! your good worships, how could they be wiser,
When both have been spoil'd in to-day's Advertiser?

OLIVER GOLDSMITH

EPITAPH ON EDWARD PURDON

Here lies poor NED PURDON, from misery freed,
Who long was a bookseller's hack;
He led such a damnable life in this world,—
I don't think, he'll ever come back.

[EPILOGUE TO *THE SISTER: A COMEDY*]

What! five long acts—and all to make us wiser!
Our authoress sure has wanted an adviser.
Had she consulted *me*, she should have made
Her moral play a speaking masquerade,
Warm'd up each bustling scene, and in her rage   5
Have emptied all the Green-room on the stage.
My life on't, this had kept her play from sinking,
Have pleas'd our eyes, and sav'd the pain of thinking.
Well, since she thus has shewn her want of skill,
What if I give a masquerade? I will.   10
But how! ay, there's the rub! (*pausing*) I've got my cue:
The world's a masquerade! the masquers, you, you, you.

[*To Boxes, Pit, Gallery*

Lud! what a groupe the motley scene discloses!
False wits, false wives, false virgins, and false spouses:
Statesmen with bridles on; and, close beside 'em,   15
Patriots, in party colour'd suits, that ride 'em.
There Hebes, turn'd of fifty, try once more,
To raise a flame in Cupids of threescore.
These, in their turn, with appetites as keen,
Deserting fifty, fasten on fifteen.   20

Miss, not yet full fifteen, with fire uncommon,
Flings down her sampler, and takes up the woman:
The little urchin smiles, and spreads her lure,
And tries to kill ere she's got power to cure.
Thus 'tis with all—Their chief and constant care   25
Is to seem every thing—but what they are.
Yon broad, bold, angry, spark, I fix my eye on,
Who seems t' have robb'd his visor from the lion,
Who frowns, and talks, and swears, with round parade,
Looking, as who should say, *Damme! who's afraid!*   [*mimicking.* 30
Strip but his vizor off, and sure I am,
You'll find his lionship a very lamb.
Yon politician, famous in debate,
Perhaps to vulgar eyes bestrides the state;
Yet, when he deigns his real shape t' assume,   35
He turns old woman, and bestrides a broom.
Yon patriot too, who presses on your sight,
And seems to every gazer all in white;
If with a bribe his candour you attack,
He bows, turns round, and whip—the man's a black!   40
Yon critic too—but whither do I run?
If I proceed, our bard will be undone!
Well then, a truce, since she requests it too;
Do you spare her, and I'll for once spare you.

THE DESERTED VILLAGE

—

TO SIR JOSHUA REYNOLDS

Dear Sir,

I can have no expectations in an address of this kind, either to add to
your reputation, or to establish my own. You can gain nothing from   5
my admiration, as I am ignorant of that art in which you are said to
excel; and I may lose much by the severity of your judgment, as few
have a juster taste in poetry than you. Setting interest therefore aside,
to which I never paid much attention, I must be indulged at present
in following my affections. The only dedication I ever made was to   10
my brother, because I loved him better than most other men. He is
since dead. Permit me to inscribe this Poem to you.

How far you may be pleased with the versification and mere mechan-
ical parts of this attempt, I don't pretend to enquire; but I know
you will object (and indeed several of our best and wisest friends con-   15
cur in the opinion) that the depopulation it deplores is no where to be
seen, and the disorders it laments are only to be found in the poet's own
imagination. To this I can scarce make any other answer than that I
sincerely believe what I have written; that I have taken all possible
pains, in my country excursions, for these four or five years past, to   20
be certain of what I alledge, and that all my views and enquiries have
led me to believe those miseries real, which I here attempt to display.
But this is not the place to enter into an enquiry, whether the country
be depopulating, or not; the discussion would take up much room,
and I should prove myself, at best, an indifferent politician, to tire the   25
reader with a long preface, when I want his unfatigued attention to a
long poem.

In regretting the depopulation of the country, I inveigh against the
increase of our luxuries; and here also I expect the shout of modern
politicians against me. For twenty or thirty years past, it has been the   30
fashion to consider luxury as one of the greatest national advantages;
and all the wisdom of antiquity in that particular, as erroneous. Still

however, I must remain a professed ancient on that head, and continue
to think those luxuries prejudicial to states, by which so many vices are
introduced, and so many kingdoms have been undone. Indeed so much   35
has been poured out of late on the other side of the question, that,
merely for the sake of novelty and variety, one would sometimes wish
to be in the right.

       I am,

           Dear Sir,   40

               Your sincere friend,

                  and ardent admirer,

                        OLIVER GOLDSMITH.

THE DESERTED VILLAGE

Sweet AUBURN, loveliest village of the plain,
Where health and plenty cheared the labouring swain,
Where smiling spring its earliest visit paid,
And parting summer's lingering blooms delayed,
Dear lovely bowers of innocence and ease,   5
Seats of my youth, when every sport could please,
How often have I loitered o'er thy green,
Where humble happiness endeared each scene;
How often have I paused on every charm,
The sheltered cot, the cultivated farm,   10
The never failing brook, the busy mill,
The decent church that topt the neighbouring hill,
The hawthorn bush, with seats beneath the shade,
For talking age and whispering lovers made.
How often have I blest the coming day,   15
When toil remitting lent its turn to play,
And all the village train from labour free
Led up their sports beneath the spreading tree,
While many a pastime circled in the shade,
The young contending as the old surveyed;   20
And many a gambol frolicked o'er the ground,
And slights of art and feats of strength went round.
And still as each repeated pleasure tired,
Succeeding sports the mirthful band inspired;
The dancing pair that simply sought renown   25
By holding out to tire each other down,
The swain mistrustless of his smutted face,
While secret laughter tittered round the place,
The bashful virgin's side-long looks of love,
The matron's glance that would those looks reprove.   30
These were thy charms, sweet village; sports like these,
With sweet succession, taught even toil to please;
These round thy bowers their chearful influence shed,
These were thy charms—But all these charms are fled.

Sweet smiling village, loveliest of the lawn,   35
Thy sports are fled, and all thy charms withdrawn;
Amidst thy bowers the tyrant's hand is seen,
And desolation saddens all thy green:
One only master grasps the whole domain,
And half a tillage stints thy smiling plain;   40
No more thy glassy brook reflects the day,
But choaked with sedges, works its weedy way.
Along thy glades, a solitary guest,
The hollow sounding bittern guards its nest;
Amidst thy desert walks the lapwing flies,   45
And tires their ecchoes with unvaried cries.
Sunk are thy bowers in shapeless ruin all,
And the long grass o'ertops the mouldering wall,
And trembling, shrinking from the spoiler's hand,
Far, far away thy children leave the land.   50

Ill fares the land, to hastening ills a prey,
Where wealth accumulates, and men decay;
Princes and lords may flourish, or may fade;
A breath can make them, as a breath has made.
But a bold peasantry, their country's pride,   55
When once destroyed, can never be supplied.

A time there was, ere England's griefs began,
When every rood of ground maintained its man;
For him light labour spread her wholesome store,
Just gave what life required, but gave no more.   60
His best companions, innocence and health;
And his best riches, ignorance of wealth.

But times are altered; trade's unfeeling train
Usurp the land and dispossess the swain;
Along the lawn, where scattered hamlets rose,   65
Unwieldy wealth, and cumbrous pomp repose;
And every want to oppulence allied,
And every pang that folly pays to pride.
These gentle hours that plenty bade to bloom,
Those calm desires that asked but little room,   70
Those healthful sports that graced the peaceful scene,
Lived in each look, and brightened all the green;

These far departing seek a kinder shore,
And rural mirth and manners are no more.

Sweet AUBURN! parent of the blissful hour,
Thy glades forlorn confess the tyrant's power.   75
Here as I take my solitary rounds,
Amidst thy tangling walks, and ruined grounds,
And, many a year elapsed, return to view
Where once the cottage stood, the hawthorn grew,
Remembrance wakes with all her busy train,   80
Swells at my breast, and turns the past to pain.

In all my wanderings round this world of care,
In all my griefs—and GOD has given my share—
I still had hopes my latest hours to crown,
Amidst these humble bowers to lay me down;   85
To husband out life's taper at the close,
And keep the flame from wasting by repose.
I still had hopes, for pride attends us still,
Amidst the swains to shew my book-learned skill,
Around my fire an evening groupe to draw,   90
And tell of all I felt, and all I saw;
And, as an hare whom hounds and horns pursue,
Pants to the place from whence at first she flew,
I still had hopes, my long vexations past,
Here to return—and die at home at last.   95

O blest retirement, friend to life's decline,
Retreats from care that never must be mine,
How happy he who crowns in shades like these,
A youth of labour with an age of ease;
Who quits a world where strong temptations try,   100
And, since 'tis hard to combat, learns to fly.
For him no wretches, born to work and weep,
Explore the mine, or tempt the dangerous deep;
No surly porter stands in guilty state
To spurn imploring famine from the gate,   105
But on he moves to meet his latter end,
Angels around befriending virtue's friend;
Bends to the grave with unperceived decay,
While resignation gently slopes the way;   110

And all his prospects brightening to the last,
His Heaven commences ere the world be past!

   Sweet was the sound when oft at evening's close,
Up yonder hill the village murmur rose;
There as I past with careless steps and slow,   115
The mingling notes came softened from below;
The swain responsive as the milk-maid sung,
The sober herd that lowed to meet their young;
The noisy geese that gabbled o'er the pool,
The playful children just let loose from school;   120
The watch-dog's voice that bayed the whispering wind,
And the loud laugh that spoke the vacant mind,
These all in sweet confusion sought the shade,
And filled each pause the nightingale had made.
But now the sounds of population fail,   125
No chearful murmurs fluctuate in the gale,
No busy steps the grass-grown foot-way tread,
For all the bloomy flush of life is fled.
All but yon widowed, solitary thing
That feebly bends beside the plashy spring;   130
She, wretched matron, forced, in age, for bread,
To strip the brook with mantling cresses spread,
To pick her wintry faggot from the thorn,
To seek her nightly shed, and weep till morn;
She only left of all the harmless train,   135
The sad historian of the pensive plain.

   Near yonder copse, where once the garden smil'd,
And still where many a garden flower grows wild;
There, where a few torn shrubs the place disclose,
The village preacher's modest mansion rose.   140
A man he was, to all the country dear,
And passing rich with forty pounds a year;
Remote from towns he ran his godly race,
Nor ere had changed, nor wish'd to change his place;
Unpractised he to fawn, or seek for power,   145
By doctrines fashioned to the varying hour;
Far other aims his heart had learned to prize,
More skilled to raise the wretched than to rise.
His house was known to all the vagrant train,
He chid their wanderings, but relieved their pain;   150

The long remembered beggar was his guest,
Whose beard descending swept his aged breast;
The ruined spendthrift, now no longer proud,
Claimed kindred there, and had his claims allowed;
The broken soldier, kindly bade to stay,   155
Sate by his fire, and talked the night away;
Wept o'er his wounds, or tales of sorrow done,
Shouldered his crutch, and shewed how fields were won.
Pleased with his guests, the good man learned to glow,
And quite forgot their vices in their woe;   160
Careless their merits, or their faults to scan,
His pity gave ere charity began.

Thus to relieve the wretched was his pride,
And even his failings leaned to Virtue's side;
But in his duty prompt at every call,   165
He watched and wept, he prayed and felt, for all.
And, as a bird each fond endearment tries,
To tempt its new fledged offspring to the skies;
He tried each art, reproved each dull delay,
Allured to brighter worlds, and led the way.   170

Beside the bed where parting life was layed,
And sorrow, guilt, and pain, by turns dismayed,
The reverend champion stood. At his control,
Despair and anguish fled the struggling soul;
Comfort came down the trembling wretch to raise,   175
And his last faultering accents whispered praise.

At church, with meek and unaffected grace,
His looks adorned the venerable place;
Truth from his lips prevailed with double sway,
And fools, who came to scoff, remained to pray.   180
The service past, around the pious man,
With steady zeal each honest rustic ran;
Even children followed with endearing wile,
And plucked his gown, to share the good man's smile.
His ready smile a parent's warmth exprest,   185
Their welfare pleased him, and their cares distrest;
To them his heart, his love, his griefs were given,
But all his serious thoughts had rest in Heaven.

As some tall cliff that lifts its awful form,
Swells from the vale, and midway leaves the storm,   190
Tho' round its breast the rolling clouds are spread,
Eternal sunshine settles on its head.

    Beside yon straggling fence that skirts the way,
With blossomed furze unprofitably gay,
There, in his noisy mansion, skill'd to rule,   195
The village master taught his little school;
A man severe he was, and stern to view,
I knew him well, and every truant knew;
Well had the boding tremblers learned to trace
The day's disasters in his morning face;   200
Full well they laugh'd with counterfeited glee,
At all his jokes, for many a joke had he;
Full well the busy whisper circling round,
Conveyed the dismal tidings when he frowned;
Yet he was kind, or if severe in aught,   205
The love he bore to learning was in fault;
The village all declared how much he knew;
'Twas certain he could write, and cypher too;
Lands he could measure, terms and tides presage,
And even the story ran that he could gauge.   210
In arguing too, the parson owned his skill,
For e'en tho' vanquished, he could argue still;
While words of learned length, and thundering sound,
Amazed the gazing rustics ranged around,
And still they gazed, and still the wonder grew,   215
That one small head could carry all he knew.

    But past is all his fame. The very spot
Where many a time he triumphed, is forgot.
Near yonder thorn, that lifts its head on high,
Where once the sign-post caught the passing eye,   220
Low lies that house where nut-brown draughts inspired,
Where grey-beard mirth and smiling toil retired,
Where village statesmen talked with looks profound,
And news much older than their ale went round.
Imagination fondly stoops to trace   225
The parlour splendòurs of that festive place;
The white-washed wall, the nicely sanded floor,
The varnished clock that clicked behind the door;

The chest contrived a double debt to pay,
A bed by night, a chest of drawers by day;   230
The pictures placed for ornament and use,
The twelve good rules, the royal game of goose;
The hearth, except when winter chill'd the day,
With aspen boughs, and flowers, and fennel gay,
While broken tea-cups, wisely kept for shew,   235
Ranged o'er the chimney, glistened in a row.

      Vain transitory splendours! Could not all
Reprieve the tottering mansion from its fall!
Obscure it sinks, nor shall it more impart
An hour's importance to the poor man's heart;   240
Thither no more the peasant shall repair
To sweet oblivion of his daily care;
No more the farmer's news, the barber's tale,
No more the wood-man's ballad shall prevail;
No more the smith his dusky brow shall clear,   245
Relax his ponderous strength, and lean to hear;
The host himself no longer shall be found
Careful to see the mantling bliss go round;
Nor the coy maid, half willing to be prest,
Shall kiss the cup to pass it to the rest.   250

      Yes! let the rich deride, the proud disdain;
These simple blessings of the lowly train,
To me more dear, congenial to my heart,
One native charm, than all the gloss of art;
Spontaneous joys, where Nature has its play,   255
The soul adopts, and owns their first born sway,
Lightly they frolic o'er the vacant mind,
Unenvied, unmolested, unconfined.
But the long pomp, the midnight masquerade,
With all the freaks of wanton wealth arrayed,   260
In these, ere triflers half their wish obtain,
The toiling pleasure sickens into pain;
And, even while fashion's brightest arts decoy,
The heart distrusting asks, if this be joy.

      Ye friends to truth, ye statesmen who survey   265
The rich man's joy's encrease, the poor's decay,

'Tis yours to judge, how wide the limits stand
Between a splendid and an happy land.
Proud swells the tide with loads of freighted ore,
And shouting Folly hails them from her shore;   270
Hoards, even beyond the miser's wish abound,
And rich men flock from all the world around.
Yet count our gains. This wealth is but a name
That leaves our useful products still the same.
Not so the loss. The man of wealth and pride,   275
Takes up a space that many poor supplied;
Space for his lake, his park's extended bounds,
Space for his horses, equipage, and hounds;
The robe that wraps his limbs in silken sloth,
Has robbed the neighbouring fields of half their growth;   280
His seat, where solitary sports are seen,
Indignant spurns the cottage from the green;
Around the world each needful product flies,
For all the luxuries the world supplies.
While thus the land adorned for pleasure all   285
In barren splendour feebly waits the fall.

As some fair female unadorned and plain,
Secure to please while youth confirms her reign,
Slights every borrowed charm that dress supplies,
Nor shares with art the triumph of her eyes.   290
But when those charms are past, for charms are frail,
When time advances, and when lovers fail,
She then shines forth sollicitous to bless,
In all the glaring impotence of dress.
Thus fares the land, by luxury betrayed,   295
In nature's simplest charms at first arrayed,
But verging to decline, its splendours rise,
Its vistas strike, its palaces surprize;
While scourged by famine from the smiling land,
The mournful peasant leads his humble band;   300
And while he sinks without one arm to save,
The country blooms—a garden, and a grave.

Where then, ah, where shall poverty reside,
To scape the pressure of contiguous pride?
If to some common's fenceless limits strayed,   305
He drives his flock to pick the scanty blade,

Those fenceless fields the sons of wealth divide,
And even the bare-worn common is denied.

    If to the city sped—What waits him there?
To see profusion that he must not share;   310
To see ten thousand baneful arts combined
To pamper luxury, and thin mankind;
To see those joys the sons of pleasure know,
Extorted from his fellow-creature's woe.
Here, while the courtier glitters in brocade,   315
There the pale artist plies the sickly trade;
Here, while the proud their long drawn pomps display,
There the black gibbet glooms beside the way.
The dome where pleasure holds her midnight reign,
Here richly deckt admits the gorgeous train,   320
Tumultuous grandeur crowds the blazing square,
The rattling chariots clash, the torches glare;
Sure scenes like these no troubles ere annoy!
Sure these denote one universal joy!
Are these thy serious thoughts?—Ah, turn thine eyes   325
Where the poor houseless shivering female lies.
She once, perhaps, in village plenty blest,
Has wept at tales of innocence distrest;
Her modest looks the cottage might adorn,
Sweet as the primrose peeps beneath the thorn;   330
Now lost to all; her friends, her virtue fled,
Near her betrayer's door she lays her head,
And pinch'd with cold, and shrinking from the shower,
With heavy heart deplores that luckless hour,
When idly first, ambitious of the town,   335
She left her wheel and robes of country brown.

    Do thine, sweet AUBURN, thine, the loveliest train,
Do thy fair tribes participate her pain?
Even now, perhaps, by cold and hunger led,
At proud men's doors they ask a little bread!   340

    Ah, no. To distant climes, a dreary scene,
Where half the convex world intrudes between,
Through torrid tracts with fainting steps they go,
Where wild Altama murmurs to their woe.

Far different there from all that charm'd before,   345
The various terrors of that horrid shore.
Those blazing suns that dart a downward ray,
And fiercely shed intolerable day;
Those matted woods where birds forget to sing,
But silent bats in drowsy clusters cling,   350
Those poisonous fields with rank luxuriance crowned
Where the dark scorpion gathers death around;
Where at each step the stranger fears to wake
The rattling terrors of the vengeful snake;
Where crouching tigers wait their hapless prey,   355
And savage men more murderous still than they;
While oft in whirls the mad tornado flies,
Mingling the ravaged landschape with the skies.
Far different these from every former scene,
The cooling brook, the grassy vested green,   360
The breezy covert of the warbling grove,
That only sheltered thefts of harmless love.

Good Heaven! what sorrows gloom'd that parting day,
That called them from their native walks away;
When the poor exiles, every pleasure past,   365
Hung round their bowers, and fondly looked their last,
And took a long farewell, and wished in vain
For seats like these beyond the western main;
And shuddering still to face the distant deep,
Returned and wept, and still returned to weep.   370
The good old sire, the first prepared to go
To new found worlds, and wept for others woe.
But for himself, in conscious virtue brave,
He only wished for worlds beyond the grave.
His lovely daughter, lovelier in her tears,   375
The fond companion of his helpless years,
Silent went next, neglectful of her charms,
And left a lover's for a father's arms.
With louder plaints the mother spoke her woes,
And blest the cot where every pleasure rose;   380
And kist her thoughtless babes with many a tear,
And claspt them close in sorrow doubly dear;
Whilst her fond husband strove to lend relief
In all the silent manliness of grief.

O luxury! Thou curst by heaven's decree,   385
How ill exchanged are things like these for thee!
How do thy potions with insidious joy,
Diffuse their pleasures only to destroy!
Kingdoms by thee, to sickly greatness grown,
Boast of a florid vigour not their own.   390
At every draught more large and large they grow,
A bloated mass of rank unwieldy woe;
Till sapped their strength, and every part unsound,
Down, down they sink, and spread a ruin round.

Even now the devastation is begun,   395
And half the business of destruction done;
Even now, methinks, as pondering here I stand,
I see the rural virtues leave the land.
Down where yon anchoring vessel spreads the sail
That idly waiting flaps with every gale,   400
Downward they move, a melancholy band,
Pass from the shore, and darken all the strand.
Contented toil, and hospitable care,
And kind connubial tenderness, are there;
And piety with wishes placed above,   405
And steady loyalty, and faithful love.
And thou, sweet Poetry, thou loveliest maid,
Still first to fly where sensual joys invade;
Unfit in these degenerate times of shame,
To catch the heart, or strike for honest fame;   410
Dear charming nymph, neglected and decried,
My shame in crowds, my solitary pride.
Thou source of all my bliss, and all my woe,
That found'st me poor at first, and keep'st me so;
Thou guide by which the nobler arts excell,   415
Thou nurse of every virtue, fare thee well.
Farewell, and O where'er thy voice be tried,
On Torno's cliffs, or Pambamarca's side,
Whether where equinoctial fervours glow,
Or winter wraps the polar world in snow,   420
Still let thy voice prevailing over time,
Redress the rigours of the inclement clime;
Aid slighted truth, with thy persuasive strain
Teach erring man to spurn the rage of gain;

Teach him that states of native strength possest,   425
Tho' very poor, may still be very blest;
That trade's proud empire hastes to swift decay,
As ocean sweeps the labour'd mole away;
While self dependent power can time defy,
As rocks resist the billows and the sky.   430

FINIS

[EPITAPH ON THOMAS PARNELL]

This tomb, inscrib'd to gentle PARNEL's name,
May speak our gratitude, but not his fame.
What heart but feels his sweetly-moral lay,
That leads to Truth thro' Pleasure's flow'ry way?
Celestial themes confess'd his tuneful aid;   5
And Heav'n, that lent him Genius, was repaid.
Needless to him the tribute we bestow,
The transitory breath of Fame below:
More lasting rapture from his Works shall rise,
While Converts thank their Poet in the skies.   10

THE HAUNCH OF VENISON
A POETICAL EPISTLE TO LORD CLARE

Thanks my Lord for your venison for finer or fatter
Never ranged in a forest or smoak'd on a platter
The haunch was a picture for painters to study
The fat was so white and the lean was so ruddy
Tho' my stomach was sharp I could scarce help regretting   5
To spoil such a delicate picture by eating
I had thoughts in my chamber to place it in view
To be shewn to my friends as a piece of virtu
As in some Irish houses where things are so so
One Gammon of Bacon hangs up for a shew   10
But for eating a rasher of what they take pride in
They'd as soon think of eating the pan it is fried in
But hold—Let us pause—Dont I hear you pronounce
This tale of the Bacon a damnable bounce
Well suppose it a bounce, sure a poet may try   15
By a bounce now and then to get courage to fly
But my Lord its no bounce I protest in my turn
It's a truth, and your Lordship may ask Mr. Burn.
To go on with my tale as I gaz'd on the haunch
I thought of a friend that was trusty and staunch   20

So I cut it and sent it to Reynolds undrest
To paint it, or eat it, just as he liked best.
Of the neck and the breast I had next to dispose
'Twas a neck and a breast that might rival Monroes
But in parting with these I was puzled again
With the how, and the who, and the where and the when
There's Howard and Coley and Haworth and Hiff
I think they love venison—I know they love beef
There's my country man Higgins Oh let him alone
For making a blunder or picking a bone
But hang it, to poets who seldom can eat
Your very good mutton's a very good treat
Such Dainties to them, their health It might hurt
Its like sending them ruffles when wanting a shirt
    While thus I debated in reverie centered
An acquaintance, a friend as he called himself entered
An under bred fine spoken fellow was he
And he smiled as he look'd at the venison and me
    What have we got here Ay this is good eating
Your own I suppose. Or is it in waiting.
    Why whose should it be cried I with a flounce
I get these things often, but that was a bounce.
Some Lords my acquaintance that settle the nation
Are pleas'd to be kind—but I hate ostentation.
    If that be the case then cried he very gay
I'm glad I have taken this house in my way
Tomorrow you take a poor dinner with me
No words I insist on't precisely at three.
We'll have Johnson and Burke, all the wits will be there
My Acquaintance is slight or I'd ask my Lord Clare
And now that I think ont, as I am a sinner
We wanted this venison to make out the dinner
What say you, a pasty—It shall, and it must
And my wife little Kisty is famous for crust.
Here porter this venison with me to mile end
No stirring I beg my dear friend, my dear friend.
Thus snatching his hat he brush'd off like the wind
And the porter and eatables followed behind.
    Left alone to reflect having emptied my shelf
And no body with me at Sea but myself.
Tho' I could not help thinking my gentle man hasty
Yet Johnson and Burke and a good venison pasty

Were things that I never disliked in my life
Tho' clogged with a coxcomb and Kisty his wife
So next day in due splendour to make my approach   65
I drove to his door in my own Hackney Coach.
   When come to the place where we all were to dine
A chair lumbered closet, just twelve feet by nine
My friend bid me welcome, but struck me quite dumb
With tidings that Johnson and Burke could not come   70
For I knew it he cried, both eternally fail
The one with his speeches the other with Thrale
But no matter I'll warrant we'll make up the party
With two full as clever and ten times as hearty
The one is a Scotchman the other a jew   75
They both of them merry and authors like you
The one writes the snarler, the other the scourge
Some think he writes Cinna, he owns to Panurge
While thus he describ'd them by trade and by name
They entered and dinner was served as they came   80
   At the top a fried liver and bacon was seen
At the bottom was tripe in a swinging Tureen
At the sides there was spinnage and pudding made hot
In the middle a place where the pasty was not.
Now My Lord as for tripe its my utter aversion   85
And your bacon I hate like a Turk or a Persian
So there I sate stuck like a horse in a pound
While the bacon and liver went merrily round.
But what vex't me most was that dam'd Scottish rogue
With his long winded speeches and smiles and his brogue   90
And Madam quoth he may this bit be my poison
A prettier dinner I never set eyes on
Pray a slice of your liver, tho may I be curst
But Ive eat of your tripe till Im ready to burst
The tripe quoth the Jew with his chocolate cheek   95
I could dine on this tripe seven days in the week
I like these here dinners so pretty and small
But your friend there the Doctor eats nothing at all
O ho quoth my friend he'l come on in a trice
He's keeping a corner for something that's nice!   100
Ther's a pasty—A pasty repeated the Jew
I don't care if I keep a corner for't too:
What the Deil Mon a pasty reechoed the Scot
Tho' splitting I'd still keep a corner for that.

We'll all keep a corner the lady cried out   105
We'll all keep a corner was echoed about
While thus we resolved and the pasty delay'd
With looks quite petrified entered the maid
A visage so sad and so pale with affright
Waked Priam by drawing his curtains by night   110
But we quickly found out for who could mistake her
That she came with some terrible news from the baker
And so it fell out for that negligent sloven
Had shut out the pasty on shutting his oven.
Sad Philomel thus—but let similes drop   115
And now that I think on't the story may stop
To be plain my good Lord its but labour misplact
To send such good verses to one of your taste
You've got an odd something, a kind of discerning
A relish, a taste sickened over by learning   120
At least its your temper, its very well known
That you think very slightly of all thats your own
So perhaps in your habits of thinking amiss
You may make a mistake and think slightly of this.

[PROLOGUE TO *ZOBEIDE*]

In these bold times, when Learning's sons explore
The distant climate and the savage shore;
When wise *Astronomers* to *India* steer,
And quit for *Venus*, many a brighter here;
When *Botanists*, all cold to smiles and dimpling,   5
Forsake the fair, and patiently—go simpling;
While every bosom swells with wond'rous scenes,
Priests, cannibals, and hoity-toity queens:
Our bard into the general spirit enters,
And fits his little frigate for adventures: 10
With *Scythian stores*, and trinkets deeply laden,
He this way steers his course, in hopes of trading—
Yet ere he lands he'as ordered me before,
To make an observation on the shore.
Where are we driven? Our reck'ning sure is lost!   15
This seems a barren and a dangerous coast.

Lord what a sultry climate am I under!
Yon ill-foreboding cloud seems big with thunder.
                                        (*to the Upper Gallery.*)
There Mangroves spread, and larger than I've seen 'em—
                                        (*to the Pit.*)
Here trees of stately size—and monkeys in 'em—   20
                                        (*to the pidgeon holes.*)
Here ill-condition'd oranges abound—   (*to the Stage.*)
And apples (*taking up and tasting*) *bitter* apples strew the ground.
The place is uninhabited I fear;
I heard a hissing—there are serpents here!
O there the natives are—a savage race!   25
The men have tails, the women paint the face!
No doubt they're all barbarians—Yes, 'tis so,
I'll try to make palaver with them though;   (*makes signs*)
'Tis best however keeping at a distance.
Good Savages, our Captain craves assistance;   30
Our ship's well stor'd;—in yonder creek we've laid her,
His honour is no mercenary trader;
To make you finer is his sole endeavour;
He seeks no benefit, content with favour.
This is his first adventure, lend him aid,   35
Or you may chance to spoil a thriving trade.
His goods he hopes are prime, and brought from far,
Equally fit for gallantry and war.
What no reply to promises so ample?
I'd best step back—and order up a sample.   40

[TRANSLATIONS FROM *AN HISTORY OF THE EARTH, AND ANIMATED NATURE*]

I

Of all the fish that graze beneath the flood,
He only ruminates his former food.

II

Chaste are their instincts, faithful is their fire,
No foreign beauty tempts to false desire:
The snow-white vesture, and the glittering crown,
The simple plumage, or the glossy down,

Prompt not their love. The patriot bird pursues   5
His well acquainted tints, and kindred hues.
Hence through their tribes no mix'd polluted flame,
No monster breed to mark the groves with shame:
But the chaste blackbird, to its partner true,
Thinks black alone is beauty's favourite hue: 10
The nightingale, with mutual passion blest,
Sings to its mate, and nightly charms the nest:
While the dark owl, to court his partner flies,
And owns his offspring in their yellow eyes.

THRENODIA AUGUSTALIS

OVERTURE a solemn Dirge

AIR. TRIO

Arise ye sons of worth, arise
And waken every note of woe,
When truth and virtue reach the skies,
'Tis ours to weep the want below.

CHORUS

When truth and virtue reach the skies,   5
'Tis ours to weep the want below.

MAN SPEAKER

The praise attending pomp and power,
The incense given to kings,
Are but the trappings of an hour,
Mere transitory things!   10
The base bestow them; but the good agree
To spurn the venal gifts as flattery.——
But when to pomp, and power, are join'd
An equal dignity of mind;
When titles are the smallest claim;   15
When wealth, and rank, and noble blood,
But aid the power of doing good,
Then all their trophies last—and flattery turns to fame!

Blest spirit thou, whose fame just born to bloom,
Shall spread and flourish from the tomb,   20
How hast thou left mankind for heaven!
Even now reproach and faction mourn,
And, wondering how their rage was born,
Request to be forgiven!
Alas! they never had thy hate;   25
Unmoved in conscious rectitude
Thy towering mind self-centered stood,
Nor wanted Man's opinion to be great.
In vain, to charm thy ravished sight,
A thousand gifts would fortune send;   30
In vain, to drive thee from the right,
A thousand sorrows urged thy end:
Like some well-fashion'd arch thy patience stood,
And purchased strength from its encreasing load.
Pain met thee like a friend that set thee free,   35
Affliction still is virtue's opportunity!
Virtue, on herself relying,
Every passion hush'd to rest,
Loses every pain of dying
In the hopes of being blest.   40
Every added pang she suffers,
Some encreasing good bestows,
And every shock that malice offers,
Only rocks her to repose.

SONG, By a Man. *Affettuoso*

Virtue, on herself relying,   45
Every passion hush'd to rest,
Loses every pain of dying
In the hopes of being blest.
Every added Pang she suffers,
Some encreasing good bestows,   50
Every shock that malice offers,
Only rocks her to repose.

WOMAN Speaker

Yet ah! what terrors frown'd upon her fate,
Death with its formidable band,

Fever, and pain, and pale consumptive care, 55
Determined took their stand.
Nor did the cruel ravagers design
To finish all their efforts at a blow;
But, mischievously slow,
They robbed the relic and defac'd the shrine.—— 60
With unavailing grief,
Despairing of relief,
Her weeping children round,
Beheld each hour
Death's growing pow'r, 65
And trembled as he frown'd.
As helpless friends who view from shore
The labouring ship, and hear the tempest roar,
While winds and waves their wishes cross;
They stood while hope and comfort fail, 70
Not to assist, but to bewail
The inevitable loss.——
Relentless tyrant, at thy call
How do the good, the virtuous fall?
Truth, beauty, worth, and all that most engage, 75
But wake thy vengeance and provoke thy rage.

> When vice my dart and scythe supply,
> How great a king of Terrors I!
> If folly, fraud, your hearts engage,
> Tremble ye mortals at my rage. 80

> Fall, round me fall ye little things,
> Ye statesmen, warriors, poets, kings,
> If virtue fail her counsel sage
> Tremble ye mortals at my rage.

MAN Speaker

Yet let that wisdom, urged by her example, 85
Teach us to estimate what all must suffer:
Let us prize death as the best gift of nature,
As a safe inn where weary travellers,
When they have journyed thro' a world of cares,
May put off life and be at rest for ever. 90

Groans, weeping friends, indeed, and gloomy sables
May oft distract us with their sad solemnity.
The preparation is the executioner.
Death, when unmasked, shews me a friendly face,
And is a terror only at a distance: 95
For as the line of life conducts me on
To death's great court, the prospect seems more fair;
'Tis nature's kind retreat, that's always open
To take us in when we have drain'd the cup
Of life, or worn our days to wretchedness.——   100
In that secure, serene retreat,
Where all the humble, all the great,
Promiscuously recline;
Where wildly huddled to the eye,
The beggar's pouch and prince's purple lie,   105
May every bliss be thine.
And ah! blest spirit, wheresoe'er thy flight,
Through rolling worlds, or fields of liquid light,
May cherubs welcome their expected guest,
May saints with songs receive thee to their rest,   110
May peace that claim'd while here thy warmest love,
May blissful endless peace be thine above.

SONG, By a WOMAN. *Amoroso*

Lovely lasting peace below,
Comforter of every woe,
Heavenly born, and bred on high,   115
To crown the favourites of the sky:
Lovely lasting peace appear,
This world itself, if thou art here,
Is once again with Eden blest,
And man contains it in his breast.   120

WOMAN SPEAKER

Our vows are heard! Long, long to mortal eyes,
Her soul was fitting to its kindred skies:
Celestial-like her bounty fell,
Where modest want and patient sorrow dwell.

Want pass'd for merit at her door,   12
Unseen the modest were supplied,
Her constant pity fed the poor,
Then only poor, indeed, the day she died.
And Oh, for this! while sculpture decks thy shrine,
And art exhausts profusion round,   13
The tribute of a tear be mine,
A simple song, a sigh profound.
There faith shall come, a pilgrim grey,
To bless the tomb that wraps thy clay;
And calm religion shall repair   13
To dwell a weeping hermit there.
Truth, fortitude, and friendship shall agree
To blend their virtues while they think of thee.

AIR. Chorus. *Pomposo*

Let us, let all the world agree,
To profit by resembling thee.   14

END OF THE FIRST PART

PART II

OVERTURE Pastorale
MAN Speaker

Fast by that shore where Thames' translucent stream
Reflects new glories on his breast,
Where, splendid as the youthful poet's dream,
He forms a scene beyond Elysium blest;
Where sculptur'd elegance and native grace   14
Unite to stamp the beauties of the place;
While, sweetly blending, still are seen
The wavy lawn, the sloping green;
While novelty, with cautious cunning,
Through every maze of fancy running,   15
From China borrows aid to deck the scene.

There sorrowing by the river's glassy bed,
Forlorn, a rural band complain'd,
All whom AUGUSTA's bounty fed,
All whom her clemency sustain'd.   155
The good old sire, unconscious of decay,
The modest matron, clad in home-spun grey,
The military boy, the orphan'd maid,
The shatter'd veteran, now first dismay'd;
These sadly join beside the murmuring deep,   160
And as they view the towers of Kew,
Call on their mistress, now no more, and weep.

CHORUS. *Affettuoso. Largo*

Ye shady walks, ye waving greens,
Ye nodding tow'rs, ye fairy scenes,
Let all your ecchoes now deplore,   165
That She who form'd your beauties is no more.

MAN SPEAKER

First of the train the patient rustic came,
Whose callous hand had form'd the scene,
Bending at once with sorrow and with age,
With many a tear, and many a sigh between,   170
And where, he cried, shall now my babes have bread,
Or how shall age support its feeble fire?
No lord will take me now, my vigour fled,
Nor can my strength perform what they require:
Each grudging master keeps the labourer bare,   175
A sleek and idle race is all their care.
My noble mistress thought not so!
Her bounty, like the morning dew,
Unseen, tho' constant, used to flow;
And as my strength decay'd, her bounty grew.   180
In decent dress, and coarsely clean,
The pious matron next was seen,
Clasp'd in her hand a godly book was borne,
By use and daily meditation worn:
That decent dress, this holy guide,   185
AUGUSTA's care had well supply'd.

And ah! she cries, all woe begone,
What now remains for me?
Oh! where shall weeping want repair
To ask for charity?
Too late in life for me to ask,
And shame prevents the deed,
And tardy, tardy are the times
To succour should I need.

But all my wants, before I spoke,
Were to my mistress known;
She still reliev'd, nor sought my praise,
Contented with her own.
But every day her name I'll bless,
My morning prayer, my evening song,
I'll praise her while my life shall last,
A life that cannot last me long.

SONG, By a WOMAN

Each day, each hour, her name I'll bless,
My morning and my evening song,
And when in death my vows shall cease,
My children shall the note prolong.

MAN SPEAKER

The hardy veteran after struck the sight,
Scarr'd, mangl'd, maim'd in every part,
Lopp'd of his limbs in many a gallant fight,
In nought entire—except his heart:
Mute for a while, and sullenly distress'd,
At last the impetuous sorrow fir'd his breast.
Wild is the whirlwind rolling
O'er Afric's sandy plain,
And wild the tempest howling
Along the billow'd main:
But every danger felt before,
The raging deep, the whirlwind's roar,
Less dreadful struck me with dismay,
Than what I feel this fatal day.

Oh, let me fly a land that spurns the brave,
Oswego's dreary shores shall be my grave;
I'll seek that less inhospitable coast,
And lay my body where my limbs were lost.

SONG by a MAN. *Basso. Spirituoso*

Old Edward's sons, unknown to yield,   225
Shall crowd from Cressy's laurell'd field
To do thy memory right:
For thine and Britain's wrongs they feel,
Again they snatch the gleamy steel,
And wish th' avenging fight.   230

WOMAN SPEAKER

In innocence and youth complaining,
Next appear'd a lovely maid,
Affliction o'er each feature reigning,
Kindly came in beauty's aid;
Every grace that grief dispenses,   235
Every glance that warms the soul,
In sweet succession charm'd the senses,
While pity harmoniz'd the whole.
The garland of beauty, 'tis thus she would say,
No more shall my crook or my temples adorn,   240
I'll not wear a garland, AUGUSTA's away,
I'll not wear a garland until she return:
But alas! that return I never shall see,
The ecchoes of Thames' shall my sorrows proclaim,
There promis'd a lover to come, but oh me!   245
'Twas death, 'twas the death of my mistress that came.
But ever, for ever, her image shall last,
I'll strip all the Spring of its earliest bloom;
On her grave shall the cowslip and primrose be cast,
And the new-blossom'd thorn shall whiten her tomb.   250

SONG by a WOMAN. *Pastorale*

With garlands of beauty the queen of the May
No more will her crook or her temples adorn;
For who'd wear a garland when she is away,
When she is remov'd, and shall never return?

On the grave of AUGUSTA *these garlands be plac't,*
We'll rifle the Spring of its earliest bloom,
And there shall the cowslip and primrose be cast,
And the new-blossom'd thorn shall whiten her tomb.

CHORUS. *Altro Modo*

On the grave of AUGUSTA *this garland be plac't,*
We'll rifle the Spring of its earliest bloom,
And there shall the cowslip and primrose be cast,
And the tears of her country shall water her tomb.

260

THE END

[SONG FOR *SHE STOOPS TO CONQUER*]

Ah me, when shall I marry me?
Lovers are plenty but fail to relieve me;
He, fond youth, that could carry me,
Offers to love but means to deceive me.

But I will rally and combat the ruiner;
Not a look, not a smile shall my passion discover;
She that gives all to the false one pursuing her
Makes but a penitent, loses a lover.

[FIRST EPILOGUE INTENDED FOR *SHE STOOPS TO CONQUER*]

Enter Mrs. Bulkley, who curtsies very low as beginning to speak. Then enter Miss Catley, who stands full before her, and curtsies to the Audience.

MRS. BULKLEY
Hold, Ma'am, your pardon. What's your business here?
MISS CATLEY
The Epilogue.
MRS. BULKLEY
The Epilogue?

Miss CATLEY

Yes, the Epilogue, my dear.　　　　　　　　　　　10

Mrs. BULKLEY

Sure you mistake, Ma'am. The Epilogue, *I* bring it.

Miss CATLEY

Excuse me, Ma'am. The Author bid *me* sing it.

Recitative　　　　　　15

Ye beaux and belles, that form this splendid ring,
Suspend your conversation while I sing.

Mrs. BULKLEY

Why sure the Girl's beside herself: an Epilogue of singing,
A hopeful end indeed to such a blest beginning.　　　　20
Besides, a singer in a comic set!
Excuse me, Ma'am, I know the etiquette.

Miss CATLEY

What if we leave it to the House?

Mrs. BULKLEY　　　　25

The House!—Agreed.

Miss CATLEY

Agreed.

Mrs. BULKLEY

And she, who's party's largest, shall proceed.　　　　30
And first I hope, you'll readily agree
I've all the critics and the wits for me.
They, I am sure, will answer my commands,
Ye candid judging few, hold up your hands;
What, no return? I find too late, I fear,　　　　35
That modern judges seldom enter here.

Miss CATLEY

I'm for a different set.—Old men, whose trade is
Still to gallant and dangle with the ladies.

RECITATIVE　　　　40

Who mump their passion, and who, grimly smiling,
Still thus address the fair with voice beguiling.

Air.—Cotillon

Turn, my fairest, turn, if ever
Strephon caught thy ravish'd eye.　　　　45
Pity take on your swain so clever,
Who without your aid must die.
　　Yes, I shall die, hu, hu, hu, hu,
　　Yes, I must die, ho, ho, ho, ho.

Da Capo　　　　50

Mrs. Bulkley

Let all the old pay homage to your merit:
Give me the young, the gay, the men of spirit.
Ye travelled tribe, ye macaroni train
Of French friseurs and nosegays justly vain,   55
Who take a trip to Paris once a year
To dress, and look like awkward Frenchmen here.
Lend me your hands.—O fatal news to tell,
Their hands are only lent to the Heinelle.

Miss Catley   60

Ay, take your travellers, travellers indeed!
Give me my bonny Scot, that travels from the Tweed.
Where are the Cheels? Ah! Ah, I well discern
The smiling looks of each bewitching bairne.

Air. A bonny young lad is my Jockey   65

I'll sing to amuse you by night and by day,
And be unco merry when you are but gay;
When you with your bagpipes are ready to play,
My voice shall be ready to carol away
    With Sandy, and Sawney, and Jockey,   70
    With Sawney, and Jarvie, and Jockey.

Mrs. Bulkley

Ye Gamesters, who so eager in pursuit,
Make but of all your fortune one *va Toute:*
Ye Jockey tribe whose stock of words are few,   75
"I hold the odds.—Done, done, with you, with you."
Ye Barristers, so fluent with grimace,
"My Lord,—your Lordship misconceives the case."
Doctors, who cough and answer every misfortuner,
"I wish I'd been call'd in a little sooner,"   80
Assist my cause with hands and voices hearty,
Come end the contest here, and aid my party.

Air.—Baleinamony

Miss Catley

Ye brave Irish lads, hark away to the crack,   85
Assist me, I pray, in this woful attack;
For sure I don't wrong you, you seldom are slack,
When the ladies are calling, to blush, and hang back.
  For you're always polite and attentive,
  Still to amuse us inventive,   90

And death is your only preventive.
        Your hands and your voices for me.

                        Mrs. BULKLEY

Well, Madam, what if, after all this sparring,
We both agree, like friends, to end our jarring?   95

                        Miss CATLEY

And that our friendship may remain unbroken,
What if we leave the Epilogue unspoken?

                        Mrs. BULKLEY

Agreed.   100

                        Miss CATLEY

Agreed.

                        Mrs. BULKLEY

And now with late repentance,
Un-epilogued the Poet waits his sentence.   105
Condemn the stubborn fool who can't submit
To thrive by flattery, though he starves by wit.

                                                    [*Exeunt.*

[SECOND REJECTED EPILOGUE TO
SHE STOOPS TO CONQUER]

There is a place,—so Ariosto sings,
A Treasury for lost and missing things.
Lost human Wits have Places there Assign'd them,
And they who lose their Senses, there may find them,
But where's this place, this Storehouse of the Age?   5
The Moon, says he: but I affirm the Stage.
At least in many things I think I see
His lunar and our Mimic World agree.
Both shine at night, for, but at Foote's alone,
We scarce exhibit till the Sun goes down.   10
Both, prone to change, no settled limits fix,
'Tis said the folks of both are lunaticks.
But in this paralell my best pretence is,
That mortals visit both to find their Senses.
To this strange spot, Rakes, Macaronis, Cits,   15
Come thronging to Collect their scatter'd Wits.
The gay Coquet, who ogles all the day,
Comes here by night, and goes a prude away.

The Gamester too, who eager in pursuit,
Makes but of all his fortune one *va toute*,   20
Whose Mind is barren, and whose words are few;
"I take the odds"—"Done, done, with you, and you,"
Comes here to saunter, having made his betts,
Finds his lost Senses out, and pays his Debts.
The Mohawk too—with angry phrases stor'd   25
As "damme Sir", and "Sir I wear a Sword:"
Here lessoned for awhile, and hence retreating,
Goes out, affronts his man, and takes a beating.
Here come the Sons of Scandal and of News,
But find no Sense—for they had none to lose.   30
The poet too—comes hither to be wiser,
And so for once I'll be the Man's Adviser.
What could he hope in this lord loving Age,
Without a brace of lords upon the Stage,
In robes and stars, unless the bard adorn us,   35
You grow familiar, lose respect, and scorn us.
Then not one passion, fury, sentiment
Sure his poetick fire is wholly spent!
Oh how I love to hear applauses shower
On my fix'd Attitude of half an hour.   40

(*Stands in an Attitude*)

And then with whining, staring, struggling, slapping,
To force their feelings and provoke their clapping.
Hither the affected City Dame advancing,
Who sighs for Opera's, and doats on dancing,
Who hums a favourite Air, and spreading wide,   45
Swings round the room, the Heinele of Cheapside,
Taught by our Art her Ridicule to pause on
Quits *Che faro* and calls for Nancy Dawson.
Of all the tribe here wanting an Adviser
Our Author's the least likely to grow wiser,   50
Has he not seen how you your favours place
On Sentimental Queens, and Lords in lace?
Without a Star, a coronet or Garter,
How can the piece expect, or hope for Quarter?
No high-life scenes, no sentiment, the creature   55
Still stoops among the low to copy Nature.
Yes, he's far gone. And yet some pity mix
The English Laws forbid to punish Lunaticks.

EPILOGUE, SPOKEN BY MR. LEE LEWES, IN THE CHARACTER OF HARLEQUIN, AT HIS BENEFIT

Hold! Prompter, hold! a word before your nonsense,
I'll speak a word or two to ease my conscience.
My pride forbids it ever shou'd be said,
My heels eclips'd the honours of my head,
That I found humour in a pyeball vest,   5
Or ever thought that jumping was a jest.

                                   [Taking off his mask

Whence, and what art thou, visionary birth?
Nature disowns, and reason scorns thy mirth;
In thy black aspect ev'ry passion sleeps,   10
The joy that dimples, and the woe that weeps.
How hast thou fill'd the scene with all thy brood,
Of fools persuing, and of fools persu'd!
Whose ins and outs no ray of sense discloses,
Whose only plot it is to break our noses;   15
Whilst from below the trap-door daemons rise,
And from above the dangling deities;
And shall I mix in this unhallow'd crew?
May rosin'd lightning blast me if I do.
No—I will act, I'll vindicate the stage;   20
Shakespeare himself shall feel my tragic rage.
Off! off! vile trappings! a new passion reigns,
The mad'ning monarch revels in my veins.
Oh! for a Richard's voice to catch the theme:
Give me another horse! bind up my wounds!—
    soft—'twas but a dream.   25
Ay, it was a dream, for now there's no retreating:
If I cease Harlequin, I cease from eating.
'Twas thus that Aesop's Stag, a creature blameless,
Yet something vain, like one that shall be nameless,
Once on the margin of a fountain stood,   30
And cavil'd at his image in the flood.
'The deuce confound (he cries) these drumstick shanks,
They neither have my gratitude nor thanks;
They're perfectly disgraceful! Strike me dead!
But, for a head, yes, yes, I have a head.   35
How piercing is that eye! How sleek that brow!

My horns! I'm told horns are the fashion now.'
Whilst thus he spoke, astonish'd! to his view,
Near, and more near, the hounds and huntsmen drew.
Hoicks! hark forward! came thund'ring from behind,   40
He bounds aloft, outstrips the fleeting wind:
He quits the woods, and tries the beaten ways;
He starts, he pants, he takes the circling maze.
At length, his silly head, so priz'd before,
Is taught its former folly to deplore;   45
Whilst his strong limbs conspire to set him free,
And at one bound he saves himself, like me.

                    [*Taking a jump through the stage door*

[LETTER TO MRS. BUNBURY]

First let me suppose what may shortly be true
The company set, and the word to be Loo.
All smirking, and pleasant, and big with adventure
And ogling the stake which is fixd in the center.
Round and round go the cards while I inwardly damn   5
At never once finding a visit from Pam.
I lay down my stake, apparently cool,
While the harpies about me all pocket the pool.
I fret in my gizzard, yet cautious and sly
I wish all my friends may be bolder than I.   10
Yet still they sit snugg, not a creature will aim
By losing their money to venture at fame.
Tis in vain that at niggardly caution I scold
Tis in vain that I flatter the brave and the bold
All play in their own way, and think me an ass.   15
What does Mrs. Bunbury? I sir? I pass.
Pray what does Miss Horneck? Take courage. Come do.
Who I! Let me see sir. Why I must pass too.
Mr. Bunbury frets, and I fret like the devil
To see them so cowardly lucky and civil.   20
Yet still I set snugg and continue to sigh on
Till made by my losses as bold as a lion
I venture at all, while my avarice regards
The whole pool as my own. Come give me five cards.
Well done cry the ladies. Ah Doctor that's good.   25
The pool's very rich. Ah. The Doctor is lood.

Thus foild in my courage, on all sides perplext,
I ask for advice from the lady that's next
Pray mam be so good as to give your advice
Dont you think the best way is to venture fort twice.   30
I advise cries the lady to try it I own.
Ah! The Doctor is lood. Come Doctor, put down.
Thus playing and playing I still grow more eager
And so bold and so bold, Im at last a bold beggar.
Now ladies I ask if law matters youre skilld in   35
Whether crimes such as yours should not come before Fielding
For giving advice that is not worth a straw
May well be call'd picking of pockets in law
And picking of pockets with which I now charge ye
Is by Quinto Elizabeth death without Clergy.   40
What justice when both to the Old Baily brought
By the gods Ill enjoy it, tho' 'tis but in thought.
Both are placed at the bar with all proper decorum
With bunches of Fennel and nosegays before em.
Both cover their faces with mobbs and all that   45
But the judge bids them angrily take of their hat.
When uncovered a buzz of enquiry runs round
Pray what are their crimes? Theyv'e been pilfering found.
But pray who have they pilfered? A Doctor I hear.
What yon solemn fac'd odd looking man that stands near.   50
The same. What a pitty. How does it surprize one
Two handsomer culprits I never set eyes on.
Then their friends all come round me with cringing and leering
To melt me to pitty, and soften my swearing.
First Sir Charles advances, with phrases well strung   55
Consider Dear Doctor the girls are but young.
The younger the Worse I return him again.
It shews that their habits are all dy'd in grain.
But then theyre so handsome, one's bosom it grieves.
What signifies handsome when people are thieves.   60
But where is your justice; their cases are hard.
What signifies justice; I want the reward.
But consider their case. It may yet be your own
And see how they kneel; is your heart made of stone?
This moves, so at last I agree to relent   65
For ten pounds in hand, and ten pound to be spent.
The judge takes the hint, having seen what we drive at
And lets them both off with correction in private.

RETALIATION
A POEM

Of old, when Scarron his companions invited,
Each guest brought his dish, and the feast was united;
If our landlord supplies us with beef, and with fish,
Let each guest bring himself, and he brings the best dish:
Our Dean shall be venison, just fresh from the plains;   5
Our Burke shall be tongue, with a garnish of brains;
Our Will shall be wild fowl, of excellent flavour,
And Dick with his pepper, shall heighten their savour:
Our Cumberland's sweet-bread its place shall obtain,
And Douglass's pudding, substantial and plain: 10
Our Garrick's a sallad, for in him we see
Oil, vinegar, sugar, and saltness agree:
To make out the dinner, full certain I am,
That Ridge is anchovy, and Reynolds is lamb;
That Hickey's a capon, and by the same rule,   15
Magnanimous Goldsmith, a goosberry fool:
At a dinner so various, at such a repast,
Who'd not be a glutton, and stick to the last:
Here, waiter, more wine, let me sit while I'm able,
'Till all my companions sink under the table;   20
Then with chaos and blunders encircling my head,
Let me ponder, and tell what I think of the dead.

Here lies the good Dean, re-united to earth,
Who mixt reason with pleasure, and wisdom with mirth:
If he had any faults, he has left us in doubt,   25
At least, in six weeks, I could not find 'em out;
Yet some have declar'd, and it can't be denied 'em,
That sly-boots was cursedly cunning to hide 'em.

Here lies our good Edmund, whose genius was such,
We scarcely can praise it, or blame it too much;   30
Who, born for the Universe, narrow'd his mind,
And to party gave up, what was meant for mankind.
Tho' fraught with all learning, kept straining his throat,
To persuade Tommy Townsend to lend him a vote;
Who, too deep for his hearers, still went on refining,   35
And thought of convincing, while they thought of dining;

Tho' equal to all things, for all things unfit,
Too nice for a statesman, too proud for a wit:
For a patriot too cool; for a drudge, disobedient,
And too fond of the *right* to pursue the *expedient*.   40
In short, 'twas his fate, unemploy'd, or in place, Sir,
To eat mutton cold, and cut blocks with a razor.

Here lies honest William, whose heart was a mint,
While the owner ne'er knew half the good that was in't;
The pupil of impulse, it forc'd him along,   45
His conduct still right, with his argument wrong;
Still aiming at honour, yet fearing to roam,
The coachman was tipsy, the chariot drove home;
Would you ask for his merits, alas! he had none,
What was good was spontaneous, his faults were his own.   50

Here lies honest Richard, whose fate I must sigh at,
Alas, that such frolic should now be so quiet!
What spirits were his, what wit and what whim,
Now breaking a jest, and now breaking a limb;
Now rangling and grumbling to keep up the ball,   55
Now teazing and vexing, yet laughing at all?
In short so provoking a Devil was Dick,
That we wish'd him full ten times a day at Old Nick,
But missing his mirth and agreeable vein,
As often we wish'd to have Dick back again.   60

Here Cumberland lies having acted his parts,
The Terence of England, the mender of hearts;
A flattering painter, who made it his care
To draw men as they ought to be, not as they are.
His gallants are all faultless, his women divine,   65
And comedy wonders at being so fine;
Like a tragedy queen he has dizen'd her out,
Or rather like tragedy giving a rout.
His fools have their follies so lost in a croud
Of virtues and feelings, that folly grows proud,   70
And coxcombs alike in their failings alone,
Adopting his portraits are pleas'd with their own.
Say, where has our poet this malady caught,
Or wherefore his characters thus without fault?

Say was it that vainly directing his view,   75
To find out mens virtues and finding them few,
Quite sick of pursuing each troublesome elf,
He grew lazy at last and drew from himself?

Here Douglas retires from his toils to relax,
The scourge of impostors, the terror of quacks: 80
Come all ye quack bards, and ye quacking divines,
Come and dance on the spot where your tyrant reclines,
When Satire and Censure encircl'd his throne,
I fear'd for your safety, I fear'd for my own;
But now he is gone, and we want a detector,   85
Our Dodds shall be pious, our Kenricks shall lecture;
Macpherson write bombast, and call it a style,
Our Townshend make speeches, and I shall compile;
New Lauders and Bowers the Tweed shall cross over,
No countryman living their tricks to discover;   90
Detection her taper shall quench to a spark,
And Scotchman meet Scotchman and cheat in the dark.

Here lies David Garrick, describe me who can,
An abridgment of all that was pleasant in man;
As an actor, confest without rival to shine,   95
As a wit, if not first, in the very first line,
Yet with talents like these, and an excellent heart,
The man had his failings, a dupe to his art;
Like an ill judging beauty, his colours he spread,
And beplaister'd, with rouge, his own natural red.   100
On the stage he was natural, simple, affecting,
'Twas only that, when he was off, he was acting:
With no reason on earth to go out of his way,
He turn'd and he varied full ten times a day;
Tho' secure of our hearts, yet confoundedly sick,   105
If they were not his own by finessing and trick,
He cast off his friends, as a huntsman his pack;
For he knew when he pleased he could whistle them back.
Of praise, a mere glutton, he swallowed what came,
And the puff of a dunce, he mistook it for fame;   110
'Till his relish grown callous, almost to disease,
Who pepper'd the highest, was surest to please.
But let us be candid, and speak out our mind,
If dunces applauded, he paid them in kind.

Ye Kenricks, ye Kellys, and Woodfalls so grave,   115
What a commerce was yours, while you got and you gave?
How did Grub-street re-echo the shouts that you rais'd,
While he was beroscius'd, and you were beprais'd?
But peace to his spirit, wherever it flies,
To act as an angel, and mix with the skies: 120
Those poets, who owe their best fame to his skill,
Shall still be his flatterers, go where he will.
Old Shakespeare receive him with praise and with love,
And Beaumonts and Bens be his Kellys above.

   Here Hickey reclines, a most blunt, pleasant creature,   125
And slander itself must allow him good-nature:
He cherish'd his friend, and he relish'd a bumper;
Yet one fault he had, and that one was a thumper:
Perhaps you may ask if that man was a miser?
I answer, no, no, for he always was wiser;   130
Too courteous, perhaps, or obligingly flat;
His very worst foe can't accuse him of that.
Perhaps he confided in men as they go,
And so was too foolishly honest; ah, no.
Then what was his failing? come tell it, and burn ye,   135
He was, could he help it? a special attorney.

   Here Reynolds is laid, and to tell you my mind,
He has not left a better or wiser behind;
His pencil was striking, resistless and grand,
His manners were gentle, complying and bland;   140
Still born to improve us in every part,
His pencil our faces, his manners our heart:
To coxcombs averse, yet most civilly staring,
When they judged without skill he was still hard of hearing:
When they talk'd of their Raphaels, Corregios and stuff,   145
He shifted his trumpet, and only took snuff.

THE END

NOTES

p. 1. **The Good Natur'd Man**

Goldsmith completed this play in 1766 or early in 1767, and submitted it first to Garrick, the famous actor-manager of Drury Lane, and then, since Garrick raised a number of objections to it, to George Colman. Colman produced it in Covent Garden late in January 1768. The play was not well received: the taste of the public inclined towards 'genteel' or sentimental comedy, and Goldsmith's play, which was a reaction against the artificiality of this mode towards the more naturalistic— and funnier—comedies of Molière and the Restoration, was only saved by the support of his friends and the cutting of the entire Bailiff scene, which was thought to be 'low'—vulgar. The scene was restored for the printed edition, which was fairly favourably reviewed; but on the whole the play was not more than a moderate success.

4.5. Bensley acted the part of Leontine.

4.12. Caesar forced his pilot to sail into a storm.

4.16. The simile refers to the coming General Election of 1768.

11.25. There had been several earthquakes in London in 1767.

12.40. *Almack's*: a suite of assembly rooms in St James's Square (the centre of fashionable London), where balls were held. *the public gardens*: Vauxhall Gardens, another fashionable centre; they were decorated by landscape paintings.

14.37. *a trip to Scotland*: a runaway marriage. The Scottish marriage laws did not require parental consent.

18.41. *another guess lover*: another kind of lover. See *Glossary*.

19.42. *Silence gives consent*: *Qui tacet, consentire videtur*; a legal maxim.

22.23-5. Quoting Congreve's masque *The Judgement of Paris*. Goldsmith was apparently uncertain who wrote this, since he first put 'Waller Congrave says', which was preserved accidentally in the printed edition. On correcting it in ed. 3, either Goldsmith or the printer made the wrong choice and struck out 'Congrave' instead of

'Waller'. I have put in the correct ascription, as Goldsmith undoubt-
edly would have wished. *the House*: the House of Commons.

22.31–2. *land carriage fishery*: a scheme proposed in 1761 for supplying
fish to London. *stamp act*: probably the tax of 1765 that was one of
the causes of the American War of Independence. *jaghire*: an Indian
word for an annuity consisting of the government's share in the
produce of a district, made over to a particular person.

23.17. *Borough interest*: indicating that she has powerful connections
that could sway elections.

28.18. *capus*: i.e. *capias*, a writ or summons.

30.12. He was probably in charge of a side-show in a fair.

30.33. *circuit*: the route taken by judges, presiding over cases in successive provincial assizes.

30.39. *Fleet*: punning on the Fleet Prison, which was principally for
debtors and bankrupts.

31.4–5. Lord Hawke, Admiral of the Fleet, had destroyed the French
fleet at the battle of Quiberon in 1759; Lord Amherst was Wolfe's
commander-in-chief at the capture of Quebec in 1759.

32.34. *before and behind*: they are escorting him as a captive.

35.23. There was a club of wits who called themselves the 'choice
spirits'.

36.20. *Pensacola*: made the capital of West Florida when the Floridas
were ceded to Great Britain in 1763.

43.10. *incendiary*: according to Johnson's *Dictionary*, 'one who sets
houses or towns on fire in malice or for robbery'. In the 1760s there
was a spate of these blackmailing letters.

43.15–16. *gunnes, experetion*: guineas, expedition. *blown up*: a colloquial
phrase for 'ruined'.

43.23. There was an earthquake in Lisbon in 1755. It caused an eight-
day fire.

44.14. *engine*: fire engine. Most houses had their own.

46.24–5. According to legend, the house of the Virgin Mary was
miraculously transferred to Loretto in Italy, in 1294.

49.24–5. *Lamb, Dolphin, Angel*: the names of rooms in the inn.

50.5. *rasberry*: raspberry wine.

56.28. *Quietus*: short for *quietus est*, 'it is discharged'.

56.39–41. Pasquale Paoli was living in London on a pension after
having led a celebrated but unsuccessful attempt to achieve Corsican
independence. The Marquis of Squilachi was Prime Minister of
Spain, who had been driven from Madrid into exile at Naples in
1766. Stanislaus Poniatowski had been made King of Poland in 1764.

57.37–9. Wildman's was a coffee-house in Covent Garden; the Merchant Tailors had the largest hall of all the City Companies. Lofty's final claim is that he had signed public documents and had had his portrait in shops selling prints.

61.18–21. Possibly the Dr George Baker mentioned in the 'Reply to an Invitation' (176). The contest in Warwick Lane was at the Royal College of Physicians, in 1767; it arose because of a dispute between the Fellows of the College and the Licentiates about the admission of some of the latter.

61.22. *manager*: George Colman.

62.8. Quoting *King Lear* III. iv. 29.

p. 63. **She Stoops to Conquer** was written by September 1771, but was not acted until 15 March 1773. During that time it was revised heavily, and probably made worse—less lively and colloquial, and more respectable—because Goldsmith found difficulty in persuading theatre-managers to accept that the public taste was ready for the 'laughing' anti-sentimental comedy. George Colman, manager of Covent Garden, was eventually prevailed on by Goldsmith's friends (among them Dr Johnson) to stage it, which he did at the end of the season, with little attention to props and costumes, and with great reluctance. It was an enormous success, and Colman was pilloried in the newspapers for his lack of confidence in it. It was published on March 25, and in three days sold the unprecedented quantity of 4,000 copies.

66.3. Henry Woodward was to have played the part of Tony Lumpkin, but he turned it down.

66.7. Parodying *Hamlet* I. ii. 77, 85: ''Tis not alone my inky cloak, good mother . . . But I have that within which passeth show.'

66.19. Edward (Ned) Shuter took the part of Hardcastle in the play.

66.24. This line is printed as a quotation, but the source has not been traced.

67.4. A sexual innuendo is intended.

69.19. *rumbling*: an old-fashioned term for 'rambling'.

69.22–3. Prince Eugene of Savoy and the Duke of Marlborough led the Austrian and British armies against the French in the War of the Spanish Succession (1701–14).

71.9. Presumably a juggler.

74.10. Quoting *I Henry IV*, V. i. 126.

74.15. As chairman ('a mallet in his hand') he will propose himself for a song.

75.18. *Water parted*: a song from the opera *Artaxerxes* (1762). Handel's *Ariadne* was first performed in 1734.

76.27. 'There needs no ghost, my lord, come from the grave / To tell us this.' *Hamlet* I. v. 124–5.

77.26. There had been a prize of £20,000 available since 1713 for the discoverer of an accurate means of ascertaining the longitude; it was won on 14 June 1773, three months after the opening of this play.

82.25–6. *dutchesses of Drury lane*: prostitutes.

83.7. Marlborough was not at the retreat from the unsuccessful siege of Denain (1712).

84.3. *sell ale*: This must have a special meaning for Hardcastle, presumably connected with the buying and selling of votes for parliamentary elections.

84.9. Hyder Ali was Sultan of Mysore; Cossim Ali Cawn was Subah of Bengal; 'Ally Croaker' was a popular Irish song.

84.28. The siege of Belgrade took place in 1717.

85.39–41. *florentine*: meat baked in a dish with a covering of paste. *a shaking pudding*: a jelly. *taffety cream*: fine silky cream (only usage). *made dish*: a dish composed of several ingredients.

86.1. *green and yellow dinner*: presumably referring to the elaborately coloured china, the food being correspondingly insubstantial.

87.6–7. This was taken by the contemporary audience as intending an attack on the unpopular and restrictive Royal Marriage Act of 1772.

91.13–14. Ranelagh Gardens in Chelsea and St James's Park were centres of fashion; Tower Wharf was decidedly not. He is mocking her.

91.18–19. The Pantheon, in Oxford Street, was a fashionable resort; the Grotto Gardens, in the Borough of Southwark, were distinctly unfashionable by 1773.

91.21. A reference to the monthly publication in the *Town and Country Magazine* of portraits, known as 'Tête-à-têtes', each of a famous man and his mistress, with a scandalous commentary.

91.25. *dégagée*: relaxed, informal. The opposite of Mrs Hardcastle's hairstyle.

91.31. *inoculation*: against smallpox.

93.4–6. The *Compleat Housewife* (1729) and John Quincy's *Compleat English Dispensatory* (1718) were still popular home-helps.

96.11. *Bully Dawson*: a famous bully, mentioned in *The Spectator*, no. 2.

98.23. *Rose*[-cut] (first usage), *table-cut*: particular, and then unfashionable, ways of cutting diamonds.

100.36. The landlord's daughter in Farquhar's play of 1707.

101.16–17. Rooms in inns were given names. Cf. *The Good-Natured Man*, p. 49.

102.42. *Ladies Club*: a satirical reference to a fashionable gathering of women, to which men were invited, that met in Albemarle Street. 'Biddy Buckskin' (103.7) is Rachael Lloyd, one of the founders.

108.11. Possibly a partisan's cry from the Wilkes riots, like 'Wilkes and Liberty'. John Williams the bookseller sold the banned No. 45 of Wilkes's *North-Briton* in Fleet Street; he was pilloried for this.

111.15–16. *Whistlejacket*: a famous race-horse that belonged to the Marquis of Rockingham.

113.5–7. Cock-fighting terms: *Shake bag*: a shake-bag is a large fighting cock. *goose-green*: refers to the bird's colour. *odd battle*: perhaps an uneven match (only usage).

115.27–8. *Yours and yours*: I have been unable to trace the origin of this phrase.

128.1. Delivered by Kate Hardcastle. For the background to this, see the 'First Rejected Epilogue', p. 206.

128.10. Cf. *As You Like It*, II. vii. 43. The rest of the speech is a parody of Jaques's 'Seven Ages of Man' speech.

128.28. Nancy Dawson was a famous horn-pipe dancer; 'Che faro senza Eurydice' is a song from Gluck's opera *Orfeo* (1764).

128.30. Anne Heinel, a dancer, had just unsuccessfully appeared at the Opera in the Haymarket.

129.5. A reference to Mr Bayes, the hero of Buckingham's play *The Rehearsal* (1672), who became a stock figure of the dramatist; but there is also a pun on 'bays', the laurel crown for poetry.

p. 133. Prologue of Laberius (?1758)
Goldsmith translated this poem as part of his attack on actors and managers of the theatre in his *Enquiry into the Present State of Polite Learning in Europe*. It is introduced as follows: 'Macrobius [*Saturnalia*, II. vii] has preserved a prologue, spoken and written by the poet Laberius, a Roman knight, whom Caesar forced upon the stage, written with great elegance and spirit, which shews what opinion the Romans in general entertained of the profession of an actor.'

p. 133. On a Beautiful Youth (printed October 1759)
Though a note in the text describes this poem as 'imitated from the Spanish', its source has not been found.

p. 134. The Gift (pr. October 1759)
An imitation—chiefly in the punch-line—of Bernard de la Monnoye's 'Etrène à Iris' (*Poesies*, 1716, p. 53). Iris's address may imply that she is an actress, or perhaps a prostitute.

p. 134. A Sonnet (pr. October 1759)

A close imitation of a seventeenth-century French poem by Denis Sanguin de Saint-Pavin. The point, which is rather obscured by the translation, is that Myra is afraid of the pain of losing her virginity. Had she followed the poet's directions, that virginity would have been a thing of the past.

8. *wanted*: here in the sense of 'lacked'.

p. 135. Elegy on Mrs Blaize (pr. October 1759)

Evidently Goldsmith's first exercise in this deflating mode, which he also used in 'On the Death of the Right Hon. ***' and in the 'Elegy on the Death of a Mad Dog' (pp. 140, 141), as here, to satirize contemporary elegies. The model is La Monnoye's 'Le Fameux La Galisse' (*Poesies*, 1716, pp. 91–102).

5. *Either*: seldom passed without being invited in; or, ironically, seldom went near.

26. Kent Street was famous for its beggars.

p. 136. The Double Transformation (pr. January 1760)

97. *nooze*: noose.

p. 139. An Author's Bed-Chamber (pr. May 1760)

Goldsmith introduced lines 7–18 of this poem in a letter to his brother Henry of *c*. 13 January 1759, as an extract from a 'heroicomical poem'. He added four extra lines: 'And Now immagine after his soliloquy the landlord to make his appearance in order to Dun him for the reckoning, / Not with that face so servile and so gay / That welcomes every stranger that can pay / With sulky Eye he smoak'd the patient man / Then pull'd his breeches tight, and thus began. &c. All this is taken you see from Nature.' The poem reappears in its present form in Goldsmith's *Chinese Letters*, where it is ironically put into the mouth of one of a club of authors, who describes it as 'an heroical description of nature'.

3. Calvert and Parsons were well-known brewers of 'entire butt beer', or porter—popularly known as 'black champagne'.

4. Drury Lane was known for its prostitutes.

11. A simple and popular board game, played with dice.

12. Twelve 'golden rules' attributed to Charles I and often printed as broadsheets.

14. The Duke of Cumberland, victor of Culloden; presumably a silhouette.

p. 139. On Seeing Mrs **** (pr. October 1760)
This poem is presented in Goldsmith's *Chinese Letters* (letter 85) as a parody on the panegyrics written for successful actors and actresses: 'should it happen to be an actress, Venus the beauteous queen of love, and the naked graces are ever in waiting, the lady must be herself a goddess bred and born'. Paphos (9) was a city in Cyprus sacred to Venus.

p. 140. On the Death of the Right Honourable *** (pr. March 1761)
This poem is part of a *Chinese Letter* attacking panegyrics on the great. It is proposed as a means 'of flattering the worthless, and yet of preserving a safe conscience'. It is another imitation of La Monnoye (see the 'Elegy on Mrs. Blaize', p. 135).

p. 141. South American Ode (pr. May 1761)
From letter cxvi of *The Citizen of the World*, where it is used to support an argument that love is a natural rather than an artificial passion: 'Even in the sultry wilds of southern America, the lover is not satisfied with possessing his mistress's person, without having her mind.' The poem follows from that.

p. 141. On the Death of a Mad Dog (?1760–2)
This poem (from *The Vicar of Wakefield*), like the 'Elegy on Mrs Blaize' (p. 135), is a satire on contemporary elegies, and similarly imitates La Monnoye's 'le fameux la Galisse'.

p. 142. Song from The Vicar (by Autumn 1762)
In the novel this is sung by Olivia, the Vicar's daughter, who has been seduced and abandoned.

p. 142. A Ballad (?1761–2)
'That poem, Cradock, cannot be amended,' said Goldsmith of his ballad. Characteristically, he left it in two distinct versions, each heavily amended. I have reproduced the text found in *The Vicar of Wakefield*, which seems to me the better, and the more carefully revised, of the two. In the novel it is presented in the course of an attack on contemporary poetry, and its simplicity is evoked as a contrast to the 'luxuriant images' and plotlessness of the latter.
31–2. 'Man wants but Little; nor that Little, long'. Young, *Night-Thoughts*, iv. 119.

p. 147. **The Captivity** (by October 1764)

This libretto earned Goldsmith ten guineas in 1764, but was never published in his lifetime. It is clearly a purely commercial product. Its theme is the conquest of Babylon by Cyrus, King of Persia, which ended the captivity of the Jews.

p. 160. **The Traveller** (pr. December 1764)

The Traveller was begun in 1755, during Goldsmith's travels on the Continent; part of it was sent to his brother from abroad. It was revised heavily, perhaps in 1762, and again while at the press and between editions: Goldsmith was conscious that it was the poem that could establish him as a man of letters, rather than a bookseller's hack, and so worked at it with inordinate care and caution. He was assisted by Dr Johnson, who contributed lines 420, 429–34 and 437–8. The poem achieved his ambition, gaining him fame and respect. The dedication to his brother Henry, an obscure clergyman, was a calculatedly unusual step: poems were usually dedicated to potential or actual patrons, who would reward what they took to be merit with money and favour. Goldsmith's patrons were, as he later remarked, the booksellers, and therefore the public: he was at once announcing his independence from 'party' (*Dedication* 36ff.) and complimenting his readers, as well as making a critical comment on the theme of the poem (*Dedication* 12ff.).

Dedication 5. Goldsmith's eldest brother, Curate-in-charge of the Parish of Kilkenny West in County Westmeath.

Poem 2. The Scheldt flows through N. France to the sea at Antwerp; the Po is the largest river in Italy.

3. Carinthia was a Duchy in the Austrian Alps.

5. Campania was in Roman times an exceptionally fertile province in W. Italy.

69. *the line*: the Equator.

84. Many suggestions as to Idra's whereabouts have been offered: the most convincing is Lonsdale's, that it is Idria, a mining town in the Austrian Alps. The Arno flows past Florence and Pisa.

105. The Appennines extend from the Alps through almost the whole length of Italy.

169–70. One of Switzerland's main exports had for a long time been mercenary soldiers.

190. *savage*: wild animal. See *Glossary*.

320. The Hydaspes was an Indian river.

411. *Oswego*: a Canadian river, running into Lake Ontario.

436. Referring to the leader of a Hungarian peasant uprising (in 1514)

who was punished by, among other things, being forced to wear a red-hot iron crown. Goldsmith confused the rebel leader, whose anglicized name was George, with his brother Luke. Robert-François Damiens attempted to assassinate Louis XV in 1757, and was chained to an iron bed during the tortures that preceded his execution.

p. 174. **A New Simile** (pr. June 1765)

Goldsmith was not directly imitating Swift, but a poem by Thomas Sheridan, *A New Simile for the Ladies*, 1732, which was answered by Swift and included in some editions of his work.

6. Andrew Tooke's *The Pantheon, Representing the Fabulous Histories of the Heathen Gods and Most Illustrious Heroes*, 1698, a popular school text, contains the engraving referred to here, but the page number is Goldsmith's invention.

64. Mercury's only 'existence' is as a stone statue.

p. 176. **Reply to an Invitation** (January 1767)

The last-minute invitation presumably asked for a verse reply: at the top of the poem as printed are the words 'This *is* a poem! This *is* a copy of verses!'—perhaps a quotation from the body of the letter, now lost, that contained the poem. The characters mentioned were all members of the circle of Sir Joshua Reynolds. Mrs Hannah Horneck (11) was the widowed mother of Mary, 'the Jessamy bride' (14), Catherine, 'little comedy' (17), and Charles, 'the Captain' (18), who enlisted a year later. Mrs Susannah Nesbitt (11) was the sister of Henry Thrale the brewer, Dr Johnson's friend. George Baker (12), the host, was Reynolds's physician. Angelica Kauffman (13) was the most famous woman painter of her day. The 'Reynoldses two' (16) were the painter and his sister Frances.

12. *bit*: mouthful. See *Glossary*.

14. *Jessamy*: probably 'fashionably dressed'. See *Glossary*. This, like 'little Comedy' (17), is a joke whose point has been lost: Mary Horneck did not marry for another ten years.

36. Reynolds, Baker, and many of their friends came from Devon.

44. A complimentary poem on the two painters, Reynolds and Angelica Kauffman, had appeared in the *Public Advertiser*, 20 January 1767.

p. 177. **On Edward Purdon** (March–April 1767)

Purdon had been at Trinity College, Dublin, with Goldsmith; he died on 27 March 1767, according to the *Gentleman's Magazine*. The point of the poem is that Goldsmith too was little more than a bookseller's hack.

p. 177. Epilogue: The Sister (February 1768)
Written for the comedy *A Sister*, by Mrs Charlotte Lennox, which had its sole performance on 18 February 1768.
16. *Patriots*: see *Glossary*. *party colour'd*: many-coloured. There is a pun on the political sense of 'party'.
17. Hebe, the handmaiden of the gods, is evoked because of her perpetual youth.

p. 179. The Deserted Village (1768–70)
Probably composed between 1768 and 1770, but Goldsmith claimed that he had spent four or five years before that collecting materials in visits to the country. Attempts have been made to locate the characters and setting of the poem in Goldsmith's own early life; but although a nostalgic impulse may have contributed to the poem, to suppose that the village is a specific place is to contradict the generalizing mood of the poem. Its events and scenery are intended, not to represent, but to be representative.
Dedication 11. *my brother*: see *The Traveller*, p. 160. Henry Goldsmith died in 1768.
Poem 1. The name is not fictitious: there are at least two real Auburns, one in Wiltshire and one in Lincolnshire.
227–36. This passage is closely based on Goldsmith's *Description of an Author's Bedchamber*, 9–20 (p. 139). For 'The twelve good rules, the royal game of goose', see the notes to that poem.
344. The Altama is a river in Georgia, N. America.
355. *tigers*: Goldsmith means cougars.
418. Torne is a river, town, and lake in Sweden; Pambamarca is a mountain in Ecuador.
419. *equinoctial fervours*: the heat at the Equator.
427–30. The last four lines of the poem were contributed by Dr Johnson.

p. 193. On Thomas Parnell (?June 1770)
Possibly Goldsmith wrote this while he was working on his *Life* of Parnell, which was published with Parnell's *Poems* in 1770. The poet had died in 1718; Goldsmith's epitaph is not on his tomb.

p. 193. The Haunch of Venison (Winter 1770–1)
Robert Nugent, Viscount Clare, was Vice-Treasurer for Ireland, a

minor poet, and a very rich man. He had offered Goldsmith his friendship as a result of reading *The Traveller*, and by 1771 Goldsmith was spending much of his time at Clare's different residences. Although the poem may have been based on an actual gift of venison, the dinner party section is based on Boileau's third *Satire*, which in turn imitates Horace, *Satires*, III. viii. This text has been taken from a manuscript in Goldsmith's own handwriting, and reproduces for the first time his light and informal punctuation of this poem.

18. Michael Byrne, Lord Clare's nephew; like Clare, he was Irish.

21. Sir Joshua Reynolds.

24. Dorothy Monroe, niece of the Earl of Ely, a famous beauty of the time.

27. All presumably obscure hack writers; only Paul Hiffernan, an Irishman, has been identified as such.

29. Possibly the Captain Higgins known only as a friend of Goldsmith's.

48. The usual time for dinner.

60. A current catch-phrase, originating in the sensational trial of the Duke of Cumberland for adultery with Lady Grosvenor. In one of his letters to her he describes a dream that she was with him on a couch: 'but alas when I woke I found it all dillusion no body by me but myself at Sea.' The Duke's illiteracy was the subject of much mockery in the newspapers.

72. Johnson was at that time spending most of his time in the family circle of Henry Thrale, the brewer, at Streatham.

77-8. Pen-names of anonymous writers to the newspapers—the last three were actually in use at the time.

95. *chocolate*: i.e. chocolate-coloured.

109-10. Quoting *II Henry IV* I. i. 70-3: 'Even such a man, so faint, so spiritless, / So dull, so dead in look, so woe-begone, / Drew Priam's curtains in the dead of night, / And would have told him half his Troy was burnt.'

p. 196. **Prologue: Zobeide** (?December 1771)
Joseph Cradock's tragedy, *Zobeide*, was first performed on 11 December 1771. The play was an adaptation of Voltaire's *Les Scythes* (see 11). The point of the prologue is a topical reference to the return of one of Captain Cook's scientific expeditions in July 1771. One of the aims of the expedition had been to observe the planet Venus (4).

20. *pidgeon holes*: seats in the upper gallery.

21-2. Referring to the habit of throwing fruit at the stage.

33-4. Cradock was a wealthy amateur: he gave the profits to Mrs Yates, the leading lady.

p. 197. From Animated Nature (1769–72)

Both these poems are used to illustrate points in Goldsmith's *Animated Nature*. The first is introduced by: 'there are numberless other animals that appear to ruminate . . . The salmon also is said to be of this number: and, if we may believe Ovid, the scarus likewise; of which he says . . .' The Latin, from Ovid's *Halieuticon*, 118–19, is given in a footnote. The second translation is introduced by: 'Addison, in some beautiful Latin lines, inserted in the Spectator [no. 412], is entirely of opinion that birds observe a strict chastity of manners, and never admit the caresses of a different tribe.'

p. 198. Threnodia Augustalis (February 1772)

Written to be performed at a concert in memory of Augusta, widow of Frederick, Prince of Wales, and mother of George III (d. 8 February 1772). It is pure hack-work, as Goldsmith admits in a note that prefaces the printed edition: 'the following may more properly be termed a Compilation than a Poem. It was prepared for the Composer in little more than two days'. The full title is 'Threnodia Augustalis Sacred to the Memory of Her late Royal Highness the Princess Dowager of Wales, Spoken and Sung in the Great Room at Soho-Square, on Thursday the 20th of February'.

126–8. The Princess was said to have given considerable sums of money in secret to private charities.

141ff. A description of the palace and gardens at Kew, which had been restyled according to the current fashion for the 'Chinese'.

222. Cf. *Traveller*, 411 (p. 172).

225. Edward III, victor of the Battle of Crécy in 1346.

p. 206. Song for She Stoops (by March 1773)

James Boswell sent a copy of this poem to the *London Magazine* (June 1774) together with a letter: 'I Send you a small production of the late Dr. *Goldsmith*, which has never been published, and which might perhaps have been totally lost had I not secured it. He intended it as a song in the character of Miss *Hardcastle*, in his admirable comedy, *She stoops to conquer*; but it was left out, as Mrs. *Bulkeley* who played the part did not sing.'

p. 206. First Epilogue: She Stoops (March 1773)

Goldsmith had some difficulty in providing an epilogue for *She Stoops to Conquer*, since the first proposal was that Miss Catley (originally cast to play Miss Neville) should deliver it; Mrs Bulkley (Kate Hardcastle)

objected, and Goldsmith attempted to use the quarrel by making it
the subject of this epilogue. Miss Catley objected to this, and Goldsmith
had to produce a second attempt, for Mrs Bulkley to recite (p. 209).
But Colman, the manager, thought this 'too bad to be spoken'. The
final version was written at the last moment, performed by Mrs
Bulkley, and printed with the play (p. 128). At some point in all this
Miss Catley walked out, and her place was taken by Mrs Kniveton.
59. Anna-Frederica Heinel, a currently successful dancer. See *She
Stoops to Conquer*, 128.30.
63. *Cheels*: now usually spelt 'chiels'. Scots dialect for 'children'.

p. 209. **Second Epilogue: She Stoops** (March 1773)
This is the epilogue, intended for Mrs Bulkley to recite alone, that
Colman thought 'too bad to be spoken'. See notes to the first rejected
epilogue.
1–6. Ariosto, in his poem *Orlando Furioso* (xxxiv. 68ff.) imagines that
all things lost on earth, including lost wits, are stored on the moon.
Pope made the conceit famous in the climax to *Rape of the Lock*
(v. 113–16).
9. In 1773 Samuel Foote was producing matinée puppet shows; other
theatres gave only evening performances.
19–22. Cf. the first epilogue, 47–50.
33–42. Goldsmith is attacking the trappings of sentimental comedy—
its titled characters, and their artificial gestures.
44–8. These lines were re-used for the epilogue finally chosen for the
play, lines 25–8. See *She Stoops to Conquer*, p. 128, and notes.
56. Possibly this line gave Goldsmith the idea for his title, chosen at
the last minute: *She Stoops to Conquer*.

p. 211. **Epilogue for Lee Lewes** (April–May 1773)
Written for Charles Lee Lewes, a pantomime actor who had played
Young Marlow in *She Stoops to Conquer*. A benefit was a performance
whose profits were the actor's perquisite. Here, the Harlequin addresses
his mask, symbol of the pantomime, and attempts to disown it, along
with his 'piebald' costume, and the acrobatics, over-use of stage
machinery, and fantastic plot associated with the Harlequinade.
19. Rosin was used to simulate fire or lightning.
22. *King Lear*, III. iv. 113: 'Off, off, you lendings! Come, unbutton
here.'
25. *Richard III*, V. iii. 177–8.
37. Referring to the cuckold's horns.

p. 212. **Letter to Mrs Bunbury** (December 1773)
This pleasant poem is part of a letter replying to an invitation from
Mrs Catherine Horneck Bunbury (see the 'Reply to an Invitation',
p. 176) to see the New Year of 1774 in at the house of her husband,
Henry Bunbury, a successful caricaturist. One of the attractions offered
by Mrs Bunbury was an evening of Loo, a popular card game resembling whist: 'you'll surely get fame / By winning our money away in a
trice, / As my sister [Mary Horneck] and I will give you advice.'
Goldsmith's mock anger at this offer, and his wry awareness of his
own disastrous addiction to gambling, are the basis of this poem. He
writes with a cheerful disregard for punctuation, which is preserved
here: since the poem was not intended for publication, it seems false
to the informality of the tone to regularize it.
6. Pam, the Jack of Clubs, trumps even the Ace of Trumps.
26. To be 'looed' is to win no tricks, and thus lose one's stake.
30. *fort*: either 'for it' or a slip for 'forth'.
36. Sir John Fielding, the famous Justice of Peace for Westminster.
40. Referring to a legal statute in the eighth (not the fifth—'quinto')
    year of Elizabeth's reign, prescribing a death sentence, without
    benefit of clergy (i.e. exemption from trial by a secular court), for
    petty theft.
44. To guard against gaol-fever, then prevalent.
45. *mobbs*: mob-caps.
55. Sir Charles Bunbury, the elder brother of Catherine's husband.

p. 214. **Retaliation** (begun by January 1774; unfinished)
Various slightly conflicting accounts exist of how this remarkable
poem came to be written. What seems to have happened is that at a
meeting of a club of wits to which Goldsmith belonged, early in 1774,
his fellow members amused themselves (rather tactlessly, since he was
then suffering from the illness which would soon kill him) by writing
mock epitaphs on Goldsmith. This eventually provoked him into a
Retaliation, dealing with each club member in turn. One of them was
Garrick, who had produced the famous couplet 'Here lies NOLLY
Goldsmith, for shortness call'd Noll, / Who wrote like an angel, but
talked like poor Poll' (*Works*, i (1854), 78). Goldsmith replies to this
in detail: the joke in the first line about his lack of height is neatly
answered (*Retaliation*, 94) by a reference to Garrick's own shortness;
and the nice tribute in 'wrote like an angel' is unkindly picked up in
line 120.
The poem, which was never finished, circulated in MS during Goldsmith's lifetime, and was published shortly after his death, presumably

from one of these MS copies. Explanatory notes were added to some
copies of the first edition, and in the third they were revised and set as
footnotes to the text. I have reproduced all of these that still seem of
use (in quotation marks, and from *ed. 1* unless it is stated otherwise),
but not the prefatory letter from the anonymous donor of the MS to
the printer.

1–2. Paul Scarron, the seventeenth-century French poet, gave brilliant
supper parties, to which each guest brought or ordered his own
favourite dish.

3. 'The master of the St. James's coffee-house, where the Doctor, and
the friends he has characterised in this Poem, held an occasional
club.'

5. 'Doctor Barnard, Dean of Derry in Ireland, author of many ingenious pieces' (*ed. 3*).

6. 'Mr. Edmund Burke, member for Wendover, and one of the greatest
orators in this kingdom' (*ed. 3*).

7. 'Mr. William Burke, late Secretary to General Conway, and Member
for Bedwin, Wiltshire.' Obscurely related to Edmund Burke.

8. 'Mr. Richard Burke, Collector of [Customs in] Grenada, no less
remarkable in the walks of wit and humour, than his brother Mr.
Edmund Burke is justly distinguished in all the branches of useful
and polite literature.'

9. 'Doctor Richard Cumberland, author of the West Indian, Fashionable Lover, the Brothers, and other dramatic pieces.'

10. 'Doctor Douglas, an ingenious Scotch gentleman, who has no
less distinguished himself as a *Citizen of the World*, than a *sound Critic*,
in detecting several literary mistakes (or rather *forgeries*) of his
countrymen; particularly Lauder on Milton, and *Bowyer's History of
the Popes*.' (See below, 89*n*.)

11. 'David Garrick, Esq; joint Patentee and acting Manager of the
Theatre-Royal, Drury-Lane. For the *other parts* of his character, *vide*
the Poem.'

14. 'Counsellor John Ridge, a gentleman belonging to the Irish bar,
the *relish* of whose agreeable and pointed conversation, is admitted
by all of his acquaintance, to be very properly compared to the above
sauce.'

'Sir Joshua Reynolds, President of the Royal Academy' (*ed. 3*).

15. Joseph Hickey, legal adviser to Burke and Reynolds.

34. 'Mr. T. Townshend Junior, Member for Whitchurch, Hampshire.'

42. *cut blocks with a razor*: use the wrong tool for the job—therefore,
to misapply one's talents.

61–72. Cumberland was a successful exponent of sentimental comedy:

these lines sum up, with succinct brilliance, Goldsmith's critique of the genre. The comparison with Terence (62) is pointed: the Latin dramatist was held to be a precursor of the sentimental mode.

86. William Dodd was a preacher, author, and notorious amorist and fraud, who was hanged for forgery in 1777. 'Mr. [William] Kenrick lately read lectures at the Devil Tavern, under the Title of "The School of Shakespeare"' (*ed. 3*). He had constantly and bitterly attacked Goldsmith in print.

87. James Macpherson, the 'translator' of the fictitious Ossian poems, had recently produced a much-criticized prose translation of Homer.

88. Townshend (see 34*n.*) had attacked the donation of a pension to Samuel Johnson in the House of Commons. Goldsmith also refers wryly to his own habit of 'compiling'—i.e. plagiarizing—in order to beat booksellers' deadlines.

89. Douglas had exposed these two Scots writers in error and deceit: William Lauder had accused Milton of deriving *Paradise Lost* from what Douglas proved to be a later Latin translation of Milton's poem; and Archibald Bowers had pretended to be a member of the Church of England while writing his *History of the Popes* (1748–66); Douglas proved him still to be a Catholic.

115. Hugh Kelly's sentimental comedy *False Delicacy* (1768) was produced (by Garrick) shortly before Goldsmith's *The Good-Natur'd Man*, and was much more successful. 'Mr. William Woodfall, Printer of the Morning Chronicle' (*ed. 3*) had been an actor and dramatic critic; he, Kelly, and Kenrick (see 86*n.*) had all at some time flattered Garrick.

118. Charles Churchill's *Rosciad* (1761) was a satire on the theatre.

124. Francis Beaumont and Ben Jonson.

135–6. 'The English reader is to be told, that the phrase "burn ye," ... tho' it may seem *forced* to rhyme to "attorney," is a familiar method of salutation in Ireland amongst the lower classes of the people.'

144–6. 'Sir Joshua Reynolds is so remarkably deaf as to be under the necessity of using an ear-trumpet in company; he is, at the same time, equally remarkable for taking a great quantity of snuff' (*ed. 3*).

TEXTUAL INTRODUCTION

This edition is based as far as possible on a fresh collation of substantive copies, and the copy-text is taken where appropriate from the copy nearest to Goldsmith's MS, and emended according to authorial revisions in later editions, if any.

There are, however, certain exceptions, appropriate to what we know or can deduce of Goldsmith's attitude to his work. Successive revisions of individual texts do two things, apart from adding authors' second thoughts: they correct errors of punctuation, or supply it where it is absent, and also make Goldsmith's punctuation heavier, stiffer and more regular. Both of these were most probably done without Goldsmith's direct authority. Since this is so, one's immediate impulse is to ignore them. But from the few autograph manuscripts that have survived, it is clear that Goldsmith's own punctuation was both extremely light and extremely careless: I have no doubt that, like a number of eighteenth-century writers, he left the punctuation to the printer, and relied on him to produce a 'correct' text. Thus if one reproduced faithfully the punctuation of the first edition, and ignored the printer's later emendations, one would be transmitting four different kinds of punctuation: Goldsmith's own light punctuation; Goldsmith's errors; the printer's heavier punctuation; and the printer's errors. The third of these is unavoidable, since for the most part it is all that we have; the first is desirable, since it fits the light conversational style of much of Goldsmith's work; but it is hard to believe that Goldsmith would have wished erroneous or misleading punctuation (erroneous, that is, by eighteenth-century standards) to emerge into printed form. Nor does it help the modern reader to preserve these errors. Therefore I have emended the punctuation in order, as far as possible, to remove these errors and give what Goldsmith intended, which is a correct eighteenth-century style of pointing; at the same time I have tried to maintain wherever possible what is left of the lightness of Goldsmith's own style. Some of these emendations are editorial, but most come from the printer's own revisions, since, clearly, this is the best guide to good eighteenth-century printer's practice.

Thus it is hoped that this text represents as nearly as possible, in spelling, punctuation, and in the words of the text, what Goldsmith finally intended as his published work. However, other purely formal aspects of the early editions, which were simply the product of individual printing houses and do not affect the text, have been normalized. These include the different founts and sizes of type used for different titles and texts, the occasional use of drop initial capitals in the poems, different styles of stage-direction, and so on. There is little point in reproducing an artificial collage of type-designs. Also quotations in the original copies of the poems which are usually indicated by double quotation marks before every line have been normalized according to modern practice, and long 's' altered to the modern form. Apart from this all emendations of words, spellings, and punctuation in the copy-text are recorded in the textual notes, except for such obvious errors as 'sentimenrs' for 'sentiments'. A brief textual note on each poem or play lists the copy-text and other substantive texts, if any, and identifies the copies used in each case.

NOTES

In the apparatus, the following abbreviations are used. (1) All unascribed quotations followed by a square bracket are editorial emendations; all others are from the copy-text. (2) The symbol $\sim$ signifies a repetition of the word already quoted; $\sim_\Lambda$ means that there is no punctuation attached to that word in the copy-text. (3) The symbols used for copies of each text are explained in the textual notes. Thus: 'lives,] 2: $\sim_\Lambda$' means that the copy-text reads 'lives' without the comma, and a comma has been introduced from the second edition. 'lives,] $\sim_\Lambda$' means that the comma is an editorial emendation. (4) Unless otherwise stated, each copy is that found in the Bodleian Library, Oxford.

TEXTUAL NOTES

p. 1. The Good-Natur'd Man

Text: The textual situation of this play is fairly simple. It was printed in 1768, and the first edition went through five impressions in that year (*1–5*). Each of these was carefully revised—usually, it is safe to assume, without consulting Goldsmith, and principally in matters of punctuation. This was done in two ways: by correcting obvious errors or confusions, and by making the punctuation stiffer and more formal. The copy-text here is the first impression of 1768; I have incorporated (and added to) the first kind of correction, but not the second; and I have adopted such substantive changes in successive impressions as appear to be authorial. (See *Textual Introduction*.)

The *Dramatis Personae* in the original text was printed after the Preface.

4.27. Crispin,] *3*: ∼∧
12.32. of?] *3*: ∼.
13.30. world!] *3*: ∼,
13.33–4. my father's] *4*: this
14.10. suspicion?] ∼.
14.28. her] ∼,
15.19. friend,] *3*: ∼∧
    Lofty] *3*: Le Bronze
19.1. dog—] *3*: ∼.
19.6. Madam!] ∼;
19.20. you] me
19.31. boy?] ∼.
21.19. honours] honour's
21.22. department!] *2*: ∼.
22.20. is eternally;] *2*: is; eternally
22.23–4. Congrave] Waller Congrave: Waller *3*
22.25. Congrave, Congrave] Waller, Waller
22.39. formidable] *4*: formal
23.13. in] *4*: a
26.25. life] ∼,
28.19. And, now] *2*: And now,

28.30. thoughts] *2*: thought
29.22. People may say] People, may say,
29.29. little] *2*: Little
    let] *2*: let little
30.13. (*Re-enter* FLANIGAN)] *2*: *om.*
32.5. spoke] *3*: speak
32.13. Justice!] *3*: ∼.
    elevens] *2*: eleven
32.15. dear] *2*: ∼,
32.23. question] ∼,
32.39. see?] *3* ∼.
33.16. house,] *2*: ∼;
33.28. becomes] *2*: become
34.22. he!] *3*: ∼.
34.27. me!] *2*: ∼.
35.4. uncle!] *2*: ∼;
35.6. Sir?] *2*: ∼∧
35.14. it?] ∼.
35.15. Madam—] *3*: ∼,
    further—] *3*: ∼;
35.22. head?] ∼.
35.28. men] *2*: *om.*

36.26. me?] ∼;
36.27. office?] *3*: ∼;
37.31. and] *2*: *om.*
37.34. will endeavour] *2*: he en-
deavours
37.35. fear] ∼,
38.11. me] *2*: *om.*
40.23. one; my] *3*: one. My
      persecution! What] *3*: per-
      secution, what
40.29. trusting] *2*: trusty
41.5. that] *3*: *om.*
42.2. Croaker—] *4*: ∼.
42.5. up] *2*: ∼.
      flame—] *2*: ∼.
42.32. by the way] *2*: in Scotland
43.16. *up.*] *3*: ∼:
44.26. Sir?] *2*: ∼∧
45.2. whom] *2*: that

45.22. loves] ∼.
      Madam] *2*: ∼.
45.26. out; tho'] *3*: out. Tho'
46.4. sentiments?] *2*: ∼.
46.24. me?] *2*: ∼.
50.9. was,] *3*: ∼∧
50.19. city has] city, has,
50.26. yet:] *3*: ∼!
51.38. got?] *3*: ∼.
51.40. hear] *3*: heard
52.12. *without,*] ∼∧
52.37. Confusion!] ∼.
56.16. friends] *3*: ∼?
56.19. years.] : ∼,
56.24. Honeywood?] ∼.
57.36, 58.15. ins] inns
61.19. What,] *3*: ∼∧
62.10. be each critick] *4*: view with
favour

p. 63. She Stoops to Conquer

Copies: MS copy made by a scribe and sent to the licenser for the stage,
shortly before the play's performance; now in the Larpent Collection at the
Huntington Library, California (*L*). The first edition of 1773 was reprinted
six times, each impression containing non-authorial revisions (*1–6*). I have
used the copy of the first impression now in the English Faculty Library,
Oxford.

Text: The printed edition differs in many details from *L*; these variants represent either authorial revisions or errors in one or the other versions. I have
used the printed edition as the basis for this text, since it contains Goldsmith's
final opinion as to his text, but have emended it against *L*. It was very carelessly printed, no doubt because of haste necessitated by the sudden and enormous popularity of the play. This shows itself in minor errors of sense, and
especially of punctuation. The first impression was particularly slip-shod:
it was apparently set in type in two printing houses, and thus exhibits two
different kinds of punctuation. This irregularity was largely normalized for
the second impression, and so I have adopted this as copy-text: there seems
to be little point in reproducing two different styles of punctuation because
of the possibility that one or the other of them might resemble Goldsmith's.
It seems best to preserve the kind of punctuation that Goldsmith would have
wished his printer to produce, had the printing been more careful. I have
therefore corrected the punctuation of *2*, usually with reference to *L*, or to
the corrections introduced in subsequent impressions, where the sense is
obscured or obviously in error—for instance, when question marks are
omitted after sentences that clearly require them. (See *Textual Introduction*.)

I have printed Garrick's prologue and Goldsmith's epilogue, but not the (rather perfunctory) epilogue contributed by Colman. Goldsmith's poem was printed among the prelims: I have put it at the end of the play. The *Dramatis Personae* in the original was printed after Garrick's prologue.

70.18. footmen's] *1*: footmens

71.25. hast] *L*: has

75.26. wench,] *L*: ~∧

76.19. these] *L*: those

77.38. what if] *L*: what—if

81.8. ones] *L*: inns

82.39. Charles] *L*: George

84.12. without] *L*: within

within] *L*: without

85.16. *Enter . . . Fare*] *L*: *om.*

87.34. my boy] *L*: boy

87.36. called] *L*: ~,

87.37. horses] *L*: ~,

88.13. ridiculous.] *L*: ridiculous. Yet, hang it! I'll take courage. Hem!

88.16–17. Yet . . . Hem!] *om.*

88.26. Yet] *L*: Yes

90.1. hypocrisy—] *L*: ~∧

92.10. Seriously?] ~.

93.14. or the] *L*: or

94.15. Anon?] ~.

94.27–8. *Set in roman type in 2*

98.12. Lady Kill-day-light] *3*: lady, Kill day light

104.13. open,] *L*: ~∧

104.13. me?] *L*: ~.

108.3. assure you] *L*, *4*: assure

109.22. *Coming*] coming

110.20. sorry] *L*: ~,

113.34. you] *L*: ~,

113.41. Goose-greens] *3*: Goose greens

114.3. gentleman?] *L*: ~.

114.26. explanations!] *L*: ~.

114.36. ridiculous?] ~.

114.39. Sir?] *L*: ~.

115.2. dispute?] ~.

115.6a. *om.*] *L*: *Enter* SERVANT.

116.24. friendship] *L*: friendships

117.24. HARDCASTLE] *L*: Miss HARDCASTLE

122.17. home?] ~.

122.19. wits?] ~.

123.25. those] *L*: these

125.26. not stir] *L*: not, Sir

125.35. Hastings?] ~.

126.3–4. HARDCASTLE. But . . . disposal] *L*: *in the printed editions, this speech is given to Mrs Hardcastle.*

126.8. MRS.] *L*: *om.*

p. 133. **Prologue of Laberius**
Text: *Enquiry into the Present State of Polite Learning*, 1759, pp. 176–7.

p. 133. **On a Beautiful Youth**
Text: *The Bee*, i, 6 October 1759.

p. 134. **The Gift**
Text: *The Bee*, ii, 13 October 1759.

p. 134. **A Sonnet**
Text: *The Bee*, iii, 20 October 1759.

p. 135. **Elegy on Mrs Blaize**
Text: *The Bee*, iv, 27 October 1759.

p. 136. **The Double Transformation**
Copies: *Weekly Magazine*, 5 January 1760 (*M*); revised for Goldsmith's *Essays*,
ed. 1, 1765, pp. 229–33 (*1*); further revised for ed. 2, 1766, pp. 241–5 (*2*).
Text: *M*, emended against *1* and *2*, except where Goldsmith has cut the poem.
These lines (7–12, 25–36, 47–52, 83–4) are better prᴉnted in the text rather
than lost in an appendix.

Title TRANSFORMATION] *1*:
  METAMORPHOSIS
2. Book-worm] *1*: Book wit
  led] *2*: liv'd
16. Our swain] *1*: Poor Jack
19. Flavia] *1*: Hetty
34. as well] well
38. frown'd, and blush'd] *1*: psha'd
  and frown'd
  was—] *1*: ∼ₐ
42. Or] *1*: And
43. Let it suffice,] *1*: Suffice to say
44. He] *1*: Jack

45. usage] *2*: visage
53. honey-moon] *1*: honey month
77. Fond . . . she] *2*: Now tawdry
  Madam *with para.*
85. While . . . were] *2*: Thus every
  hour was
87. Thus . . . day] *2*: Each day the
  more her faults
  were] *1*: are
97. Now] *2*: Thus
98. As] *2*: While
99. sullen] *1*: sulky

p. 139. **An Author's Bed-Chamber**
Copies: *Public Ledger*, 2 May 1760 (BM copy), reprinted in *The Citizen of the
World*, i (1762), 121; the texts are identical except for an indentation in the
Ledger (here omitted) before line 19.

p. 139. **On Seeing Mrs ****
Text: *Public Ledger*, 21 October 1760; reprinted without change in *The
Citizen of the World*, ii (1762), 87–8.
6. face.] ∼ₐ

p. 140. **On the Death of the Right Honourable ***
Copies: *Public Ledger*, 4 March 1761 (*P*); *Citizen of the World*, ii (1762), 164–5.
Text: *P*
17. throng] ∼;

p. 141. **South American Ode**
Copies: *Public Ledger*, 13 May 1761 (*L*); *Citizen of the World*, ii (1762), 209 (*C*).
Text: *L*; roman substituted for italic; the title from a footnote of uncertain
origin in *C*.

p. 141. **On the Death of a Mad Dog**
Text: *The Vicar of Wakefield*, ed. 1, i (1766), 175–6; emended to incorporate
the one revision in ed. 2 (1766):
19. some] *2*: his

p. 142. **Song from The Vicar**
Text: *The Vicar of Wakefield*, ed. 1, ii (1766), 78.

p. 142. A Ballad

Copies: *The Vicar of Wakefield*, 1766, pp. 70–7 (*1*); revised in the second edition, 1766 (*2*); alternative version in *Edwin and Angelina* [1765], revised in *Poems for Young Ladies*, 1767, pp. 91–8.

Text: *1*, incorporating authorial revisions from *2*, as follows:

11. faithless phantom] *2*: phantom only
30. All] *2*: For
31–2. *single quotation marks added from 1765 version*
35. modest] *2*: grateful
37. in a wilderness] *2*: shelter'd in a glade
38. lonely] *2*: modest
43. wicket] *2*: door just
45. busy] *2*: worldly
46. take their evening] *2*: revels or to
78. modern] *2*: haughty
84. His love-lorn] *2*: The bashful
85. Surpriz'd he sees new] *2*: He sees unnumber'd
86. Swift mantling] *2*: Expanding
87. colours o'er] *2*: clouds that deck
89. The bashful look, the rising] *2*: Her looks, her lips, her panting
109. hour a mercenary] *2*: morn the gay phantastic
115. Wisdom and worth were]: A constant heart was
116a–d. *Percy, in his edition of Goldsmith's* Works, *ii (1801), 25, printed at this point the following stanza, which he claimed had been presented to one Richard Archdal by Goldsmith himself*: 'And when, beside me in the dale, / He carol'd lays of love, / His breath lent fragrance to the gale, / And music to the grove.'
116. these were] *2*: that was
141. Forbid it heaven!] *2*: Thou shalt not thus,
152. My life] *2*: O thou

p. 147. The Captivity

Copies: two autograph MSS, containing two distinct versions, each prepared for a publisher but neither of them printed during Goldsmith's lifetime. One was given to Dodsley (*D*), and is now in the Free Library of Philadelphia; the other was for Newbery, and is now in the Pierpont Morgan Library, New York. Friedman (iv, 209–12) plausibly suggests that each represents an independent revision of an earlier MS.

Text: *D*, though neither version is definitely superior. The MSS are punctuated sparsely and irregularly. Since the poem was intended for publication I have punctuated it, as Goldsmith would have expected his printer to do. The musical directions are italicized and placed consistently after the name of the singer—in the MS they sometimes precede and sometimes follow the name.

p. 160. The Traveller

Copies: first edition (*1*), printed in December 1764, in four states: the text is

invariant, but the prelims are expanded in the second state from one sentence
to six paragraphs; the third and fourth states vary only in the half-title. I have
used the BM copy of the fourth state. Second edition, 1765, revised (*2*); 'the
sixth edition' (actually the fifth) containing Goldsmith's final revisions (*6*).
There also exists an early version of the poem, entitled *A Prospect of Society*,
in the form of four proof-sheets; the first 72 lines are missing, or were never
printed, and a further 24 were apparently added in revision. This copy is
distinctive in that it was printed backwards, in sections of (on average) 36
lines, beginning with 351–92, and ending with 73–90. It was repunctuated
to make it sound (somewhat) like sense. Furthermore, the last four pages
were printed without spacing-material between the lines. I believe the
explanation for all this is that, as Quiller-Couch proposed in 1902, when
'Goldsmith finished writing out each page of his poem for press he laid it
aside, on top of the page preceding', and forgot to re-order them.[1] The
discrepancy in the number of lines per page of MS that this presupposes
(the nine sections, which I take to correspond in length with pages of copy,
include two of 42 and one of 28 lines [2]) can easily be accounted for by authorial deletions and insertions in the MS: this poem was heavily revised on at
least two other occasions, with just such deletions and additions. The un-
leaded lines on the last sheet can most simply be explained by assuming that
the printing shop ran out of spacing material (a not uncommon phenomenon),
and so proof-sheets were pulled from type temporarily imposed without
spaces, in order that proof-correction could go on without waiting for fresh
supplies. At this point perhaps a new MS bearing the revised version arrived
from the author, the *débâcle* was discovered, and the whole thing rearranged,
repunctuated, and revised. There is no reason to believe that Goldsmith read
proof on the early version, or, if my hypothesis is correct, that it is any more
tean a printer's botch that did not progress beyond the proof stage—luckily
for Goldsmith's reputation. There is therefore no reason to use it (as Friedman has done) as copy-text, particularly if *1* was set from a fresh MS, as I
propose.[3]

Text: *1*, emended according to Goldsmith's revisions in *2* and *6*.

Preface 20–2. what from . . . of party,] *6*: as things are now circumstanced,
    perhaps

22. wildest.] *6*: wildest. What from the encreased refinement of the times,
    from the diversity of judgments produced by opposing systems of criti-
    cism, and from the more prevalent divisions of opinion influenced by party,
    the strongest and happiest efforts can expect to please but in a very narrow
    circle. Though the poet were as sure of his aim as the imperial archer of
    antiquity, who boasted that he never missed the heart; yet would many

[1] *Daily News*, 31 March 1902.

[2] The last section, 18 lines long, is clearly incomplete, since the compositor finished
the sheet before finishing the section.

[3] Friedman's view of *A Prospect of Society* is based on another and most ingenious
hypothesis concerning its origin, offered by W. B. Todd in *Studies in Bibliography* vii
(1955), 103–11. This theory was (to my mind) refuted by L. W. Hanson (*Library*, 5th
Ser. x (1955), 297–8; Todd's reply can be seen in *Library* xi (1956), 123–4.

of his shafts now fly at random, for the heart is too often in the wrong
place.

25. As these] *6*: And as they
27. that . . . her] *6*: favour to themselves
35. say; . . . talkative.] *6*: say.
37–8. When the mind is] *6*: A mind capable of relishing general beauty, when
38. it] *6*: *om.*
45. tawdry] *6*: *om.*
49. solicitous] *6*: much solicitous
52. states, that are] *6*: other states, though
53. every] *6*: each   particular] *6*: peculiar
54. each] *6*: each state, and in our own in particular,
57. dear] *6*: *om.*
Poem
6. expanding] *2*: expanded   skies:]*6*: ∼.
17. with . . . crown'd] *6*: where mirth and peace abound
25. Impell'd, . . . unceasing,] *2*: Impell'd with steps, unceasing
35. extending] *6*: extended
38–40. should . . . vain?] *2*: 'twere thankless to repine. / 'Twere affectation
all, and school-taught pride, / To spurn the splendid things by heaven
supply'd.
58. hoard] *6*: sum
63. But] *6*: Yet,
66. proclaims . . . spot] *2*: asserts that country for
68. his long] *2*: live-long
73. Such is] *6*: Nor less
75–6. countries . . . share;] *2*: states with states we scan, / Or estimate their
bliss on Reason's plan,
77–9. still . . . different] *2*: and though fools contend, / We still shall find uncertainty suspend, / Find that each
80. different . . . even.] *2*: these or those, but makes the balance even:
80a–b. *om.*] *2*: Find that the bliss of all is much the same, / And patrioric
boasting reason's shame.
83–4. With . . . side] *2*: *om.*
84. cliffs] *6*: cliff *2*
85. the . . . summits] *2*: rough rocks or gloomy summits
88. commerce] *6*: splendours
91–2. where . . . fails] *6*: *om.*
99. try] *2*: view
107. Its] *6*: Her
124. the] *6*: this
126. Man seems] *6*: Men seem
127. his] *6*: their
132. departed] *6*: ∼,
139. Till] *6*: But
140. Commerce . . . display'd] *6*: Soon Commerce turn'd on other shores

141–2. While . . . slave:] 2: *om.*

142. slave:] 6: ~. 2

144. Its] 6: Their   but] 6: now

145–6. still . . . splendid] 2: though to fortune lost, here still abide / Some splendid arts, the

147. these] 2: which

154a–b. *om.*] 6: At sports like these, while foreign arms advance, / In passive ease they leave the world to chance.

155. Each . . . represt] 6: When struggling Virtue sinks *with para.*

156. Now sinks] 6: She leaves

161. There in] 6: Amidst

173. sues] 6: sooths

196. her] 6: the

200. heart,] 2: ~ᴧ

201–2. 2: *om. 1*

205. child] 6: babe

209. Such] 6: These

210. but] 6: are

213. For] 6: Since

215. Whence] 6: Hence

222. Unquench'd . . . unfann'd] 6: Nor quench'd . . . nor fan'd

232. heart.] 6: ~,

236. the] 6: our

240. I] 6: We

263. courts,] 6: ~ᴧ

286. pride.] 6: ~,

287–90. Onward . . . shore.] 2: *order of these couplets reversed in 1*

288. grow] 6: go

289. Spreads its long] 2: That spreads its

291. the pent ocean] 2: ocean pent, and

292. smile;] 2: ~.

299. bosom reign] 2: breast obtain

312. slumber in] 6: sleep beneath

318. courts] 6: broods

320. glide.] 2: ~,

327–8. Pride . . . by] 2: *order reversed in 1*

328. by,] 2: ~ᴧ

331. their] 2: a

332. right,] 2: ~ᴧ

341–2. 2: *om. in 1*

343. Here . . . feebly] 2: See, though by circling deeps together

347. Till] 6: Whilst

348. fire] 6: fires

349. nature's ties] 6: social bonds

356. The . . . the] 6: That . . . that

358. Where . . . wrote] 6: And monarchs toil, and poets pant

361. not, thus] *2*: not thus,
363–80. Ye . . . warms] *2*: Perish the wish; for, inly satisfy'd, / Above their pomps I hold my ragged pride
368. proud] *6*: cold
375. Hence] *6*: Much on the low, the rest, as rank supplies, / Should in columnar diminution rise; / While *2*
416. marks with murderous] *6*: takes a deadly
421. long] *6*: fond

p. 174. **A New Simile**
Copies: Essays, ed. 1, 1765, pp. 234–6 (*1*); ed. 2, 1766, pp. 246–8 (*2*).
Text: *1*, emended according to revisions in *2*.
1. Long . . . vain] *2*: I long had rack'd my brains
50. too,] to
59. all modern] *2*: our scribling

p. 176. **Reply to An Invitation**
Text: From a letter, now lost; the poem was printed by Prior in Goldsmith's *Works*, iv (1837), 132–3. Lonsdale points out that the printed title—'at Sir George Baker's'—is inaccurate, since Baker had not yet been knighted. I have followed his emendation.

p. 177. **On Edward Purdon**
Copies: Weekly Magazine, xxi (12 August 1773), 224; Works, 1777, p. 79.
Text: *Works*, with the last line emended in accordance with the *Magazine* text (*M*) since that reading has the partial support of an anecdote quoted in Forster's *Life* of Goldsmith [1848], p. 423, which quotes it as 'I think he will never come back'.
4. ever] *M*: wish to

p. 177. **Epilogue: The Sister**
Text: Charlotte Lennox, *The Sister*, 1769.
4. masquerade,] ∼.
12. *Gallery*] *Gall.*
29. parade,] ∼.

p. 179. **The Deserted Village**
Copies: First (*1*), second (*2*), and fourth (*4*) editions, all published in 1770.
Text: *1*, emended against *2* and *4*. I have used the BM copies of *1* and *2*.
67. oppulence] *2*: luxury
80a–b. *om*] *4*: Here, as with doubtful, pensive steps I range, / Trace every scene, and wonder at the change,
87. To . . . at] *4*: My anxious day to husband near
88. the] *4*: life's
99. happy] *2*: blest is
106. the] *2*: his
109. Bends] *2*: Sinks

123. sweet] *4*: soft
128. For] *4*: But
145. Unpractised] *4*: Unskilful
148. skilled] *4*: bent
182. steady] *2*: ready
189. form,] *2*: ～ₐ
266. joy's] joys
304. pride?] *2*: ～;
313. those joys] *2*: each joy
325. thoughts?] *4*: ～ₐ
343. Through] *4*: To
378. for a] *4*: for her
384. silent] *4*: decent
401. move,] *4*: ～ₐ
412. crowds,] *2*: ～ₐ

p. 193. **On Thomas Parnell**
Text: *The Haunch of Venison*, 1776, p. 9.

p. 193. **The Haunch of Venison**
Copies: First published in 1776; a revised edition (*2*), taken from a second MS, was published in the same year. This MS, in Goldsmith's hand, is now in the Berg Collection, New York Public Library.
Text: From the MS, thanks to the kindness of the Curators of the Berg Collection. Since the poem was not intended for publication, I have kept the informal spelling and punctuation of the MS, only emending it when the sense is obscured. Title from *2*; the MS has no title.
31. it,] ～,
73. I'll] Ill
120. relish,] ～ₐ
121. temper,] ～ₐ

p. 196. **Prologue: Zobeide**
Copies: Joseph Cradock's *Zobeide* (1771) (*Z*); autograph MS in Newberry Library (*MS*).
Text: *Z*. Since Goldsmith intended this poem for publication, the punctuation and spelling of the published version have been adopted; but the MS has been followed in substantives, since the published alterations are probably not Goldsmith's.
5. When] *MS*: While
7. While] *MS*: When
18. *to the*] *MS*: *om.*
19. *to the*] *MS*: *om.*
20. monkies] *MS*: turtles
   to the pidgeon holes] *MS*: *Balconies*
21. *to the*] *MS*: *om.*
22. *taking . . . tasting*] *MS*: *takes up one and tastes it*

25. savage] *MS*: dreadful
28. *makes*] *MS*: *making*
33–4. To make . . . favour] *MS* (*punctuation added*): *om.*

p. 197. From Animated Nature
Text: from Goldsmith's *Animated Nature*, 1774, iii, 6, and v, 312.

p. 198. Threnodia Augustalis
Text: *Threnodia Augustalis*, 1772 (Harvard copy).
185. decent] decent decent

p. 206. Song for She Stoops
Text: from Goldsmith's autograph, preserved in the Boswell Papers at Yale
and reproduced in facsimile in *Boswell for the Defence*, ed. William K. Wimsatt
and Frederick A. Pottle, 1960, facing p. 218. The MS has no punctuation; I
have therefore punctuated it lightly.

p. 206. First Epilogue: She Stoops
Copies: *Works*, ii (1801), 82–6, probably printed from a holograph; BM Add.
MS 42515, ff. 81–2, which contains some probably non-authoritative variants.
Text: *Works*, with punctuation editorially emended as follows:
The stage directions (*other than the first and last*) *are not italicized in the copy-text.*
12. Epilogue,] ~$_\wedge$
22. etiquette.] ~,
41. smiling,] ~$_\wedge$
55. friseurs] ~,   nosegays] ~,
65. *A . . . Jockey*] *printed in lower case roman as part of preceding speech.*
79. Doctors, who] Doctors. Who
80. *Quotation marks added.*

p. 209. Second Epilogue: She Stoops
Copies: BM Add. MS 42515, ff. 83–4. This is probably the MS in the handwriting of Mrs Bulkley that Goldsmith gave to Percy. A copy of this, heavily
corrected by Percy, was used for the text in Goldsmith's *Works*, 1801, pp.
87–8.
Text: MS. Since the punctuation is neither Goldsmith's, nor very clear, I
have emended it as follows:
9–10. *these lines crossed out in MS.*
9. night, for, but . . . alone,] night For but . . . alone
11. Both,] ~$_\wedge$
29–42. *crossed out in MS.*
36. familiar, . . . us.] familiar . . . us
46. room,] ~$_\wedge$
52. lace?] ~;
54. Quarter?] ~.

p. 211. Epilogue for Lee Lewes

Copies: *London Chronicle*, 28–30 April 1774, p. 416 (*C*); *Universal Magazine*, liv (May 1774), 261; *Works*, i (1780), 112–14 (*W*).

Text: *C*, which was carelessly printed but probably textually superior to the others. I have corrected some obvious faults against the (probably unauthoritative) revisions in *W*.

Title: from W
20. I will] *W*: I'il
35. yes, yes] *W*: yes
37. My . . . are] *W*: And, my horns! I'm told that horns are all
42. beaten] *W*: beating
48. *not italicized in copy-text.*

p. 212. Letter to Mrs Bunbury

Text: from a holograph letter, now in the Pierpont Morgan Library.

p. 214. Retaliation

Copies: there are several witnesses to the text, all published in 1774: first edition (*1*); errata-list accompanying some copies of *1* (*1E*); second edition (*2*)—in fact an emended second impression of *1*; errata-list accompanying *2* (*2E*); third edition (*3*).

Text: since all of these witnesses are posthumous, and probably derive their texts from non-authorial MSS, none are particularly authoritative. The text here is taken from *1*, emended when the corrections in successive witnesses appear to make better sense. I have used the BM copy of *2* and *2E*.

9. bread] *3*: ∼,
37. unfit] *1E*: he's fit
41. place] *1E*: play
69. lost] *2E*: left
73. where] *1E*: when
83. When] *3*: Where
89. Lauders] *1E*: Landers
99. judging] *2E*: judge in
118. beroscius'd] *2E*: berossia'd
123. Shakespeare] ∼,   him] ∼,
125. *no para. in ed. 1*   reclines,] *3*: ∼ₐ
135. his] *1E*: *om.*

GLOSSARY

Note on the Glossary: I have supplied here, wherever appropriate, the definition from Johnson's *Dictionary* of 1755. I have also given after each gloss the date of the first use of the word in the sense given as recorded in the *Oxford English Dictionary*. It will be at once clear that Goldsmith uses a number of words for the first time, or soon after their first use in print — not because he was a word-coiner, but because his language is lively and colloquial, and many of his colloquialisms had not yet found their way into books. It is also interesting, in this connection, to note how scathing Johnson is about the words in this glossary: the description 'low' appears quite often in his definitions.

AMES ACE: 'A double ace; so called when two dice turn up the ace'. *The lowest possible throw* (1297).

ANGLE: fishing rod. *Archaic.* (880).

ANON: what did you say? (1553).

ANOTHERGUESS: 'this word . . . though rarely used in writing, is somewhat frequent in colloquial language. . . . Of a different kind' (1625).

ARTIST: artisan (1633).

ATTORNEY, SPECIAL: legal representative in a specified cause. Attorney *also carried the pejorative sense of* unscrupulous rogue (1330).

BANDBOX: container of showy trivia; hence, showy, trivial (1773: *first usage*).

BASKET: (1) single-stick with protective basket hilt (1773: *first usage*); (2) the outside back seat of a stage coach (1773: *first usage*).

BIT: 'as much meat as is put into the mouth at once' (1200).

BLOCK: (1) 'a heavy piece of timber' (1305); (2) a wooden head, used as a wig-stand (1688). *Both also carry a further sense:* blockhead.

BOB: 'a pendant; an ear-ring' (1648).

BOBBIN: spindle carrying thread, allowed to dangle and dance about during lace-making (1530).

BOUNCE: 'a boast . . . in low language' (1714).

BRONZE: impudence, unblushingness (1728).

BRUSH: 'to move with haste: a ludicrous word, applied to men' (1690).

CARO: dear (*Italian*), *thence* excellent, superb.

CASE, SET IN: suppose (1400).

CHOP-HOUSE: 'a mean house of entertainment, where provision ready dressed is sold' (1690).

CIPHER: 'to practise arithmetick' (1633).

CIRCUMBENDIBUS: roundabout process (1681).

CIT: 'a pert low townsman' (1644).

CLEVER: 'a low word, scarcely ever used but in burlesque or conversation; and applied to any thing a man likes, without a settled meaning' (1738).

CLOSET: 'a small room of privacy and retirement' (1730).

CONCATENATION: 'an uninterrupted unvariable succession'—*here, meaningless* (1622).

CONTIGUOUS: 'a meeting so as to touch' (1611).

COUNTRY: 'a region', district, locality (1275).

CRACK: 'a boast', exaggeration, lie (1450).

CUP: wine sweetened and flavoured (1773: *first usage*).

CURIOUS: taking a connoisseur's interest in (1577).

CURTAIN-LECTURE: 'a reproof given by a wife to her husband in bed' (1633).

DANGLE: *Johnson defines* dangler *as* 'a man that hangs about women only to waste time'. *Goldsmith's usage may have the connotation of sexual impotence.*

DEPARTMENT: 'business assigned to a particular person' (1735).

DIRECTION: address of a letter (1524).

DIZEN: 'to dress; to deck; to rig out. A low word.' Usually contemptuous (1619).

DOME: 'a building; a house'. *Poetic.* (1513).

ELEVENS, BY THE: heavens? Apostles (minus Judas)? *No-one knows. Only found in Goldsmith.*

FATHER-IN-LAW: step-father (1522).

FEEDER: trainer of fighting-cocks (1773: *first usage*).

FLAT: 'insipid' (1573).

FLOUNCE: a quick movement expressing disdain (1751).

FONDLING: 'something regarded with great affection' (1640).

FRIEZE: (1) mantelpiece (*Lonsdale*); (2) 'a coarse warm cloth' (1418).

FRISEUR: hairdresser (1750).

FROWARD: 'peevish; ungovernable' (1300).

GAUGE: 'to measure with respect to the contents of a vessel' (1483).

GELID: refreshingly cold (1659).

GESTIC: pertaining to bodily movement, especially dancing (1764: *first usage*).

GLOOM: (1) *intransitive:* to have a dark or sombre appearance (1770: *first usage*); (2) *transitive:* to make melancholy (1745).

GOTHIC: barbarous, unpolished (1695).

GREEN-ROOM: room used by actors when not on stage (1701).

GROOM-PORTER: officer of the Royal Household (1502).

GRUMBLETONIAN: grumbler (1773: *first usage*).

HACK: to make common, vulgar, stale (1745).

HASPICHOLLS: harpsichord; *a Lumpkinism*.

HOIKES: tally-ho (1607).

INDURATE: 'to make hard' (1594).

INVEST: 'to enclose', besiege (1600).

IZZARD: *the letter* Z (1738).

JESSAMY: foppish (1756).

JOCKEY: 'a cheat; a trickish fellow' (1683).

JORUM: bowl of punch (1730).

KNOWING: cunning (1503).

KNOWING ONE: one well up in sporting matters (1749).

LISTING: a border made of a strip of cloth (1766: *first usage*).

MACCARONI: fop, dandy (1764).

MANNERS: 'general way of life; morals; habits' (1589).

MANTLE: 'to froth . . . ferment' (1626).

MASQUED BATTERY: concealed set of guns: ambush (1759).

MASQUERADE: a masked ball (1597).

MEAUVAISE HONTE: painful self-consciousness (1721).

MEMORIAL: diplomatic instructions usually sent to ambassadors (1536).

MERCER: 'one who sells silks' (1123).

MIFF: petty quarrel (1623).

MISTRUSTLESS: 'unsuspecting' (1586).

MOHAWK: 'the name of a cruel nation in America given to ruffians who infested, or rather were imagined to infest, the streets of London' (1711).

MORRICE: get out! (1765).

MUMP: 'to talk low and quick' (1586).

NICK: make a winning throw at dice (1598).

OBSTROPALOUS: obstreperous (1773: *only usage*).

OUTRAGEOUS: 'tumultous; turbulent' (1375).

PALAVER: a parley with natives (1735).

PASSING: exceedingly. *Poetic.* (1387).

PATRIOT: 'sometimes used for a factious disturber of the government', *i.e. ironically* (1644).

PHIZ: 'the face, in a sense of contempt' (1688).

PLACE: 'employment' (1588).

PLASHY: marshy, swampy (1552).

PLETHORIC: swollen 'from debauch or feeding higher or more in quantity than the ordinary powers of the viscera can digest' (1644).

POUND: an enclosure for stray animals (1425).

PRANCE: *presumably* move out! (1773: *only usage*).

PROTEST: refuse to cash, said of bills (1655).

PUFF: advertise, publicize, *usually excessively* (1735).

RABBET: *like* drat, *a meaningless oath* (1742).

RALLY: make fun of (1691).

RAMPIRE: rampart. *Archaic.* (1548).

RATTLE: a lively, empty chatterer (1744).

REGULAR: qualified; approved by the College of Physicians (1755).

RELISH: 'sense; power of perceiving excellence; taste' (1607).

RENT-ROLL: income from rents (1534).

ROPES, ALL UPON THE HIGH: on his high horse (1700).

ROUTE/ROUT: a large fashionable evening party (1742).

SAVAGE: wild beast (1682).

SCOUT: reject with scorn, dismiss (1710).

SENTIMENT: sentimental epigrammatic phrase (1773: *only usage*).

SHAVE: fleece (1399).

SHED: a hut, cottage, poor dwelling. *Poetic.* (1600).

SHELVY: 'shallow; rocky; full of banks' (1598).

SHY-COCK: a fighting-cock that refuses to fight; *thence* one who evades the bailiffs by staying indoors (1768: *first usage*).

SMOKE: observe, look at (1715).

SOLICITOR: one who negotiates on behalf of another (1741).

SPADILLE: 'the ace of spades at ombre', a card game (1728).

SPARK: 'a lively, showy, splendid, gay man. It is commonly used in contempt' (1600).

SPUNGING-HOUSE: 'a house to which debtors are taken before commitment to prison' (1700).

SUE: woo, court. *Poetic.* (1596).

SWINGING/SWINGEING: 'great, huge. A low word' (1590).

TABLETS: notebook (1611).

TALLY: 'to be fitted; to conform' (1705).

TASTE: 'to relish intellectually; to approve' (1605).

TEMPT: 'to try; to attempt', to venture. *Poetic.* (1667).

TERM: day of the year fixed for payment of wages, rents, etc. (1426).

TÊTE: a tall elaborate hair-piece (1756).

THRENODIA: (*Latin*) a lament for the dead.

THUMPER: anything strikingly big of its kind. *Colloquial.* (1660).

TIDE: saint's day, holiday (900).

TILLAGE: ploughed land, as distinct from grazing land (1543).

TORPID: motionless . . . not active', inert (1613).

TRAFFIC: social life, business (1548).

TRAIN: 'a retinue; a number of followers or attendants'. *Poetic.* (1440).

TROLL: 'to fish for a pike with a rod which has a pulley towards the bottom' (1606).

UNDERSTRAPPER: 'an inferior agent', underling (1704).

VACANT: 'being at leisure; disengaged' (1617).

VARMENT: vermin; *here*, objectionable person (1773: *first usage*).

VENTRE D'OR: gold-fronted.

WAUNS: wounds, *short for* God's wounds (1694).

VIRTÙ, PIECE OF: a curio, antique, collector's item (1770: *first usage*).

VIZOR: a mask or disguise (1532).

WHIP: suddenly, instantly (1460).

WINNOW: 'to fan; to beat as with wings'. *Poetic.* (1764: *first usage*).

WITNESS, WITH A: 'effectually; to a great degree . . . A low phrase' (1575).

WORK: 'to embroider with a needle' (1250).

GOLDSMITH AND HIS CRITICS

This section offers a selection of the best early criticism of Goldsmith, revealing the rich context of debate in which he wrote, and more than that, something of the mentality of late-eighteenth-century literary culture. The section is heavily weighted towards the work of Goldsmith's contemporaries and near contemporaries: not only is there more of this material, and therefore more to choose from, but it is also simply better, and more interesting, than what came after it. After Romanticism became commonplace the periodical essays became less specific and less sharp, and a different reading of Goldsmith, stressing the naive, the childish, the beautiful, and in fact the sentimental aspects of his work arose. This reading now seems one-sided and rather vapid: their Goldsmith could not, one feels, have written *She Stoops to Conquer*.

Goldsmith's contemporaries were, like Goldsmith, like Samuel Johnson, literary journalists: they shared his values, and if they disagreed with him, even violently, they inhabited a terrain that each of them knew in detail. The critics' essays had two functions. Firstly, they served somewhat as a trailer does for a film: they quote long representative passages from the poems they discuss, or give close paraphrases of the action of the plays, in order to appetise (or disgust) the potential reader or play-goer. But in addition to this they give very detailed and very critical analyses of the texts themselves. As an indication of the detailed attention with which Goldsmith must have expected to be read, and with which therefore he must himself have written, this is fascinating: a unique insight into the immediate context of his work — the professional journalism of literary London.

The texts quoted are given in date order of the work discussed; within that, they are given in chronological order.

The Traveller

John Langhorne, 1735-79, was a clergyman, poet, and translator. His translation of Bion was warmly reviewed by Goldsmith in 1759. He was a regular reviewer for the *Monthly Review*, and wrote this early review of *The Traveller* for the issue of January 1765 (47-55). His quotations are all from the first edition of the poem.

The *Traveller* is one of those delightful poems that allure by the beauty of their scenery, a refined elegance of sentiment, and a correspondent happiness of expression. Thus the Author addresses his brother, to whom the poem is inscribed:

> Wherever I roam, whatever realms I see,
> My heart untravelled fondly turns to thee;
> Still to my brother turns, with ceaseless pain,
> And drags at each remove, a lengthening chain.

[7-10]

It is impossible not to be pleased with the 'untravelled heart,' and the happy image of 'lengthening chain;' nevertheless, it may be somewhat difficult to conceive how a heart *untravelled*, can, at the same time, make farther removes.

The following simile is equally just and magnificent; and is one of those real beauties in imagery, which have the power of pleasing universally, by being at once obvious to the mind, and, at the same time, possessing native dignity enough, to secure them from that indifference with which things frequently contemplated are beheld.

> Impelled with steps unceasing to pursue
> Some fleeting good that mocks me with the view,
> That, like the circle bounding earth and skies,
> Allures from far, yet, as I follow, flies.

[25-8]

The Traveller *sits him down* (as he sometimes inelegantly expresses it) on an eminence of the Alps, and from thence takes a view of the several kingdoms that lie around him; not with the contracted eye of a Monastic, but with the liberal spirit of a man, who rightly considers, and embraces, the general blessings of Providence:

[Quotes *The Traveller*, lines 37-50]

He then enquires whether superior happiness be the lot of any particular country; but concludes that, though every man thinks most favourably of his own, Nature has, in general, observed an equality in the distribution of her bounties:

[Quotes *The Traveller*, lines 63-80]

Yet though this patriotic Boasting may not have its foundation in truth, it is amongst those pleasing errors that contribute to our happiness; and he who should labour to undeceive us in this instance, would be employed in the *triste Ministerium* [sad duty] of making us miserable. We ought, indeed, never so far to cherish an attachment to our native country, as to shut out the inhabitants of different nations from our benevolence or good opinion, but while our innocent enthusiasm only indulges a preference of suns and soils, it will always be our prudence to retain it.

> Nature, a mother kind alike to all,
> Still grants her bliss at Labour's earnest call;
> And though rough rocks, or gloomy summits frown,
> These rocks, by custom, turn to beds of down.
>
> [81-2, 85-6]

Nothing is more true; but is not the Author's proposition controvertible, in which he maintains, that there is in every state a peculiar principle of happiness?

> Hence every state to one lov'd blessing prone,
> Conforms and models life to that alone.
> Each to the favourite happiness attends,
> And spurns the plan that aims at other ends;
> 'Till, carried to excess in each domain,
> This favourite good begets peculiar pain.
>
> [93-98]

It is certain that every individual has a peculiar principle of happiness; but does it therefore follow, that a state composed of these individuals should have the same? rather the contrary, where there must necessarily be so many different opinions concerning the very existence of happiness. It is, in truth, with states as with private men; they appear to be actuated rather by casual circumstances, than to pursue the general good upon any established principle. We find that what is the object of public

attention in one reign, is totally changed in another; and that as
interest, power, and caprice prevail, political sagacity is for ever
varying its principles and practice. The character of a people is
not always the same: as they vary, their ideas of happiness are
varied too, and that in so great a degree, that they can scarcely
be said to have any fixed or determined principle. But though
our Author makes no great figure in political Philosophy, he
does not fail to entertain us with his poetical descriptions:

[Quotes *The Traveller*, lines 105-164]

The description of the people of Italy is not less just than that
of their country is picturesque and harmonious: but has not the
Author, towards the conclusion, laid open a redoubt which the
Moralist ought never to give up, when he represents the Italians
as a happier people when fallen from their virue?

> When struggling virtue sinks by long controul,
> She leaves at last, or feebly mans the soul;
> While low delights succeeding fast behind,
> In happier meanness occupy the mind.
>
> [155-8]

How very unfavourable to the interests of Virtue to conclude,
that low delights have power, even in their meanness, to make
us happier; for if happiness be the end and aim of our Being,
who would not seek it through those paths by which it
appeared most accessible? The truth, however, is, that
Happiness, like everything else, is to be estimated according to
its quality. The Author has declared, that sensual bliss is all
that the Italians know; but will he consequently maintain, that
those low delights, this meanness of enjoyment, could make the
Italians happier that the conscious pleasures of that virtue
which they had lost, and the higher and more rational
satisfactions of the mind?—We are sorry to find such an
argument deducible from his poem. The instance he adduces of
a peasant's finding himself happy in a cottage formed out of the
ruins of an imperial palace affords no proof in this case; for it
doth not appear, that the peasant had fallen from his virtue:
moreover, there is not the least similitude in the circumstances.

Let us now accompany the Traveller in his prospect of a very
different people:

[Quotes *The Traveller,* lines 165-238]

It would be superfluous to point out the beauties of this
description: they are so natural and obvious, that no eye can
overlook them—Whether the severity of a Helvetian winter
chills the lap of May, when no Zephyr soothe the breast of the
mountain; whether the hardy Swiss sees his little lot, the lot of
all; breasts the keen air, and carols as he goes; drives his
plowshare to the steep, or drags the struggling savage into
day—the whole is beautiful. Whether he sits down the
monarch of a shed, and surveys his childrens looks, that
brighten at the blaze; or entertains the pilgrim, whose tale
repays the nightly bed—the whole is still beautiful—but the
simile of the babe is something more; there is a grandeur as
well as beauty in the application of it.

Those moral and intellectual refinements, which at once
embellish and add to the happiness of life in cultivated
societies, could not be expected among such a people as this:
the want of them, and of those various inferiour pleasures they
bring along with them, is very properly considered in this
elegant description.

But behold a people almost of a different species!

[Quotes *The Traveller,* lines 239-280]

There is something whimsical in the former part of this
description, where the Author represents himself as playing
upon some instrument, and the French dancing to it: but
whether this were fact or fancy, is of little consequence. The
characteristics in the passage beginning with 'so blest a life,'
[255] are very just, and ingeniously struck out; yet neither is the
description of the French nation, nor that of any other
introduced in this poem, full, or perfect. The Author has
contented himself with exhibiting them in a single point of
view; such an one, indeed, in which they are generally beheld:
but the lights are much strengthened by the powers of poetic
genius.

The Poet next makes a transition to Holland, and from thence
proceeds to Britain; but we must now refer the Reader to the
poem itself, which we cannot but recommend to him as a work
of very considerable merit.

The Good Natured Man

This anonymous review (Critical Review 25. (February 1768): 147-8) ably exposes the faults of the play.

This play has much merit, and many faults. The chief merit, as well as principal aim of the author, seems to be the delineation of character: but surely he has fallen into an error by supposing, that, in the composition of a comedy, 'no more would be expected from him.'[1] Much more may be, and always will be, expected from a comic writer; and if the author's prepossession in favour of our old poets had led him to a more studious imitation of them, he would have thought the fable as worthy his attention as the characters. Not that we would infer that this writer has wholly failed in the construction of his fable, or entirely succeeded in the delineation of character. Croker himself, whom the poet seems to have originally designed for a whimsical mixture of melancholy and humanity, is sometimes divested of the singularities which identify his character, and dwindles into the mere avaricious old curmudgeon, who appears in so many of our comedies. On the whole, his part is well sustained, and the circumstances of the fable naturally bring out the peculiarities of his mind. The scene on his first appearance, and that relative to the incendiary letter in the fourth act, are admirable. The Good-natur'd Man himself is not accurately drawn; nor is the part he sustains in the action made sufficiently capital, considering him as the hero of the piece. The weakness of super-abundant good-nature might be represented as carrying a virtue to a ridiculous excess, but should never appear to degenerate into absolute vice. Honeywood is in some instances a compostion of vanity and injustice, which are by no means the ingredients of good-nature. A series of comic distresses, brought on by his easiness of temper, might have been imagined, and have been so conducted as to display his character to much more advantage, than as it stands in this comedy, wherein his difficulties are neither sufficiently varied nor multiplied. There are many happy traits in the draught [ie drawing] of Lofty's character; but it is not made sufficiently clear what rank he really fills in society: nor is it probable that a family, like that of Croker, whose fortune is avowedly large, and whose connections are

[1] The quotations are from Goldsmith's Preface to The Good-Natured Man

apparently creditable, should be so easily imposed on by an
arrogant pretender, who knows neither persons of fashion, nor
men in power. From the character of Mrs Croker we are
taught to expect entertainment; but expectation is raised
without being gratified: from the other ladies we are led to
expect but little, and but little is performed. 'The scene of the
bailiffs, retrenched in the representation, and here restored by
the author, in deference to the judgment of a few friends, who
think in a particular way,' we neither wholly approve nor
condemn. Coarse characters should be touched by a delicate
pencil, and forcible situations should be rather softened than
aggravated. 'Humour (it is true) will sometimes lead us into
the recesses of the mean;' but in pursuing humour into those
recesses, the author, like Jove under Philemon's roof, should
not wholly abandon the dignity of his own character.

The Deserted Village

John Scott 1730-83, Quaker poet and critic, and (said Johnson) 'a very
sensible plain man' [1] wrote an essay in 1785 on Goldsmith's poem
which deserves quoting at some length for its stimulating, balanced,
and acute analysis. ("On Goldsmith's Deserted Village," *Critical
Essays on Some of the Poems of Several English Poets*, (1785) 247-
94.)

Goldsmith's Deserted Village, the work now under
consideration, is a performance of distinguished merit. The
general idea it inculcates is this; that commerce, by an
enormous introduction of wealth, has augmented the number
of the rich, who by exhausting the provision of the poor,
reduce them to the necessity of emigration. This principle is
exemplified in the description of Auburn, a Country Village,
once populous and flourishing, afterwards deserted and in
ruins.

Modern poetry has, in general, one common defect, viz. the
want of proper arrangement. There are many poems, whose
component parts resemble a number of fine paintings, which
have some connexion with each other, but are not placed in
any regular series. The Deserted Village would have pleased me
better, if all the circumstances relative to Auburn the inhabited,

.¹ *Johnsonian Miscellanies* ii, 47.

had been grouped in one picture; and all those relative to Auburn the deserted, in another. The Author's plan is more desultory; he gives us, alternately, contrasted sketches of the supposed place in its two different situations:

The Poem opens with an apostrophe to its subject:

[Quotes The Deserted Village, lines 1-34]

This passage is one of that kind, with which the imagination may be pleased, but which will not fully satisfy the judgement. The four lines, 'Dear lovely bowers,' &c. might perhaps have been spared. The village diversions are insisted on with too much prolixity. They are described first with a puerile generality, redundance, and confusion: they are sports, and pastimes, and gambols, and flights of art, and feats of strength; and they are represented sometimes as passive, the 'sports are led up;' sometimes as active, the 'pastimes circle,' and the gambols 'frolick,' and the 'flights and feats go round.' But we are perhaps fully recompensed for this, by the classical and beautiful particularity and conciseness of the context, 'the dancing pair,' 'the swain mistrustless of his smutted face,' the 'bashful virgin's looks, &c.' The paragraph in general has much inaccuracy, especially a disgusting identity of diction; the word 'bowers,' occurs twice, the word 'sweet,' thrice, and 'charms,' and 'sport,' singular or plural, four times. We have also 'toil remitting,' and 'toil taught to please,' 'succeeding sports,' and 'sports with sweet succession.'

[Quotes The Deserted Village, lines 35-50]

The passage already examined, and this, have both the same character of verbosity. There is a repetition which indicates intention, and maintains regularity; and there is a repetition which discovers either carelessness, or poverty of language. Auburn had before, l. 1. been termed 'sweet,' and 'the loveliest village of the plain;' it is now termed 'sweet,' and 'smiling,' and 'the loveliest of the lawn.' We had been told, l. 34. that 'all its charms were fled;' and we are now told that 'its sports are fled, and its charms withdrawn.' The 'tyrant's hand,' seems mentioned rather too abruptly; and 'desolation saddening the green,' is common place phraseology. The eight lines, 'No more the glassy brook, &c.' are natural and beautiful; but the next two, 'And trembling, shrinking, &c.' are ill-placed, for they prematurely introduce the subject of emigration.

[Quotes The Deserted Village, lines 63-74]

The first of these paragraphs, 'Ill fares the land, &c.' with all its merit, which is great, for the sentiment is noble, and the expression little inferior, seems rather out of place; after the affair of depopulation had been more fully described, it might have appeared to advantage as a concluding reflection. The second asserts what has been repeatedly denied, that 'there was a time in England, when every rood of ground maintained its man.' If however such a time ever was, it could not be so recent as when the Deserted Village was flourishing, a circumstance supposed to exist within the remembrance of the poet; consequently the idea had no business in the poem.

[Quotes The Deserted Village, lines 75-82]

This passage is a mere superfluity. The first six lines, 'But times are alter'd,' might have been reserved for introduction in some other part of the piece. The next, 'These gentle hours, &c.' should have been totally suppressed: 'gentle hours that are bade to bloom,' and 'healthful sports that live in looks, and brighten a green;' is certainly not vindicable language. The 'hours,' and the 'sports,' also, are said to 'seek a kinder shore,' which 'kinder shore,' is inconsistently described in the sequel of the poem, as fraught with every inconvenience and every danger. The mention of the 'sports,' and of the emigration, 'These far-departing, &c.' is here again unnecessarily repeated. The adjective 'sweet,' is frequently, and very properly, in use as a substitute for agreeable or pleasant, but it displeases in this work by perpetual repetition. The obscure and indefinite idea of a 'Tyrant,' recurs also unnecessarily here again. There is pathos in the lines, 'And many a year, &c.' but they are as evidently misplaced as some of their predecessors: we wish to hear more of the Village in its prosperity, before we hear so much of its desolation.

Subsequent to the above, we have an expatiation on the Author's fallacious hope of concluding his days at his favourite Auburn, and a paragraph in praise of retirement; both well written, but rather episodical.

[Quotes The Deserted Village, lines 113-136]

This is indeed a passage of uncommon merit. The circumstances it describes are obvious in nature, but new in poetry; and they are described with great force and elegance. . . .

The Matron gathering water-cresses, is a fine picture; but there is unnatural exaggeration in representing her as 'weeping,' every night, 'till morning;' sudden calamity occasions violent emotions, but habitual hardship will not produce incessant sorrow; time reconciles us to the most disagreeable situations. Our Author's language in this place, is also very defective in correctness. After mentioning the general privation of the 'bloomy flush of life,' the exceptionary, 'all but,' includes, as part of that 'bloomy flush,' an 'aged decrepid matron;' that is to say, in plain prose, 'the bloomy flush of life is all fled but one old woman.'

The Poet now recurs again to the past. When Auburn is described as flourishing, its Clergyman as a principal inhabitant, is very properly introduced. This supposed Village Pastor, is characterized in a manner which seems almost unexceptionable, both for sentiment and expression. His contentment, hospitality, and piety, are pointed out with sufficient particularity, yet without confusion or redundance.

Poetry attains its full purpose, when it sets its subjects strongly and distinctly in our view. This is the case here: we behold the good old man attended by his venerating parishioners, and with a kind of dignified complacence, even permitting the familiarities of their children. The concluding simile [ll. 179-80] has been much admired, and so far as immaterial objects can be illustrated by material, it is indeed a happy illustration.

As every parish has its Clergyman, almost every parish has its Schoolmaster. This secondary character is here described with great force and precision. The Muse, in part of her description, has descended to convey village ideas, in village language, but has contrived to give just so much dignity to the familiar, as prevents it from disgusting. . . .

[Quotes The Deserted Village, lines 193-216]

The description of the Village Alehouse, contains domestick minutiae, of a kind, which must necessarily have pleased in the original, but which the hand of a master alone, could have made to please in the copy. That learned and judicious Critick, Dr. Warton, in his Essay on the Writings and Genius of Pope, justly observes, that 'The use, the force, and the excellence of language, consists in raising clear, complete, and circumstantial images, and in turning readers into spectators.' This theory he exemplifies, by quoting two passages from his author, in which, he says, that 'every epithet paints its object, and paints it distinctly.' he same may be said with equal justice of the following:

> Near yonder thorn, that lifts its head on high,
> Where once the sign-post caught the passing eye;
> Low lies that house, where nut-brown draughts inspir'd,
> Where grey-beard mirth, and smiling toil retir'd . . .
>
> [219-222]

This fine poetical inventory of the furniture, is fully equalled by the character of the guests, and the detail of their amusements. The negative mode of expression, 'Thither no more, &c.' by fixing the mind on the past, adds a kind of pleasing regretful pathos:

> Vain transitory splendors ! could not all
> Reprieve the tottering mansion from its fall
> Obscure it sinks, nor shall it more impart
> An hour's importance to the poor man's heart . . .
>
> [237-240]

This is not poetical fiction, but historical truth. We have here no imaginary Arcadia, but the real country; no poetical swains, but the men who actually drive the plough, or wield the scythe, the sickle, the hammer, or the hedging bill. But though nothing is invented, something is suppressed. The rustick's hour of relaxation is too rarely so innocent; it is too often contaminated with extravagance, anger, and profanity: describing vice and folly, however, will not prevent their existing; and it is agreeable to forget for a moment, the reality of their existence.

The Deserted Village

William Mudford 1782-1848, a professional writer and critic, praised the poem with justice and intelligence. (*Essays on Men and Manners*, 1804).

I never read this poem but with increased delight; its sentiments speak to the heart; and I know no author more capable of seizing upon the feelings of his reader than Goldsmith. It is in this that he excels, if he excel in any thing; for in his poetry we can admire neither the plaintive sublimity of Gray; the concise elegance, apothegmatical morality, or caustic severity of Pope; the diffuse variety of Dryden; or the compact energy of Johnson; the characteristics of his muse are simplicity, pathos, and sentiment; an exquisite delicacy of delineation; and a happy felicity in adorning with the appearance of novelty reflections that are natural to every bosom. It will, I believe, readily be confessed, that he could not have chosen a more fit subject on which to exercise his peculiar powers, and that he appears with unrivalled excellence, as

'The sad historian of the pensive plain.'

[136]

This poem appears to have occupied his attention a long time, and to have been sent into the world at last, finished with all the accuracy he was capable of. Every line is laboured with uncommon exactness, and every expression weighed with nice precision; such exactness and such precision, as perhaps Goldsmith alone could have given.

There is nothing in our language which can surpass his descriptions of the *parish priest*, of the *country school-master*, and of the *village alehouse*. They are full without exaggeration, correct without minuteness, and animated without extravagance. They are drawn from the sacred fountain of truth, without any of the ordinary embellishments of poetry, or hyperboles of fiction. The reader, as he peruses them, feels the throbbing of assent beat in his bosom; and he recognises, with a mixture of wonder and delight, the scenes of reality moulded into the cadences of poetry. Goldsmith shews most of his genius in these delineations; for, he does not avail himself of the bold and invariable characteristics which are alike open to the observation of the careless and the attentive; but with the true discrimination of the poet, he seizes on those minute, yet distinctive circumstances which appear least susceptible of poetical dignity . . .

It was the object of Goldsmith, in this poem, to speak to the judgment, through the medium of the affections. He perceived, or thought he perceived, a national calamity; a calamity which he would willingly have been instrumental in redressing; and in order to rouse the energies of those who were capable of acting decisively, he probably thought he could not adopt a better plan to engage their moral feelings in the task, by painting, in strong colours, the prevalent misery. But two objections may be urged against the availability of this plan: first, poetry is not the proper vehicle for producing extensive reformation; poetry may shame a man out of a petty fault, or it may ridicule a woman into virtue; but it never yet redressed a public grievance. Men in general read poetry for amusement; they do not expect serious argumentation; and if they find it, they regard it only as the sportive sallies of imagination, or the fictitious embellishments of an ardent fancy.

Secondly it may be said, that a poem does not admit of that which is necessary in a serious attempt toward convincing mankind. Force of reasoning, accuracy of deduction, and strength of application, can rarely, if ever, be attained within the magic circle of poetry; or if any pedagogue were to succeed in it, its inevitable repulsive rigidity would deter those from reading for whom it was intended, and thus defeat its own purpose. But it may justly be doubted whether Goldsmith seriously believed what he wished to inculcate; or if he believed, whether he cared that his poem should be regarded as a stimulus to the dormant energies of men in power; he probably excogitated the subject in the usual course of reflection; found it suitable to his powers, and capable of that kind of embellishment he was best able to bestow.

Considered, however, without any reference to its ultimate object, it certainly stands without a rival, though it has engendered a host of imitations. It has some weak lines, and some lax expressions; but they bear so small a proportion to the blaze of excellence that is every where visible, that I should pity that man who was pedantic, or malignant enough to point them out as objects of censure.

The Deserted Village

Thomas Babington Macaulay (1800-1859), the famous historian, penetratingly exposes the dreamlike inconsistency of *The Deserted*

Village ("Life of Goldsmith," *Encyclopedia Britannica*, 8 ed. (1856)
10: 705-9).

In 1770 appeared the *Deserted Village*. In mere diction and
versification this celebrated poem is fully equal, perhaps
superior to the *Traveller* and it is generally preferred to the
Traveller by that large class of readers who think, with Bayes in
the *Rehearsal*, that the only use of a plan is to bring in fine
things. More discerning judges, however, while they admire the
beauty of the details, are shocked by one unpardonable fault
which pervades the whole. The fault which we mean is not that
theory about wealth and luxury which has so often been
censured by political economists. The theory is indeed false: but
the poem, considered merely as a poem, is not necessarily the
worse on that account. The finest poem in the Latin language,
indeed the finest didactic poem in any language, was written in
defence of the silliest and meanest of all systems of natural and
moral philosophy. A poet may easily be pardoned for reasoning
ill; but he cannot be pardoned for describing ill, for observing
the world in which he lives so carelessly that his portraits bear
no resemblance to the originals, for exhibiting as copies from
real life monstrous combinations of things which never were
and never could be found together. What would be thought of
a painter who should mix August and January in one
landscape, who should introduce a frozen river into a harvest
scene? Would it be a sufficient defence of such a picture to say
that every part was exquisitely coloured, that the green hedges,
the apple-trees loaded with fruit, the waggons reeling under the
yellow sheaves, and the sun-burned reapers wiping their
foreheads were very fine, and that the ice and the boys sliding
were also very fine? To such a picture the *Deserted Village*
bears a great resemblance. It is made up of incongruous parts.
The village in its happy days is a true English village. The
village in its decay is an Irish village. The felicity and the misery
which Goldsmith has brought close together belong to two
different countries, and to two different stages in the progress
of society. He had assuredly never seen in his native island such
a rural paradise, such a seat of plenty, content, and tranquillity,
as his *Auburn*. He had assuredly never seen in England all the
inhabitants of such a paradise turned out of their homes in one
day and forced to emigrate in a body to America. The hamlet

he had probably seen in Kent: the ejectment he had probably seen in Munster; but by joining the two, he has produced something which never was and never will be seen in any part of the world.

She Stoops to Conquer

William Woodfall, 1746-1803, actor, dramatic critic, publisher of Goldsmith's Threnodia Augustalis (1772), and editor of The London Packet published this rather reasoned attack in favour of Sentimental Comedy in the *Monthly Review* (48. (March 1773): 306-314). Goldsmith retaliated (mildly) in *Retaliation*, line 115.

A writer so much, and so justly, in favour with the Public, as the Author of this play, is entitled to more than mere candor for his imperfections. When, therefore, we meet with any thing to disapprove in his compositions, it is really with some degree of concern, and we are under a difficulty in discharging our duty to the Public.

Comedy has been defined by all theatrical Critics, from Aristotle down to the correspondents of a News-paper. We do not, however, remember a definition exactly in the following terms: Comedy is a dramatic representation of the prevailing manners of people not in very high or very low life. It must therefore vary, as those manners vary; and be wholly regulated by them. Hence the difference between Plautus and Menander; (as Menander is represented by Terence) and between all those original writers, who at different periods of time have written immediately from the manners passing in review before them. Few of our English writers of Comedy have aimed at being originals. Some exception may be made in favour of Vanbrugh, Congreve, and Farquhar; the great merit of whose Comedies is, that they represent the manners of the times. Sir Richard Steel, Mr. Cibber, &c. did little more than translate; they were happy, however, in the choice of their plays, and in accommodating them to the customs which it was the business of the stage to regulate or correct.—Our customs and manners have undergone a gradual alteration. A general correspondence arising from trade, and the progress of the arts, has brought the nation, as it were, together, and worn off those prepossessions and habits which made every little neighbourhood a separate community, and marked every community with its peculiar character. The business of comedy is therefore changed; and a man who would now exhibit a Lady Bountiful, a Lord Foppington, or an Abel Drugger, would be considered as copying from history or from old comedies. Such characters do not now exist; at least not in the general walks of men. Some of our late writers have therefore very judiciously had recourse to what is called *Sentimental Comedy*, as better suited to the principles and manners of the age. A general politeness has given a sameness to our external appearances; and great degrees of knowledge are every where diffused. An author, therefore, has not that variety of character, and that simplicity and ignorance to describe, which were the capital ingredients in the old Comedy. Modern writers may indeed have carried the matter too far, and perhaps kept their eyes too much on French models. They may have neglected some remains of English oddities which are still left, and would have very much enlivened their writings. They have erred however only in the execution: they are right in their general principle. The business of the old Comedy, and that of the present, are as different as the people they represent; and persons who have renounced the manners and religion of their fathers, and who would laugh at that wit which was their terror or delight, are affected and influenced by what is called sentiment. Some of our late plays might be mentioned, on this occasion, with great honour.

But Dr. Goldsmith does not seem to have been of this opinion. Having read more about even his own countrymen' than he had ever seen of them, and recollecting that the comedies he had perused were very different from those which now prevailed, he imagined the Comic Muse had fled the land. He determined to call her back, and employ her first in introducing the *Good-natured Man*, and afterwards the present Comedy.

The fable of *She Stoops to Conquer* is a series of blunders, which the Author calls the *Mistakes of a Night*; but they are such mistakes as never were made, and, we believe, never could have been committed.

Some modern wits have endeavoured to render this kind of offence venial. They have said, that the fable is of no consequence; and that it is immaterial how the incidents are introduced, provided they are pleasing.

' All the subjects of the British government are countrymen

To support this strange opinion, they refer to several of our plays, in which the finest circumstances have been forced in against probability. We could give instances, in moral life, where the happiest consequences have attended a falsehood; and yet lying is a crime; and a man would be laughed at, if not detested, who would plead, from any accidental advantage, against the general principles of truth. All the general principles of nature are sacred; and we offend against them, in all cases, at our peril. When the temptation is great, and the advantages such as could not be obtained in any other way, we pardon the offender, and perhaps applaud the offence; but still we retain our attachment to the principles of nature. Hence the *virtuous lie* of Tasso; and hence the applauded licences of some fine writers. This, however, does not excuse a man who gives into a *habit* of immorality, or an author who writes a *series* of improbabilities.

In this light we are obliged to consider Dr. Goldsmith's play, as most of its incidents are offences against nature and probability. We are sorry for it, because he certainly has a great share of the *vis comica* [comic force]; and when he has thrust his people into a situation, he makes them talk very *funnily*. His merit is in that sort of dialogue which lies on a level with the most common understandings; and in that low mischief and mirth which we laugh at, while we are ready to despise ourselves for so doing. This is the reason why the Reader must peruse the present Comedy without pleasure, while the representation of it may make him laugh . . .

We wish, however, that the ingenious Author could employ his talents, so as to divert the galleries, without offending others who have a right to his attention. This he might do, by taking some story of a distant date, when the manners were generally such as he chuses to represent. He would then find characters and circumstances to his hand; and his language and dialogue would have all their effect: we should put ourselves back in imagination, and have the same kind of pleasure which is now given us by the best of our old comedies.

She Stoops to Conquer

Horace Walpole (1717-1797), author of *The Castle of Otranto*, made a similar point rather more forcibly in a letter to William Mason (27 March 1773).

Dr. Goldsmith has written a comedy—no, it is the lowest of all farces; it is not the subject I condemn, though very vulgar, but the execution. The drift tends to no moral, no edification of any kind—the situations however are well managed, and make one laugh in spite of the grossness of the dialogue, the forced witticisms, and total improbability of the whole plan and conduct. But what disgusts me most, is that though the characters are very low, and aim at low humour, not one of them says a sentence that is natural or marks any character at all. It is set up in opposition to sentimental comedy, and is as bad as the worst of them. Garrick would not act it, but bought himself off by a poor prologue.

She Stoops to Conquer

This anonymous letter, printed *St. James's Chronicle* (March 1773) under the pen-name 'Bossu', weighed into the critical controversy around the play with admirable gusto and sharp textual observation.

. . . We could admit this in a Farce, but in a Comedy we cannot. But there is one Circumstance which completes the Improbability of this: Marlow on his Arrival calls for a *Bill of Fare ! Is* it then usual to call for a *Bill of Fare* in a Gentleman's Family? Is it possible that Hardcastle should not put this very Question to his impudent Guest? It is at least the only natural Reply that could be made to so extraordinary a Demand.

The Doctor, aware perhaps of these Improprieties, has called in the Assistance of several Circumstances to their Support, and even wrested them to his Purpose. Among these I place the Incident of Miss Hardcastle's changing her Dress. In the Morning she is allowed to dress in a gay Stile, to make her Visits, and to please herself; in the Evening she puts on a humbler Garb, to please her Father. Now, let us be informed what the Visits are, which a young Lady living in a remote and retired Country has to repeat every Day. When I heard her talk of paying her Morning-Visits, my Mind recurred to the Streets and the Inhabitants at the West End of the Town; but when I compared the Idea with the Circumstances of a young Lady's Life, whom we cannot suppose (from what we are told) to be situated in the Neighbourhood of any People of Fortune or Fashion, and who, at any Rate, could not have Visits to repeat every Day. When I reflected upon this, I conceived the Affair in its true Light, and was convinced that the Circumstance of the Change of Dress was dragged in, on purpose to give the Lady a more plausible Pretext of passing upon her Lover as a Bar-Maid. But another Reflection greatly heightened the Inconsistency of the Thing. Allowing the Motives of the Change of Dress to be as they are stated; allowing that the Lady visited in the Morning, and pleased her Father in the Evening—is it probable that she would assume a mean Dress *this* Evening, when she was formally to meet a Lover, and when the House had Strangers in it, and another was still expected? This is a whimsical Idea, which, I think, is not accounted for.

I have observed that Faults of this Nature are too common in the Practice of our Dramatic Writers. Instead of tracing Nature Step by Step, and following her by the Line of their Fable, till the last Period, they convert it from its natural Channel, on Purpose to cover their Errors, or to surprize us with something which we do not, and which we ought not, to expect. This is trifling with our Judgment, in order to dazzle our Imagination.

It is to such Inclinations as these we must attribute the following Inconsistency among several others:—Hardcastle, in order no Doubt to heighten the Extravagance of Marlow's Behaviour, informs us, that he had not only taken Possession of his great Chair, but *taken off his Boots* in the Parlour. Now this sounds very well to the Ear; but when we appeal to the Eye, and find that Marlow had no Boots *on* him to be *taken off*, how can we excuse the old Man for telling *Lyes*?

The Characters in this Piece have but little of Originality to boast of. With respect to these, the Author's chief Merit consists in having carried the Humour of them farther than his Predecessors. This is more particularly applicable to the 'Squire and to Marlow. And yet the Character of the latter is extremely similar to that of Young Philpot, in the Farce of the *Citizen*; I mean only in regard to his Bashfulness in the Company of modest Women. The first Scene between Marlow and Miss Hardcastle is almost a Transcript of a Scene of the same Nature between Young Philpot and Maria. Marlow faithfully copies the Words and Behaviour of Philpot, and Miss Hardcastle displays to us not a few of the Features of the lively and agreeable Maria.

In this Comedy the Unity of Time is repeatedly violated in the second or third Act (I do not remember which). Half an Hour is mentioned for the Time of an Appointment which takes Place in very few Minutes after; and Tony desires Hastings to meet him "two Hours Hence" at the Back of the Garden, tho' they both take Care to meet there very punctually at the End of a short Half Hour. In these thirty *Minutes*, however, we are desired to suppose that a Chaise has been got ready, the Horses harnessed, and a Company prepared themselves for a Journey, and that they actually did travel so much Road as appeared to Mrs. Hardcastle to be forty *Miles*. All this Business is supposed to be finished in the *Half Hour*; for a Half Hour it actually was, though Tony, on his Return, informs us, that he had been absent *three Hours*. To believe this, our *Conscience* must move in as wide a Latitude as the Author's who wrote it.

I do not mention, to aggravate these Lapses of the Judgement, the utter Improbability of a timid old Lady setting off with a young one, at Midnight, upon a journey of forty Miles, through imperious Roads, impassable Ditches, and Heaths frequented by Robbers; though the Journey could have been with greater Convenience performed the next Day, and all Danger removed in the mean Time, by securing the Lady from the Reach of the Lover.

I regard these Incongruities in Comedy as the Errors of a Man who is either too hasty, or too unequal to the Task of writing one. It appears not well, when the Poet, instead of bending his Fancy to the Fable, bends the Fable to his Fancy. I honour Dr. Goldsmith when he writes a *Poem*; but when he writes a *Comedy*, I lose Sight of the Man of Genius.

She Stoops to Conquer

The paradoxes of the play were still alive in 1846, when Leigh Hunt, 1784-1859, the poet and critic, wrote about it in his *Wit and Humour, Selected from the English Poets.*

. . . in reality the production is merely a large farce with the name of comedy. Tony Lumpkin is certainly a most original personage; his subjection at home and his domination abroad, his uncouth bashfulness at the gallantries of his female cousin, and his love of mischievous fun, present an inimitable picture of broad rusticity: the natural contempt which he shews for his mother, who has indulged him till he is too old to play the child, enforces an excellent moral in the midst of the most laughable caricature. But the characters are exaggerated throughout, and most of the incidents are inconsistent and improbable. It is from this play and the grinning comedies of O'KEEFFE, I have arisen those monstrous farces of the present stage, which may, for ought I know, attain the end of comedy, for they are certainly satires on human nature together.

SUGGESTIONS FOR FURTHER READING

EDITIONS

Goldsmith, Oliver. *The Collected Works of Oliver Goldsmith*. Ed. Arthur Friedman. Oxford: Clarendon Press, 1966.

Goldsmith, Oliver. *She Stoops to Conquer*. Ed. Tom Davis. The New Mermaids. London: A & C Black/W W Norton, 1979.

Goldsmith, Oliver. *The Grumbler: an Adaptation*. Ed. Alice Ida Perry Wood. Huntington Library Publications. Cambridge, Mass.: Harvard University Press, 1931.

Lonsdale, Roger H., ed. *The Poems of Thomas Gray, William Collins, Oliver Goldsmith*. Harlow: Longmans, 1969.

GENERAL READING

Boswell, James. *The Life of Samuel Johnson, L.L.D.* 1791. *The essential context to Goldsmith's life and work.*

Forster, John. *The Life and Adventures of Oliver Goldsmith*. London: Bradbury and Evans, 1848. *With Prior, the classic early biographies: minor works of art in their own right.*

Ginger, John. *The Notable Man*. London: Hamilton, 1977. *Interesting biography; supersedes Wardle in some respects.*

Hopkins, Robert Hazen. *The True Genius of Oliver Goldsmith*. Baltimore: Johns Hopkins University Press, 1969. *Stimulating and individual reading of Goldsmith.*

Prior, Sir James, *The Life of Oliver Goldsmith M.B.*, London: John Murray, 1837.

Quintana, Ricardo. *Oliver Goldsmith: a Georgian Study*. Masters of World Literature. London: Weidenfeld & Nicolson, 1967. *Some worthwhile insights; a valuable critical appreciation. Contains a full bibliography.*

Rousseau, G. S., ed. *Goldsmith; the Critical Heritage*. London: Routledge and Kegan Paul, 1974. *A useful collection of critical work.*

Swarbrick, Andrew, ed. *The Art of Oliver Goldsmith*. London: Barnes & Noble, 1984. *Some of the best writing on Goldsmith is in this collection. In*

*particular, Donald Davies' exhilarating and stylish essay on
Goldsmith's politics; a stimulating, suggestive, and densely-argued
study of the imagery patterns in* The Traveller *by Pat Rogers; an
equally important contribution from W. J. McCormack that places a
necessary, and much neglected, emphasis on Goldsmith's Irishness;
and, finally, a useful study of* The Good-Natur'd Man *in Bernard
Harris's piece 'Goldsmith in the Theatre'.*

Wardle, Ralph Martin. *Oliver Goldsmith.* Lawrence: University of
Kansas Press, 1957.
The standard biography.

SPECIALIST READING

Bell, H. J. 'The Deserted Village, and Goldsmith's Social Doctrines.'
Publications of the Modern Language Association of America, 59
(1944): 747-772.

Brooks, Christopher. 'The Political Sub-Text of Goldsmith's The
Good-Natur'd Man.' *English Language Notes* 26.3 (1989): 25-29.

Brooks, Christopher. 'Goldsmith's Political Drama: The Good Natur'd
Man, Lofty, and Bute.' *Restoration and 18th Century Theatre
Research* 3.2 (1988): 23-37.

Donoghue, Frank. ' "He never gives us nothing thats low":
Goldsmith's Plays and the Reviewers.' *English Literary History* 55-3
(1988): 665-684.

Ferguson, Oliver W. ''Goldsmith as Ironist.' *Studies in Philology* 81 2
(1984): 212-228.

Hamlyn, Susan. *She Stoops to Conquer: the Making of a Popular
Success.* M.A. Thesis (unpublished). University of Birmingham,
1975.

Hawthorn, Jeremy. *Multiple personality and the disintegration of
literary character: from Oliver Goldsmith to Sylvia Plath.* London:
Edward Arnold, 1983.

Heilman, R. B., 'The Sentimentalism of Goldsmith's The Good-
Natur'd Man.' *Studies for W.A. Read,* 235-53, 1940.

Jeffares, A. Norman. *Oliver Goldsmith. Writers and their Work.*
London: Longmans, Green, 1959. 107.

Lucy, Sean. 'Who was Oliver Goldsmith?' Sean Lucy ed. *Goldsmith:
The Gentle Master.* Cork: Cork UP, 1984. 13-25.

McCarthy, B. Eugene. 'The Theme of Liberty in She Stoops to
Conquer.' *University of Windsor Review* 7.1 (1971): 1-8.

McGuinness, Arthur E. 'Goldsmith's *The Traveller*: A Christian
Perspective.' *Forum* 17 (Winter 1979): 52-58.

McVeagh, John. 'Goldsmith and Nationality'. *660-1780: All the
World Before Them.* Ed. John McVeagh. London: Ashfield, 1990.
217-33. London: Ashfield; 1990. 217-33.

Miner, Earl. 'The Making of the Deserted Village.' *Huntington Library Quarterly* 22 (1958-9): 125-141.

Nicoll, Allardyce. *A History of English Drama, 1660-1900.* Cambridge: Cambridge University Press, 1952. 3.

Piper, William Bowman. 'The Musical Quality of Goldsmith's The Deserted Village.' *Studies in Eighteenth-Century Culture* 14 (1985): 259-274.

Prior, Sir James, *The Life of Oliver Goldsmith M.B.*, John Murray, London, 1837.

Sampson, H. Grant. 'Comic Patterns in Goldsmith's Plays.' *English Studies in Canada* 10.1 (1984): 36-49.

Sherbo, Arthur. 'From the Westminster Magazine: Swift, Goldsmith, Garrick, et al.' *Studies in Bibliography* 41 (1988): 270-283.

Todd, W. B. 'The First Editions of The Good-Natur'd Man and She Stoops to Conquer.' *Studies in Bibliography* 2 (1958): 133-142.

Traugott, John. 'Heart and Mask and Genre in Sentimental Comedy.' *Eighteenth-Century Life.* 3 (1986): 122-144.

Williams, Raymond. *The Country and the City.*London: Chatto & Windus, 1973.

Woods, Samuel H. *Oliver Goldsmith, a reference guide.* Boston, Mass.: G. K. Hall, 1982.